IMAGES of America

MADISON PARISH

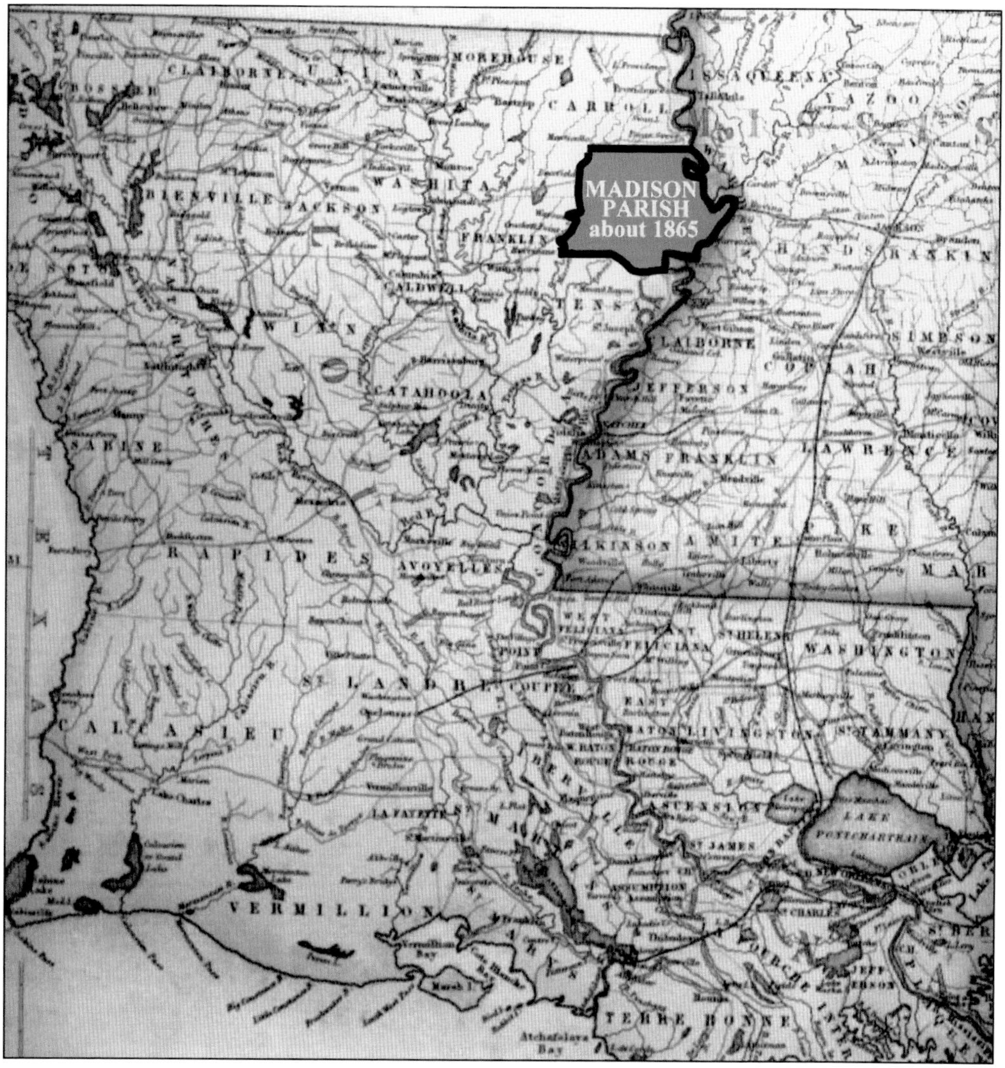

Louisiana Index Map Showing Location of Madison Parish. This old map shows the location and shape of Madison parish relative to the states of Louisiana and Mississippi. The city of Vicksburg is immediately to the east of the parish. This map was printed in Scotland c. 1865 and is scaled in "British" miles. (From *A&C Black*, Edinburgh, Scotland.)

IMAGES
of America

MADISON PARISH

Richard P. Sevier

ARCADIA
PUBLISHING

ISBN 978-0-7385-1510-6

Published by Arcadia Publishing
Charleston SC, Chicago IL, Portsmouth NH, San Francisco CA

Printed in the United States of America

Library of Congress Catalog Card Number: 2002117623

For all general information contact Arcadia Publishing at:
Telephone 843-853-2070
Fax 843-853-0044
E-Mail sales@arcadiapublishing.com
For customer service and orders:
Toll-Free 1-888-313-2665

Visit us on the Internet at www.arcadiapublishing.com

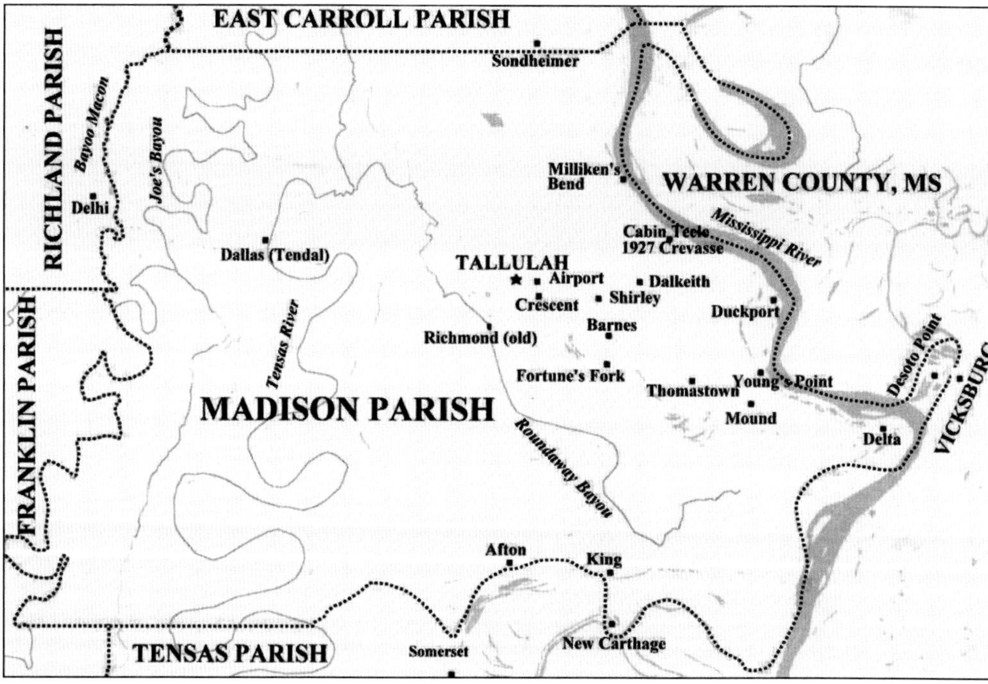

Madison Parish Index Map. This index map of Madison Parish shows the location of almost every town, settlement, or plantation mentioned. Tallulah, the parish seat, is fairly centrally located. Richmond, the first parish seat, was burned to the ground during the Civil War. Two other important towns, Milliken's Bend and New Carthage, are no longer in existence since they were heavily damaged during the Civil War and, later, totally destroyed by the Mississippi River.

Contents

Acknowledgments

Many people supplied the pictures that made this book possible. Foremost among these are Haw Kirkpatrick and Perry Glick, both long since deceased. These gentlemen worked for the United States Department of Agriculture Experiment Station in Tallulah, and their detailed pictures of the 1927 flood, supplied by Scott Moore, superbly chronicled that devastating event. Because of size limitations, many of their fine photographs could not be included here.

Thanks also to Marion Lawrence Walker Lott for use of her stereopticon pictures on Theodore Roosevelt's 1907 bear hunt and to Marilyn Bedgood for pictures and data on the Bear Lake Hunting Club, about which she is writing a book scheduled to go to press shortly. Special thanks go to Frances (Boo) Bettis Eiland who allowed the use of her one-of-a-kind collection of the 1841–1844 *Richmond Compiler* and provided several interesting pictures. Also, Cody Ray and Geneva Rountree Williams of the Madison Historical Society have been especially helpful. Others contributing photographs to this publication are my wife, Barbara P. Sevier; my son, William R. Sevier; my sisters, Dorothy Sevier Elliott and Sherrill Sevier Pirone; Martha Yerger André; Mary Jo Provine Briggs; Louis Buckner; Charles Michael Finlayson; Reid Foster; Sally Jo Foster Gibson; Mary Gregg; Judy Kell Morris; Bea Neill; Henry C. Sevier Jr.; Ken Smith; and Jeanne Yerger. Probably the most interesting contributor was Jeremy Prescott of Leicester, England who happened upon *The John Perkins Family of Northeast Louisiana* on the Madison Parish historical/genealogical website. Jeremy is John Perkins Sr.'s great-great-great-grandson and has been a tremendous help with data and photographs.

David Bastian's book *Grant's Canal The Union's Attempt to Bypass Vicksburg* was the source of much data and pictures on the Civil War subject. Thanks to A'Lelia Perry Bundles for pictures of "Madam Walker," her great-great-great-grandmother. A'Lelia's two recent books, *Madam C.J. Walker* and *On Her Own Ground*, are required reading for information on the Madam. Thanks also goes to Tallulah's *Madison* Journal, whose Centennial Issue of August 14, 1975 provided much information; to William M. Murphy's 1927 *Notes from the History of Madison Parish, Louisiana*; and to Robert L. Moncrief's 1937 *The Economic Development of the Tallulah Territory*. Additional information on Madison Parish may be found on the Internet at http://www.rootsweb.com/~lamadiso/index.htm and http://www.rootsweb.com/~usgenweb/la/madison.htm. Many of the maps in the book came from the Library of Congress and can be accessed at the Louisiana and/or Mississippi historical map sites at http://www.rootsweb.com/~usgenweb/maps/louisiana/ and http://www.rootsweb.com/~usgenweb/maps/mississippi/, respectively.

INTRODUCTION

Madison Parish, Louisiana is located in extreme northeastern Louisiana across the Mississippi River from the city of Vicksburg, Mississippi. It played an important role during the Civil War at the time of the Siege of Vicksburg, as it was a troop staging area and the site of two abortive attempts by General Grant to bypass or divert the flow of the Mississippi River so he could storm the city in 1863. These were the Duckport and "Grant's" canals. It was also the site of the Battle of Milliken's Bend and the Battle of Richmond.

Named for the fourth President of the United States, James Madison, Madison Parish was created in 1838 and reduced to its current boundaries in 1861. Prior to that time it had been a part of the New Orleans District (1721), Ouachita "County" (1805), Concordia "County" (1809), Warren "County" (1811), Ouachita and Concordia Parishes (1814), and Carroll Parish (1832).

The lands of Madison Parish are composed entirely of alluvial deposits of the Mississippi River and its tributaries and are outstanding farming and hardwood timber areas. During the 1830–1860 period, many people were attracted to the rich, fertile soils here. Although most of Madison Parish's immigrants came from other Southeastern states, many came from Ireland, some of whom built the first major levees along the Mississippi River. In fact, the Madison "Tips," a group of Irishmen originally from County Tipperary, fought for the Confederacy when they weren't fighting among themselves. In addition, many Union soldiers and officers liked what they saw in Madison Parish and returned after the war. Among these were Elias S. Dennis, a Brigadier General under U.S. Grant, who became a Parish judge and later a sheriff. Another newcomer was Maj. Gen. Francis Preston Blair. A former Congressman and Senator from Missouri, Blair was Horatio Seymour's running mate in the 1868 Presidential election against General Grant, Blair's former commander at Milliken's Bend. Blair is credited with introducing the "sharecropping" or "tenant-farming" system when his own ridiculous system of "farming by military commands" failed.

The first parish seat was established in 1838 at the town of Richmond, which was located about two miles south of the current parish seat, Tallulah. During the Civil War, Richmond was burned to the ground by General Grant's troops. Not a single building was left standing, and today there is no visual evidence that it ever existed. In fact, after the War only two or three buildings were left standing in the entire parish.

The only other Madison Parish towns of note that existed before the Civil War were Milliken's Bend, New Carthage, and Delta. Milliken's Bend was the site of a little-publicized, fierce, hand-to-hand bayonet battle involving one of the Union's first deployments of black troops. At one period, over 30,000 soldiers were stationed in the Milliken's Bend-Young's Point area, which also functioned for a time as headquarters for Generals Grant, McClernan, and Sherman. Milliken's Bend was also a fairly important steamboat port. Unfortunately, with the demise of steamboat traffic and the increasing importance of Tallulah, Milliken's Bend was abandoned. Also, much of Milliken's Bend was consumed by the Mississippi River as it continued to shift its channel westward, leaving a portion of Madison Parish east of the river and contiguous to the state of Mississippi. Delta, a small village located directly across the River from Vicksburg, was the parish seat from 1868 until 1882 when a group of "vigilantes" in the dead of night raided the courthouse and moved all the records to Tallulah. New Carthage was located at the extreme southern end of the parish and was partly destroyed by the Union Army and totally destroyed by the Mississippi River. Other smaller sites, all steamboat ports, were located along the Mississippi River at Duckport, Young's Point, and Tuscumbia Bend.

Tallulah, the current parish seat, was established as a railroad watering station during the late 1850s, but did not reach a level of importance until after the Civil War. Legend has it that Tallulah's name and possibly its very existence resulted from a story of romantic intrigue. It seems that a railroad was to be built during this period and was scheduled to pass through Richmond, which was then the largest town in this part of the country. Apparently the engineer in charge of constructing the railroad became enamored with an attractive widow who owned land near the current site of Tallulah. She persuaded him to reroute the railroad through her property, thus greatly enhancing its value. However, after the railroad was completed the widow immediately lost interest in the engineer who then named the station Tallulah after a former sweetheart in Georgia.

In a pictorial history such as this it is impossible to discuss all of the important Madison Parish events that have occurred. Many significant events have necessarily been left out because no pictures were available. I have tried to make the format of this book read as chronologically as possible from 1800 to about 1927. However, if an event was related to an older event, it was included with the older event in the interest of clarity.

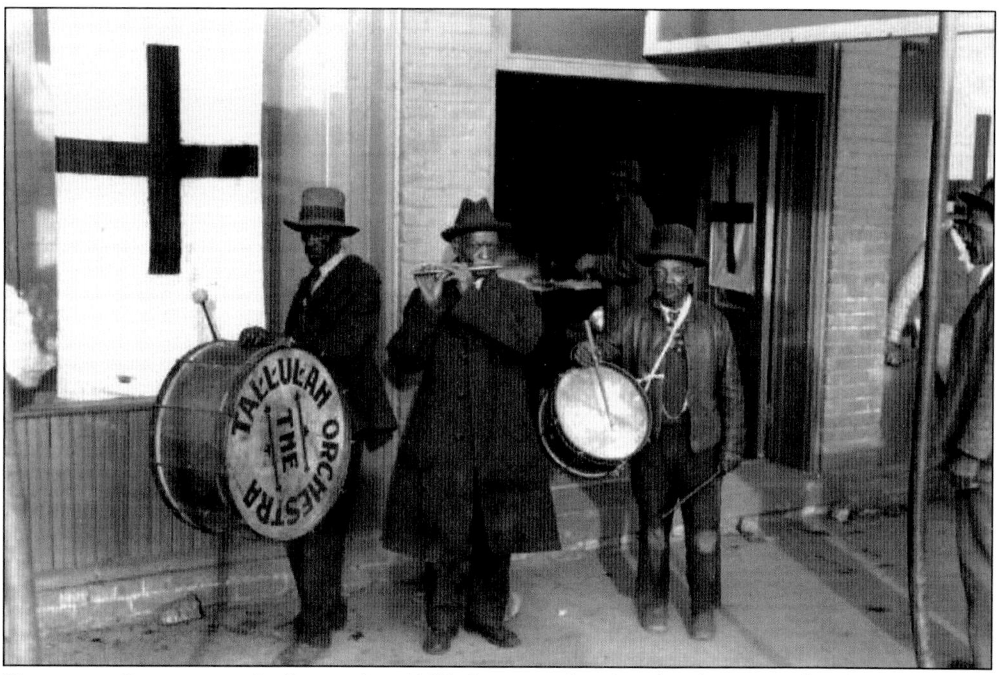

TALLULAH ORCHESTRA. In September 1927, five months after the disastrous flood, the Tallulah Orchestra played at a Red Cross benefit where clothing and furniture were issued to the needy. The only person identified is the drummer, Tom Byrd. Tom was the first black undertaker in Madison Parish. The drum will be recognized later in a 1915 photograph of the orchestra, then a 12-piece, all-white group. (Courtesy of the USDA.)

One

1800–1860

From 1800 to about 1835, the land that was later to become Madison Parish in 1838 had little activity. Prior to 1800 the only occupants were members of the Taensas Native American tribes. The first European settlers in the area came about 1803, the year of the Louisiana Purchase. Most of these people were hunters and trappers. By 1834 there were only three settlements in Madison Parish, two on Walnut Bayou and one on the Tensas River. The depression following 1837 and the "wearing out" of the older Southeastern states' farmland caused accelerated immigration into Madison Parish, especially to the fertile lands along the Mississippi River. By 1850, 25 percent (185) of the white residents over age 20 in Madison Parish were born in Mississippi, 14 percent (104) in Virginia, 9 percent (68) in Tennessee, and 9 percent (66) in states which later were to become the Union. Only 8.4 percent (63) were born in Louisiana, while 5.7 percent (43) were born overseas. The 1860 Census shows that Mississippi still held the lead with 25 percent (228), foreign-born residents now had 14 percent (104), followed by Virginia and Louisiana with 10 percent each (97 and 94, respectively). It is interesting to note that in 1860 there were more white residents aged 20 and older born overseas than born in Louisiana. Most came from Ireland (31), England (17), Bavaria (15), and Germany (12).

During the period from 1840 to 1860, Louisiana was considered the richest of the Southern states, and Madison was among the top parishes. Fortunes were made quickly during this time. The rich alluvial land, steamboat access to cotton markets in New Orleans, and an abundance of slave labor made men wealthy as demonstrated by the beautiful mansions that began to rise. Unfortunately, this would all change soon.

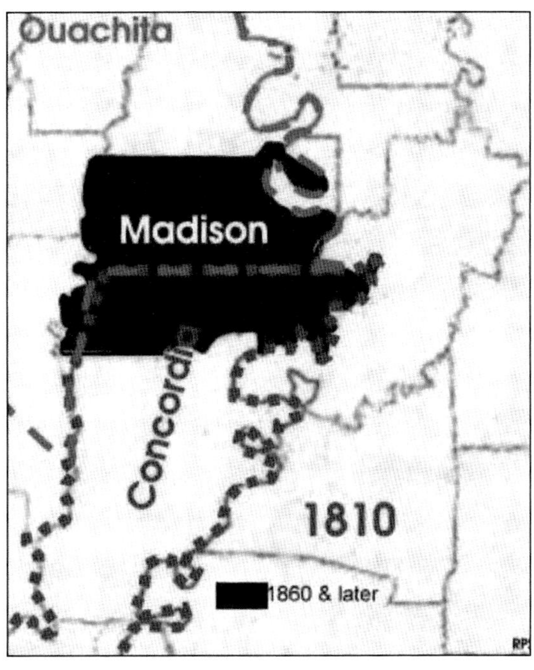

1810 Boundaries. Madison (present boundaries shown in black) did not become a parish until 1838. In 1805, just after the Louisiana Purchase, what is now Madison Parish became part of the "County" of Ouachita. In 1809 the southern portion was added to Concordia "County."

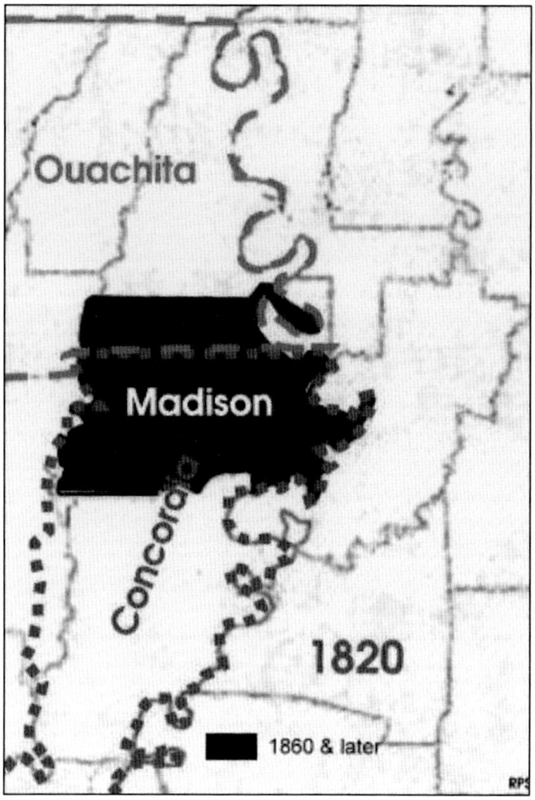

1820 Boundaries. In 1811 all land south of an east-west line through Vicksburg, Mississippi was given to Concordia and all land north of this line, all the way to the state of Arkansas, became a new "county" called Warren. In 1814 Warren County was abolished, with its northern portion reverting to Ouachita and the southern to Concordia. At this time the "county" designation was abolished and "parish" was substituted and used from that point forward.

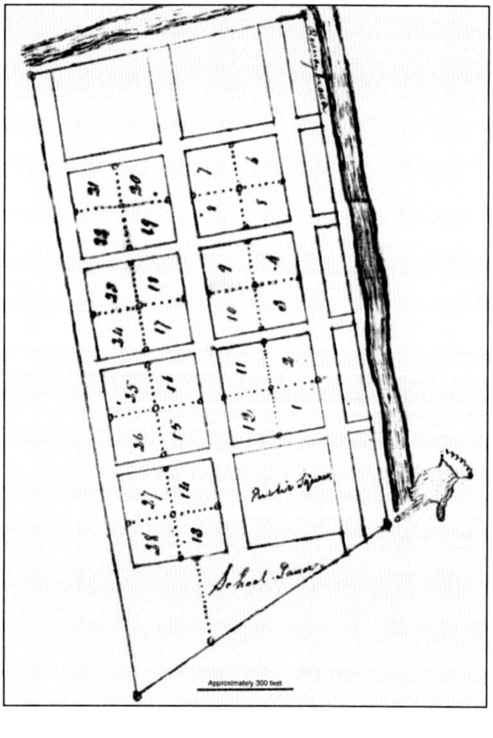

Plat of Richmond. Madison Parish was officially born in 1838 with Richmond as its county seat. This old plat of Richmond shows it located on Roundaway "Bioua." In this part of Louisiana, "bayou" is usually pronounced "bio" or "biya" rather than "biou," as in the southern part of the state. Richmond was burned to the ground by Union troops and abandoned in 1863 during the Civil War. (Courtesy of Louis Buckner.)

1840 BOUNDARIES. The 1840 parish boundaries (the gray and black areas) are essentially the same as when it was formed in 1838. In 1846, a strip three miles wide was cut from the southern part of Carroll and attached to Madison. A year later some of this was given back to Carroll.

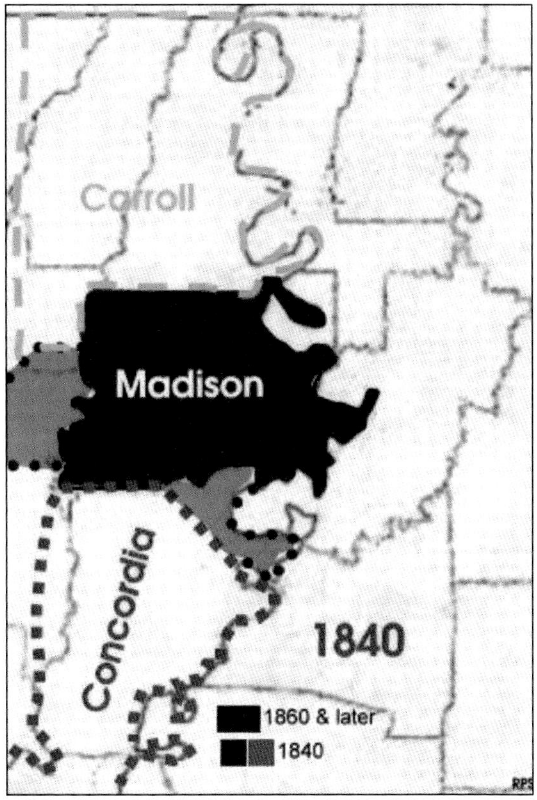

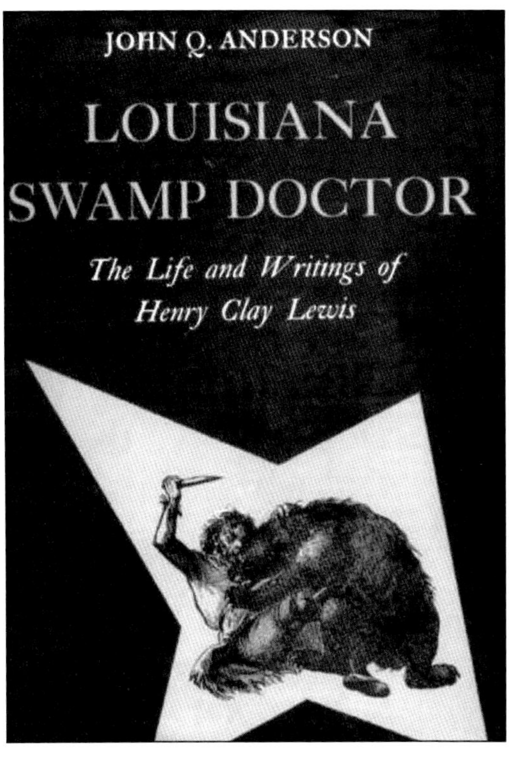

LOUISIANA SWAMP DOCTOR. In the 1840s a series of humorous stories began to appear in the *Spirit of the Times*, a New York weekly. The author of these stories signed his name as "Madison Tensas, M.D., the Louisiana Swamp Doctor." In 1850 these stories were collected and published in a book called *Odd Leaves from the Life of a Louisiana Swamp Doctor*. However, very few people knew the true identity of the author. After an extensive search in the early 1960s, John Q. Anderson, an English professor at Texas A & M, was able to identify the author as Henry Clay Lewis, a young Madison Parish physician living in Richmond. Anderson republished the *Swamp Doctor* in 1962. Lewis met an unfortunate death in August 1850 when he and his horse attempted to cross a flood-swollen stream near Richmond (probably Roundaway Bayou). Both drowned.

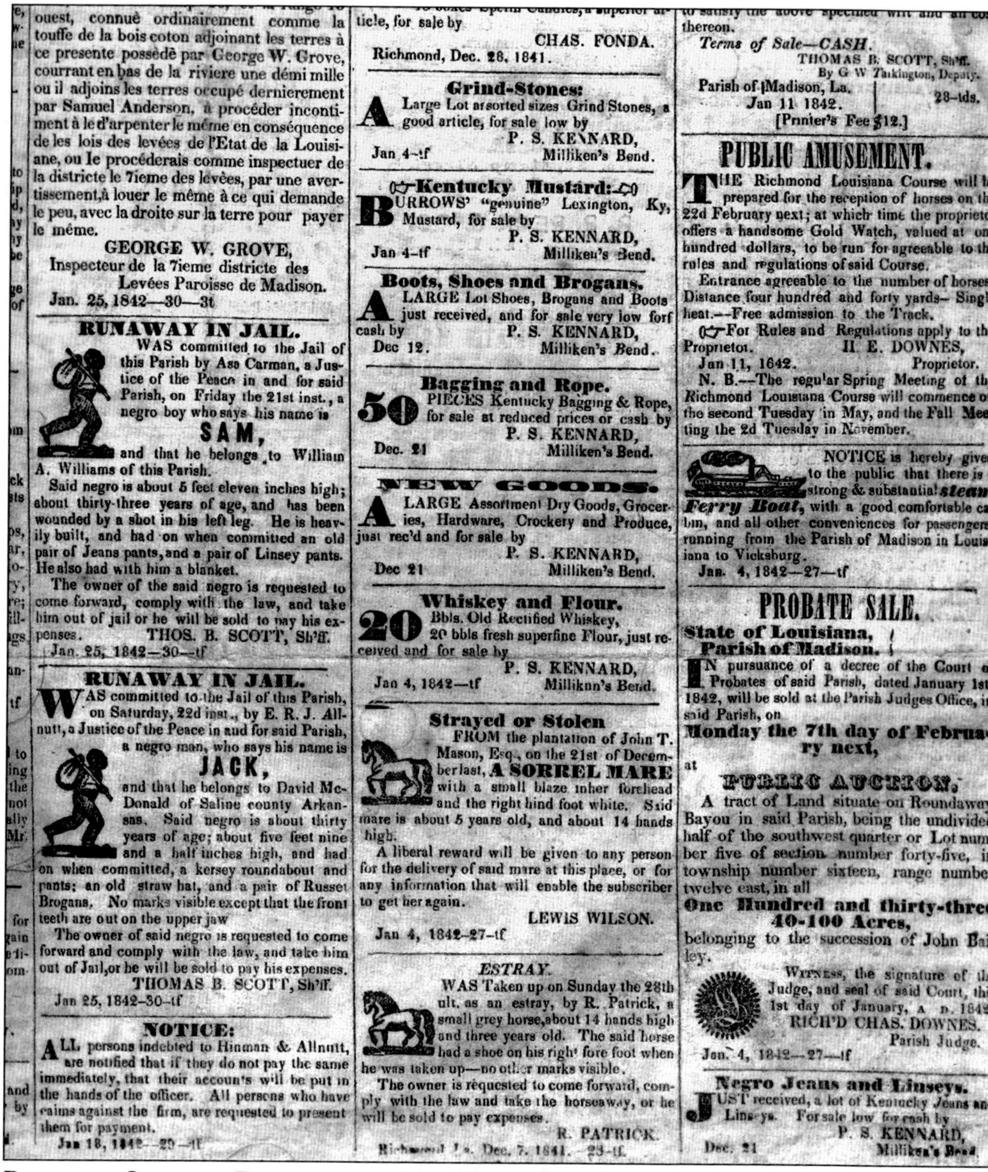

ouest, connuè ordinairement comme la touffe de la bois coton adjoinant les terres à ce presente possédè par George W. Grove, courrant en bas de la riviere une démi mille ou il adjoins les terres occupé dernierement par Samuel Anderson, à procéder incontiment à le d'arpenter le même en conséquence de les lois des levées de l'Etat de la Louisiane, ou Ie procéderais comme inspectuer de la districte le 7ieme des levées, par une avertissement, à louer le même à ce qui demande le peu, avec la droite sur la terre pour payer le même.

GEORGE W. GROVE,
Inspecteur de la 7ieme districte des Levées Paroisse de Madison.
Jan. 25, 1842—30—3t

RUNAWAY IN JAIL.

WAS committed to the Jail of this Parish by Asa Carman, a Justice of the Peace in and for said Parish, on Friday the 21st inst., a negro boy who says his name is

SAM,

and that he belongs to William A. Williams of this Parish.

Said negro is about 5 feet eleven inches high; about thirty-three years of age, and has been wounded by a shot in his left leg. He is heavily built, and had on when committed an old pair of Jeans pants, and a pair of Linsey pants. He also had with him a blanket.

The owner of the said negro is requested to come forward, comply with the law, and take him out of jail or he will be sold to pay his expenses. THOS. B. SCOTT, Sh'ff.
Jan. 25, 1842—30—tf

RUNAWAY IN JAIL.

WAS committed to the Jail of this Parish, on Saturday, 22d inst., by E. R. J. Allnutt, a Justice of the Peace in and for said Parish, a negro man, who says his name is

JACK,

and that he belongs to David McDonald of Saline county Arkansas. Said negro is about thirty years of age; about five feet nine and a half inches high, and had on when committed, a kersey roundabout and pants; an old straw hat, and a pair of Russet Brogans. No marks visible except that the front teeth are out on the upper jaw

The owner of said negro is requested to come forward and comply with the law, and take him out of Jail, or he will be sold to pay his expenses.
THOMAS B. SCOTT, Sh'ff.
Jan 25, 1842—30—tf

NOTICE:

ALL persons indebted to Hinman & Allnutt, are notified that if they do not pay the same immediately, that their accounts will be put in the hands of the officer. All persons who have claims against the firm, are requested to present them for payment.
Jan 18, 1842—29—tf

ticle, for sale by
CHAS. FONDA.
Richmond, Dec. 28, 1841.

Grind-Stones:

A Large Lot assorted sizes Grind Stones, a good article, for sale low by
P. S. KENNARD,
Jan 4—tf Milliken's Bend.

Kentucky Mustard:

BURROWS' "genuine" Lexington, Ky, Mustard, for sale by
P. S. KENNARD,
Jan 4—tf Milliken's Bend.

Boots, Shoes and Brogans.

A LARGE Lot Shoes, Brogans and Boots just received, and for sale very low for cash by P. S. KENNARD,
Dec 12. Milliken's Bend.

Bagging and Rope.

50 PIECES Kentucky Bagging & Rope, for sale at reduced prices or cash by
P. S. KENNARD,
Dec. 21 Milliken's Bend.

NEW GOODS.

A LARGE Assortment Dry Goods, Groceries, Hardware, Crockery and Produce, just rec'd and for sale by
P. S. KENNARD,
Dec 21 Milliken's Bend.

Whiskey and Flour.

20 Bbls. Old Rectified Whiskey, 20 bbls fresh superfine Flour, just received and for sale by
P. S. KENNARD,
Jan 4, 1842—tf Milliken's Bend.

Strayed or Stolen

FROM the plantation of John T. Mason, Esq., on the 21st of December last, **A SORREL MARE** with a small blaze in her forehead and the right hind foot white. Said mare is about 5 years old, and about 14 hands high.

A liberal reward will be given to any person for the delivery of said mare at this place, or for any information that will enable the subscriber to get her again.
LEWIS WILSON.
Jan 4, 1842–27–tf

ESTRAY.

WAS Taken up on Sunday the 28th ult. as an estray, by R. Patrick, a small grey horse, about 14 hands high and three years old. The said horse had a shoe on his right fore foot when he was taken up—no other marks visible.

The owner is requested to come forward, comply with the law and take the horse away, or he will be sold to pay expenses.
R. PATRICK.
Richmond, La. Dec. 7, 1841. 23-tf.

thereon.

Terms of Sale—CASH.
THOMAS B. SCOTT, Sh'ff.
By G W Tarkington, Deputy.
Parish of Madison, La.
Jan 11 1842. 28-tds.
[Printer's Fee $12.]

PUBLIC AMUSEMENT.

THE Richmond Louisiana Course will be prepared for the reception of horses on the 22d February next; at which time the proprietor offers a handsome Gold Watch, valued at one hundred dollars, to be run for agreeable to the rules and regulations of said Course.

Entrance agreeable to the number of horses. Distance four hundred and forty yards—Single heat.—Free admission to the Track.

For Rules and Regulations apply to the Proprietor. H. E. DOWNES,
Jan 11, 1842. Proprietor.

N. B.—The regular Spring Meeting of the Richmond Louisiana Course will commence on the second Tuesday in May, and the Fall Meeting the 2d Tuesday in November.

NOTICE is hereby given to the public that there is a strong & substantial *steam Ferry Boat*, with a good comfortable cabin, and all other conveniences for passengers, running from the Parish of Madison in Louisiana to Vicksburg.
Jan. 4, 1842—27—tf

PROBATE SALE.

State of Louisiana, Parish of Madison.

IN pursuance of a decree of the Court o Probates of said Parish, dated January 1st, 1842, will be sold at the Parish Judges Office, in said Parish, on

Monday the 7th day of February next,

at

PUBLIC AUCTION,

A tract of Land situate on Roundaway Bayou in said Parish, being the undivided half of the southwest quarter or Lot number five of section number forty-five, in township number sixteen, range number twelve east, in all

One Hundred and thirty-three 40-100 Acres,

belonging to the succession of John Bailey.

WITNESS, the signature of the Judge, and seal of said Court, this 1st day of January, A. D. 1842.
RICH'D CHAS. DOWNES.
Parish Judge.
Jan. 4, 1842—27—tf

Negro Jeans and Linseys.

JUST received, a lot of Kentucky Jeans and Linseys. For sale low for cash by
P. S. KENNARD,
Dec. 21 Milliken's Bend

RICHMOND COMPILER FEBRUARY 1, 1842. The *Richmond Compiler* was Madison Parish's first newspaper founded by John O. Stewart on July 6, 1841. It was a four-page weekly printed on cotton fiber paper and contained mostly excerpts from other newspapers, but had many legal notices, advertisements, parish ordinances, etc., and surprisingly little local news. The page depicted is typical and, among other things, shows runaway slaves, a Vicksburg ferry, a horse race at the "Richmond Louisiana Course," and other advertisements. The extreme top left shows a levee announcement in French. All levee announcements were presented in both English and French. (Courtesy of Frances [Boo] Bettis Eiland.)

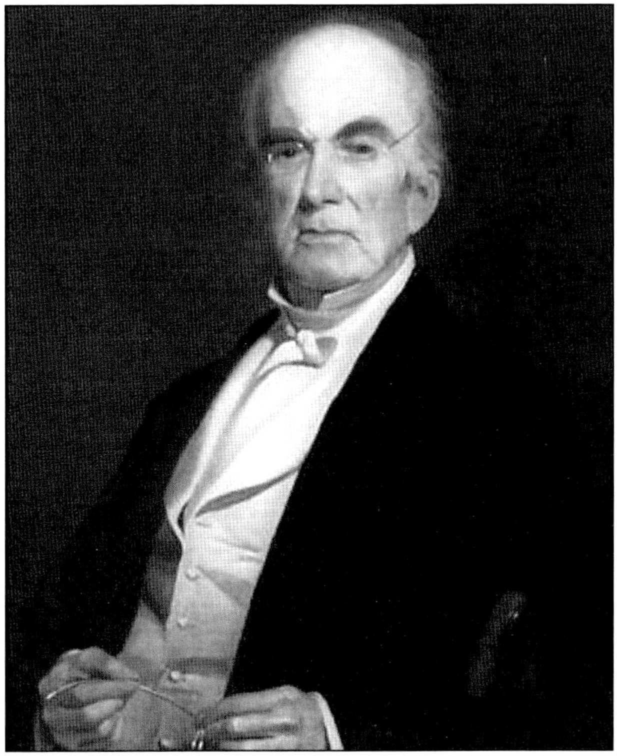

PORTRAIT OF JOHN PERKINS SR. In the 1840s "Judge" Perkins was by far the wealthiest person in Madison Parish. Perkins moved to the Deep South c. 1803. He once owned "The Briars" in Natchez, the home where some time later Jefferson Davis would marry Varina Howell. Between 1815 and 1840 he acquired several plantations in Madison Parish. His property totaled 17,500 acres, included 250 slaves, and was consolidated into "Somerset" Plantation in honor of Perkins's boyhood home in Maryland. (Courtesy of Jeremy Prescott.)

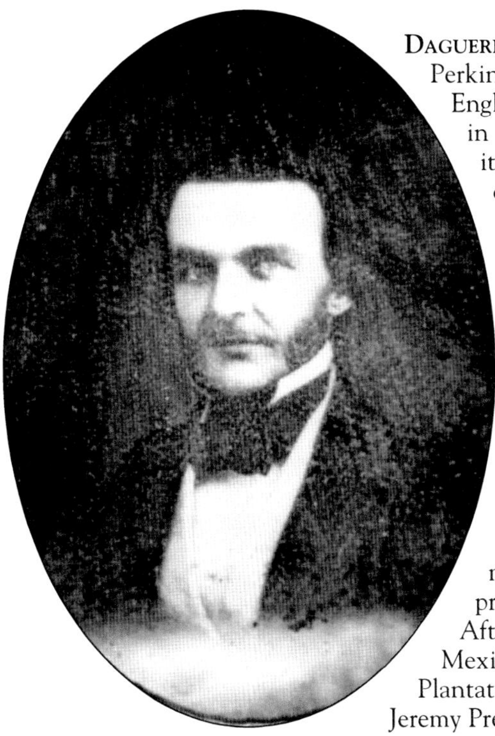

DAGUERREOTYPE OF WILLIAM PERKINS c. 1850. John Perkins's youngest son, William, was married in England but drowned returning to the United States in 1854 when his boat, the *Arctic*, sank. However it was John Perkins Jr. who was the better known of the brothers. John Perkins Jr. was a graduate of Yale and Harvard and had a New Orleans law practice until 1851, when he returned to Madison Parish to be Parish Judge. In 1861 he was made Chairman of the Committee of 15, which was to prepare the ordinance for the withdrawal of Louisiana from the Union. The ordinance Perkins's committee drew up was adopted by the convention on his motion on January 26 by a vote of 113 to 17. He later was elected to the Confederate House of Representatives from the Northeast Louisiana District. He is best known for setting fire to his magnificent home and 2,000 bales of cotton to prevent them from being used by the Yankees. After the Civil War he escaped to Cordova, Mexico, but ultimately returned to his Hapaka Plantation in Madison Parish in 1878. (Courtesy of Jeremy Prescott.)

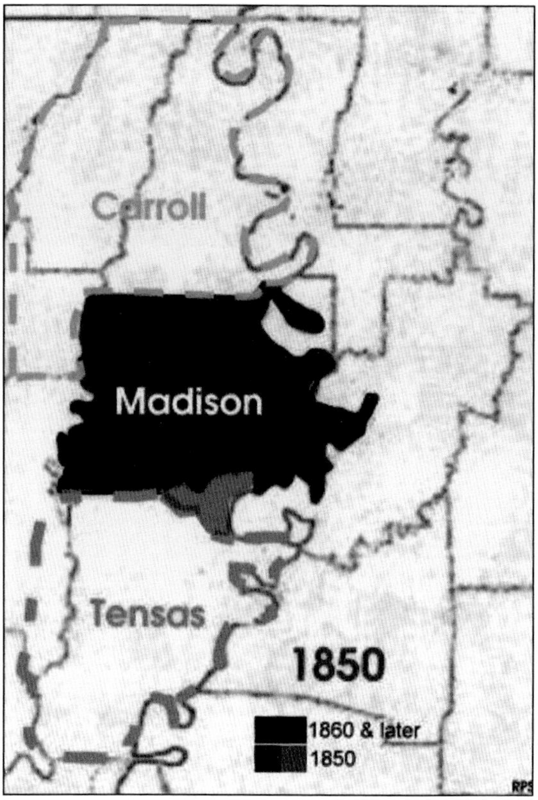

1850 Boundaries. The 1850 boundaries were essentially as depicted to the left. However in 1861 all of Madison's lands south of Bayou Vidal were given to Tensas Parish, which was formed in 1843. From this point forward Madison Parish's boundaries have remained the same.

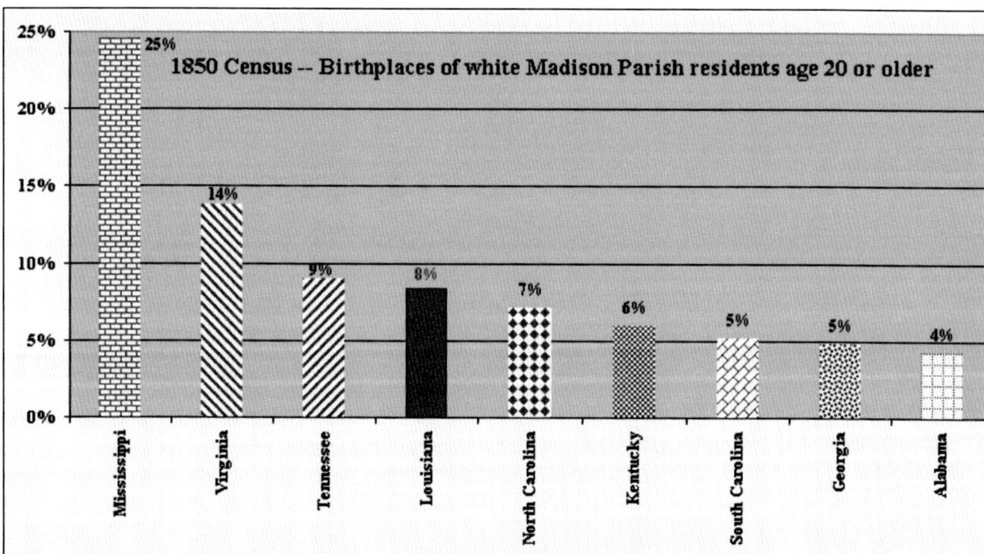

Birthplace Chart. Based upon the 1850 census, this chart shows the birthplaces of white Madison Parish residents aged 20 years or older. Note that over three times as many were born in Mississippi (25 percent) as in Louisiana (8 percent). In fact both Virginia (14 percent) and Tennessee (9 percent) were ahead of Louisiana, and North Carolina (7 percent) and Kentucky (6 percent) were close behind.

Two

THE CIVIL WAR

The Civil War in Madison Parish must have been a horrible experience. For the first two years of the war, farmers were able to continue raising crops although sales became difficult because the port of New Orleans was blockaded. By late 1863 Grant had arrived with Generals Sherman and McClernan and made his headquarters at Milliken's Bend. Soon the entire area was overrun with 30,000 or more troops scattered from Milliken's Bend to Young's Point, all gathered for the inevitable assault on Vicksburg. During this time the plantation owners' mansions were burned and pillaged by Union troops and former slaves. Many of the plantation owners sought safety in northwestern Louisiana, and some went to Texas for the duration.

Grant made two attempts to find a way around the big guns on the hills of Vicksburg. The first, Grant's Canal, was an attempt to cut a canal across Desoto Point deep and wide enough to cause the river to change its course and bypass Vicksburg. Although this turned out to be a disaster, nature did the trick on its own 23 years later in 1876, when the Mississippi flooded across DeSoto Island and cut a new channel two miles from downtown Vicksburg. The second attempt, the Duckport Canal, was not a cut-off but rather a bypass whereby a canal was cut to Walnut Bayou, which ultimately emptied into the Mississippi at New Carthage. This also failed.

On March 29, 1863, Grant's troops left Milliken's Bend and marched down the eastern side of Madison Parish, finally crossing the Mississippi River near Bruinsburg, Mississippi in late April. From there the troops went as far northeast as Jackson, then doubled back to Vicksburg, which was under siege from May 19 until it surrendered on July 4. During this time the Battle of Milliken's Bend was fought and the little town of Richmond was burned to the ground. From this point until the end of the war Madison Parish was a no-man's land occupied by thieves, Yankees, roaming bands of ex-slaves, Northern carpetbaggers, and Southern scalawags.

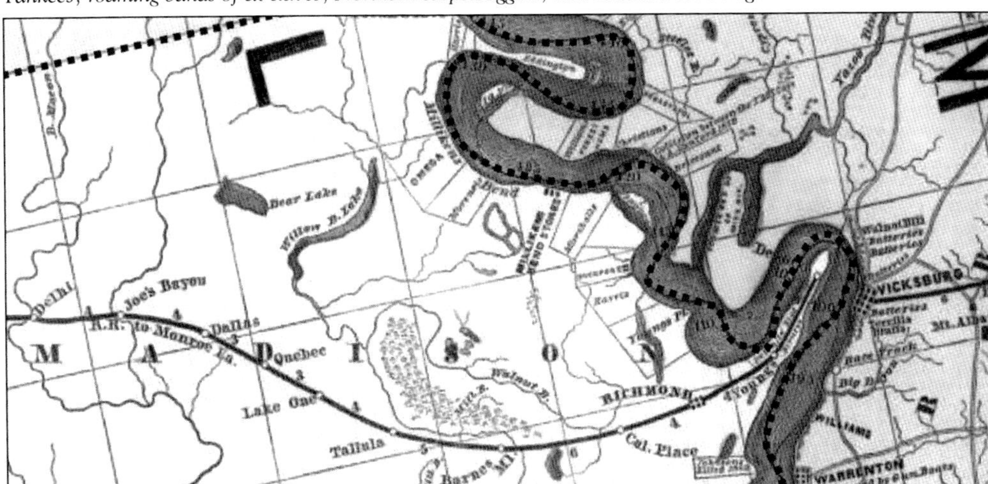

1862 MAP. This 1862 map of Madison Parish was made just before Generals Grant, Sherman, and McClernan came to Madison Parish in preparation for the Siege of Vicksburg. On the map Richmond, the Madison Parish seat, is totally misplaced and "Tallula" (Tallulah) is misspelled, but located correctly. Richmond was in reality situated about two miles south of Tallulah. The map is actually a portion of a three-map series that paralleled the Mississippi River from Cairo, Illinois to the Gulf. Madison Parish's boundaries are shown with a dotted line. (From *Library of Congress*.)

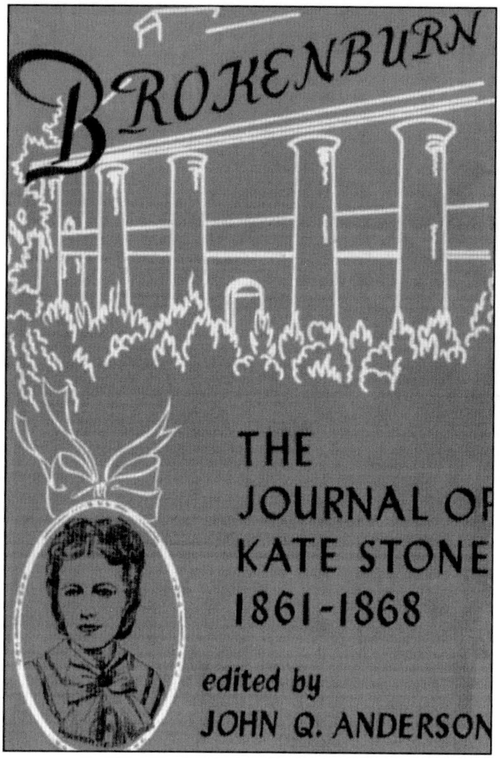

BROKENBURN. In May 1861, 20-year-old Kate Stone, daughter of a young widowed Madison Parish plantation owner, began her diary that would continue until 1868. This diary would turn out to be one of the most important chronicles of the Civil War in Louisiana in general and Madison Parish in particular. After the war Kate married Henry Bry Holmes, later sheriff of Madison Parish. In 1954 the diary was published in book form by Dr. John Q. Anderson, a Texas A & M English professor, as *Brokenburn, The Journal of Kate Stone 1861–1868*. The book was widely acclaimed and became a "Book-of-the-Month" selection.

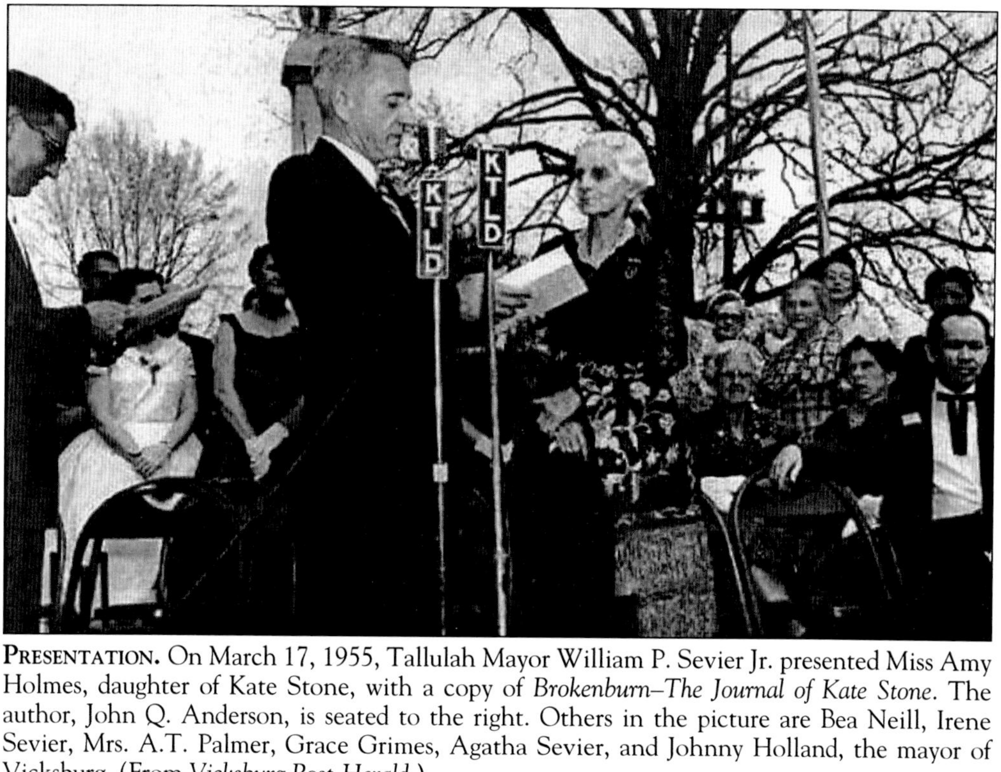

PRESENTATION. On March 17, 1955, Tallulah Mayor William P. Sevier Jr. presented Miss Amy Holmes, daughter of Kate Stone, with a copy of *Brokenburn–The Journal of Kate Stone*. The author, John Q. Anderson, is seated to the right. Others in the picture are Bea Neill, Irene Sevier, Mrs. A.T. Palmer, Grace Grimes, Agatha Sevier, and Johnny Holland, the mayor of Vicksburg. (From *Vicksburg Post-Herald*.)

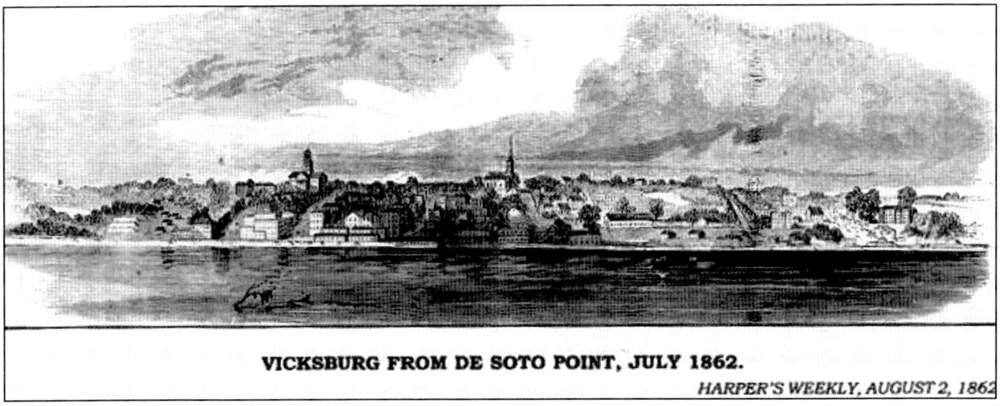

Desoto Point. This drawing shows the view from Desoto Point in Madison Parish, southeastward across the Mississippi River to Vicksburg. Because of the hairpin bend in the Mississippi River at Desoto Point, and the resultant gunfire from the hills of Vicksburg, the capture of this area was one of the Union's toughest chores and resulted in the Siege and Battle of Vicksburg. (From *Harper's Weekly*.)

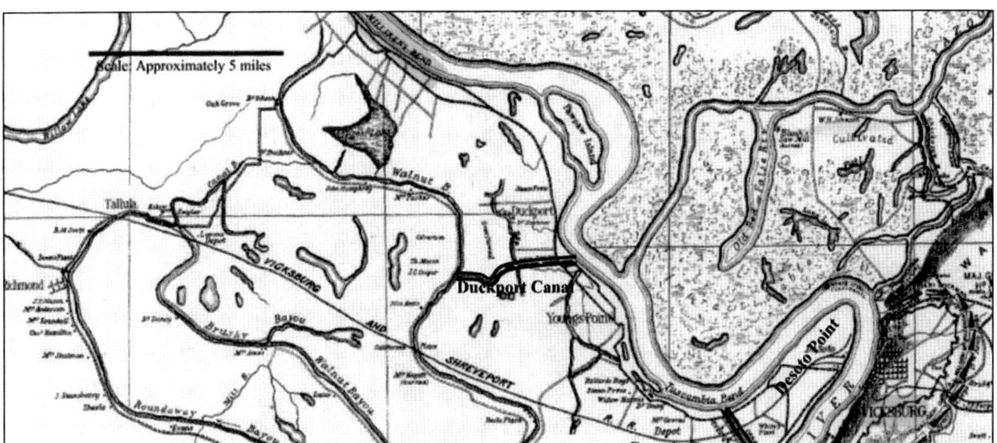

Vicksburg Area 1862. This 1862 map of the Vicksburg area shows the relation of Desoto Point to Vicksburg. The canal shown as "Grant's Canal" was at this time known as the Williams Canal. The Duckport Canal was attempted later in 1863. (From *Library of Congress*.)

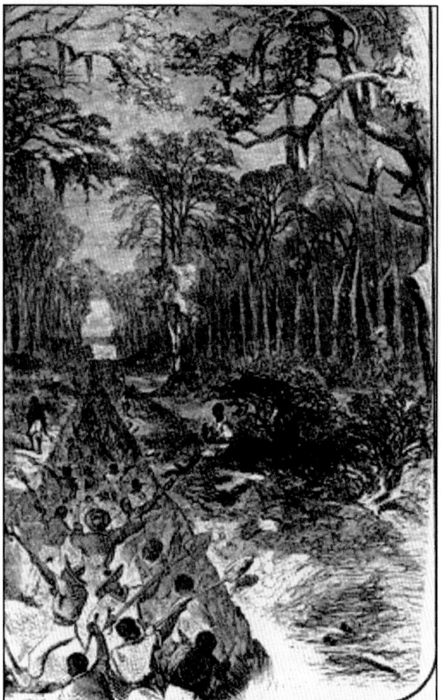

SLAVES WORKING ON THE CUTOFF.
HARPER'S WEEKLY, AUGUST 2, 1862

SLAVES WORKING ON CUTOFF. In order to divert the Mississippi River from Vicksburg, two attempts were made to cut off the hairpin turn at Desoto Point. The first was made in 1862 by the Union's commanding general at the time, Brig. Gen. Thomas Williams. To dig the canal, Williams initially commandeered as many as 1,200 slaves from the surrounding plantations. This number later expanded to 3,200 soldiers and slaves. The canal had to be dug under miserable conditions. In addition to occasional gunfire from the Confederates, the humidity and temperature were unbearable, and the mosquitoes inflicted excruciating pain and disease on slaves and soldiers alike. Rations were inadequate and clean drinking water was unavailable. Sickness finally reduced the force of 3,200 to 700. To make matters worse, the River continued to fall faster than the canal could be dug. The Williams's Canal, later to be reopened as Grant's Canal, was a failure. (From *Harper's Weekly*.)

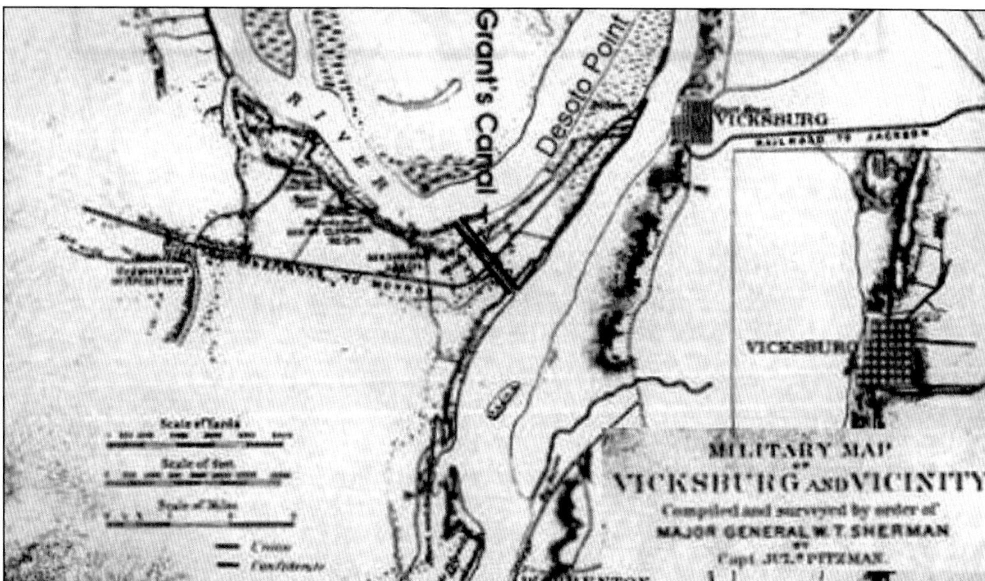

GRANT'S CANAL. In January 1863, Grant began an attempt to reopen and enlarge the canal started by Williams because no attempt had been made by the Confederates to fill it in. Since water from the river had already entered about 75 yards into the upper canal, and water stood in pools throughout the canal's length, an attempt was made to broaden it in hopes that natural erosion would deepen it. (From *Library of Congress*.)

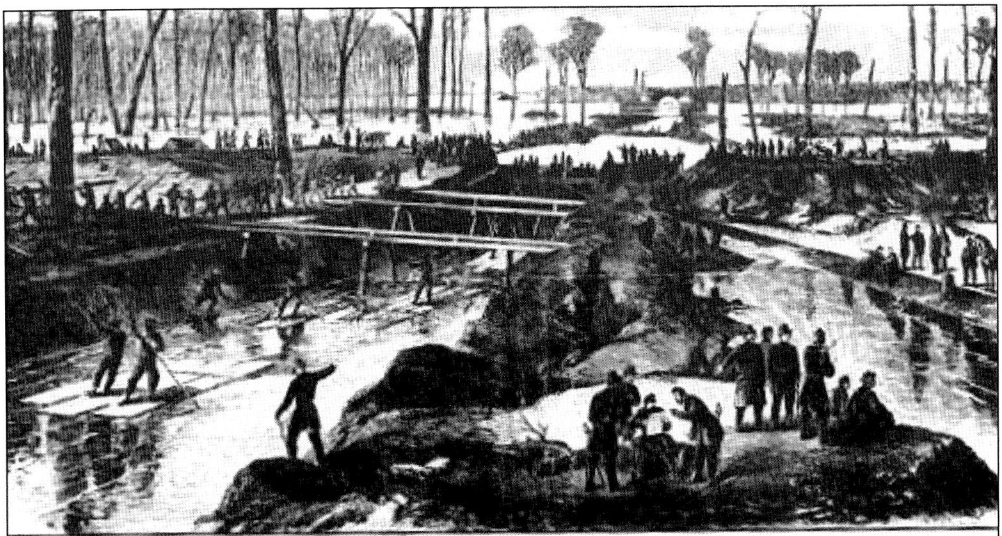

HEAD OF CUTOFF SHOWING CLOSURE.

HEAD OF CUTOFF. By February the canal was finally dammed with closures at each end so it could be drained and more easily deepened. At this point the river began to rise faster than the workers could handle it, and soldiers and slaves worked around the clock to keep the project from failing. Of the 35,000 troops stationed in the area, only about 3,000 worked on the canal. Torrential spring rains and inoperative pumps caused the area (including the campsites) to flood, preventing the soldiers from working on the canal for all but two hours a day. (From *Frank Leslie's Illustrated.*)

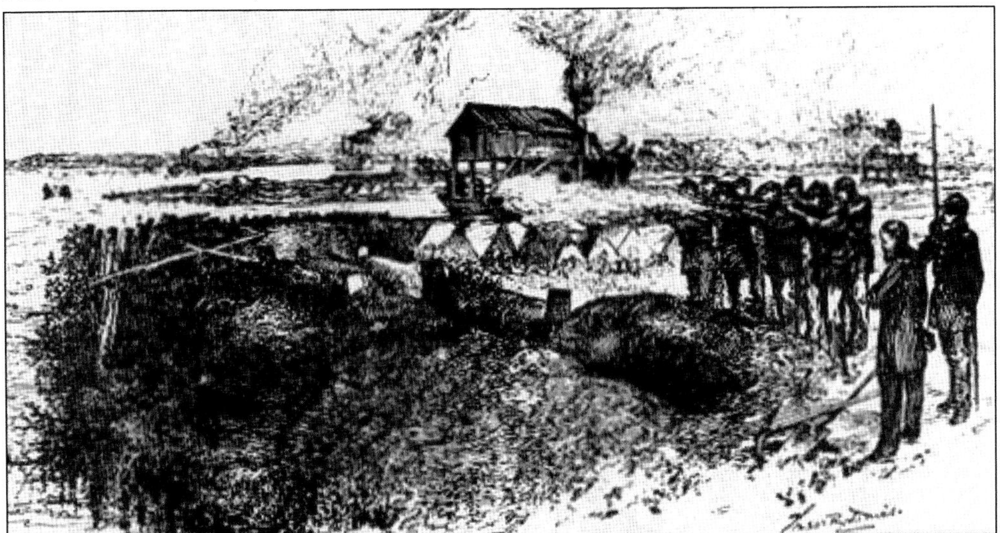

FUNERAL ON THE LEVEE WITH THE MISSISSIPPI RIVER, CANAL AND DREDGES IN THE BACKGROUND.

LEVEE FUNERAL. As before, miserable conditions and sickness, especially diarrhea, claimed their toll. Of the total troops in the area, about 85 died each day from disease and were usually buried in levees—the only high ground available. (From *Battles and Leaders.*)

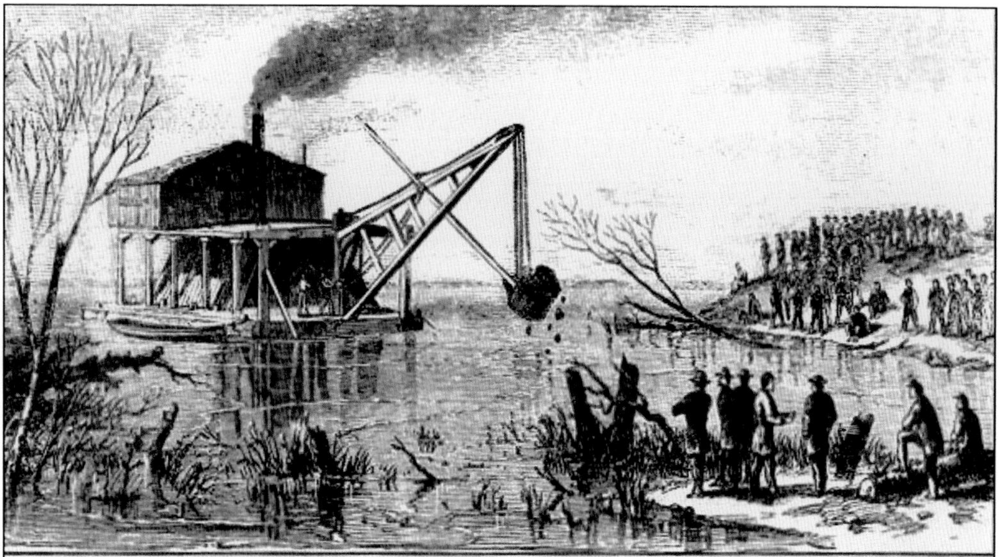

THE DIPPER DREDGE *SAMPSON* WORKING ON THE ENTRANCE TO THE CANAL.
FRANK LESLIE'S, APRIL 4, 1863

DIPPER DREDGE. On March 1, much-needed dredges arrived to help with the cleanout and digging tasks. Unfortunately for the Union, the upper dam gave way on March 5, and the area again flooded to the point that several of the campsites had to be evacuated to Milliken's Bend. After the crevasse was plugged with confiscated timbers ripped from buildings on local plantations, dredges resumed their cleanout work, and stumps were blasted out with black powder. By March 19, accurate shelling from Confederate batteries forced the barges to work only at night. The dredges were withdrawn on March 24, and Grant's Canal was pronounced a failure. (From *Frank Leslie's Illustrated*.)

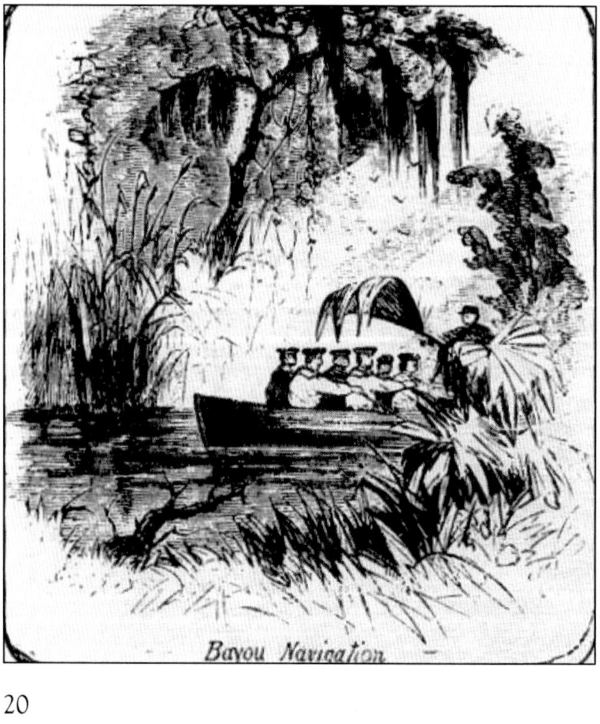

WALNUT BAYOU. Grant had his troops reconnoiter Walnut Bayou and ordered a canal cut at Duckport from it to the Mississippi. If successful, this would allow supply boats to travel from the Mississippi River through the canal and down Walnut Bayou, then back to the Mississippi at New Carthage, 20 miles south of Vicksburg. (From *Harper's Weekly*.)

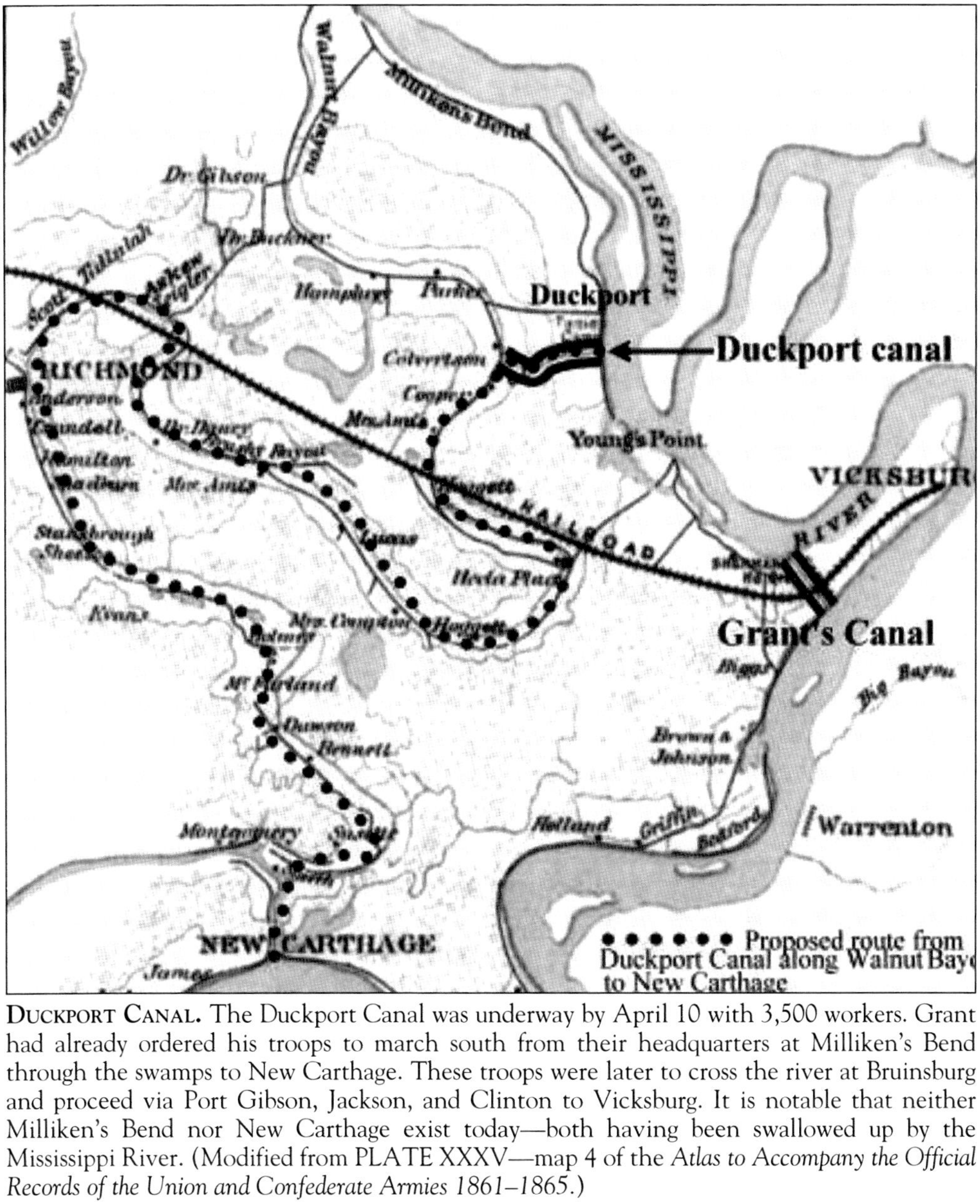

DUCKPORT CANAL. The Duckport Canal was underway by April 10 with 3,500 workers. Grant had already ordered his troops to march south from their headquarters at Milliken's Bend through the swamps to New Carthage. These troops were later to cross the river at Bruinsburg and proceed via Port Gibson, Jackson, and Clinton to Vicksburg. It is notable that neither Milliken's Bend nor New Carthage exist today—both having been swallowed up by the Mississippi River. (Modified from PLATE XXXV—map 4 of the *Atlas to Accompany the Official Records of the Union and Confederate Armies 1861–1865.*)

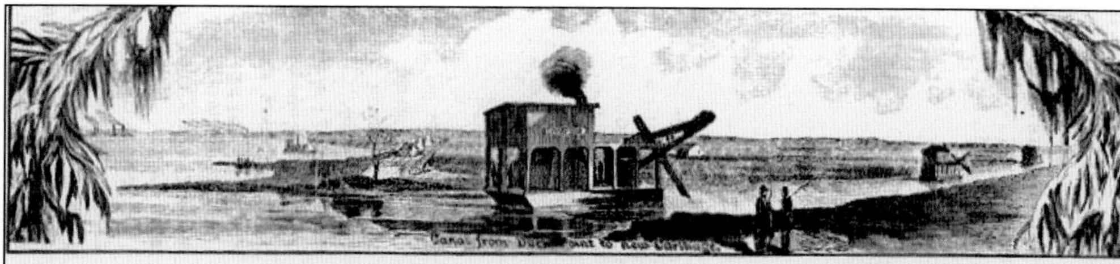

THREE DIPPER DREDGES WORKING ON THE DUCKPORT CANAL.

HARPER'S WEEKLY, MAY 16, 1863

DIPPER DREDGES AT DUCKPORT. By April 22, at least four floating dipper dredges were working on the canal. (From *Harper's Weekly*.)

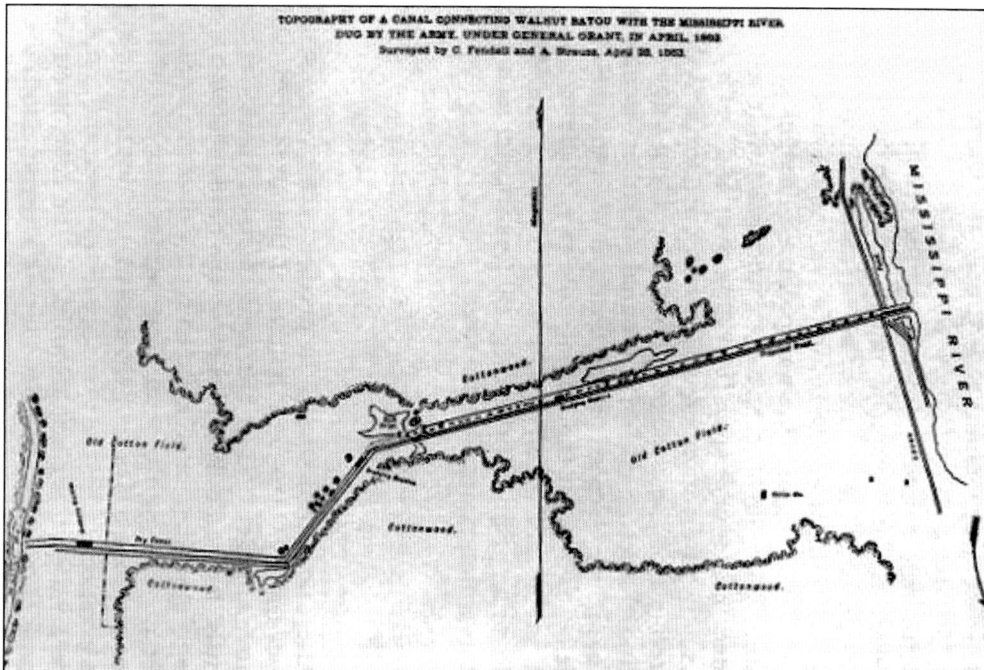

MAP OF DUCKPORT CANAL.

ORN, 24:59

DUCKPORT CANAL DETAIL. By the end of April, it was apparent that the Duckport Canal was not to be. Again, the river fell rapidly to the point that the dredges could not keep up with it. With the water depth in the canal reduced to less than a foot in some places, the boats that were running the route at the time were trapped and grounded between Duckport and New Carthage. They were abandoned and left to decay in the mud. As were the other canal projects, this project was discarded. Ironically, nature later accomplished what the Yankee troops could not when on April 26, 1876, the Mississippi flooded across DeSoto Island and cut a new channel two miles from downtown Vicksburg. What is left of Grant's Canal is now part of the Vicksburg National Military Park. (From *ORN*.)

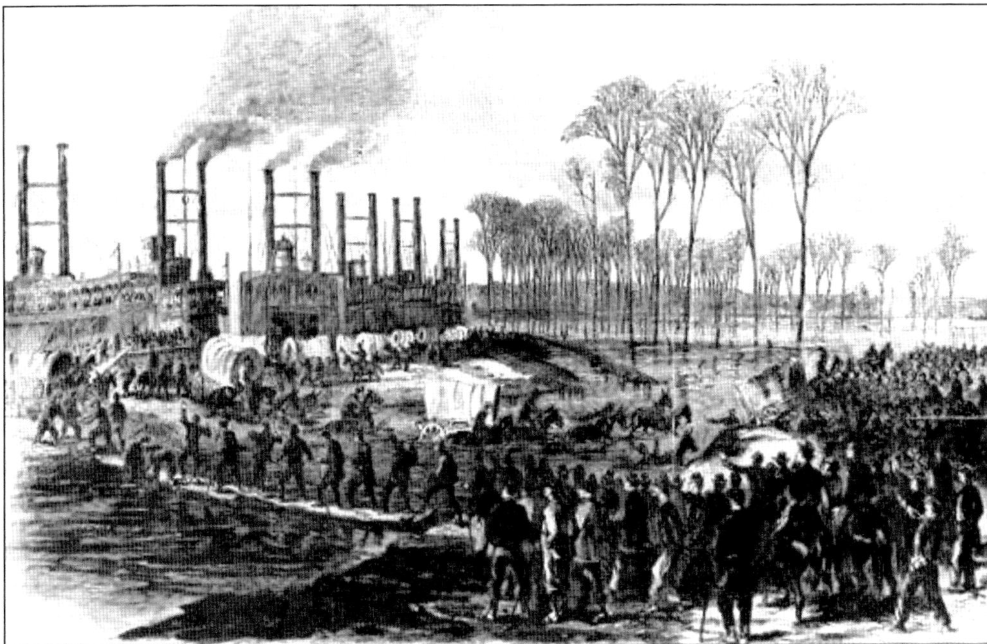

TROOPS LANDING AT YOUNG'S POINT.

Troops Landing at Young's Point. Troops landed at Young's Point and Duckport to prepare to join Grant's circuitous march through Madison Parish to Vicksburg. (From *Frank Leslie's Illustrated.*)

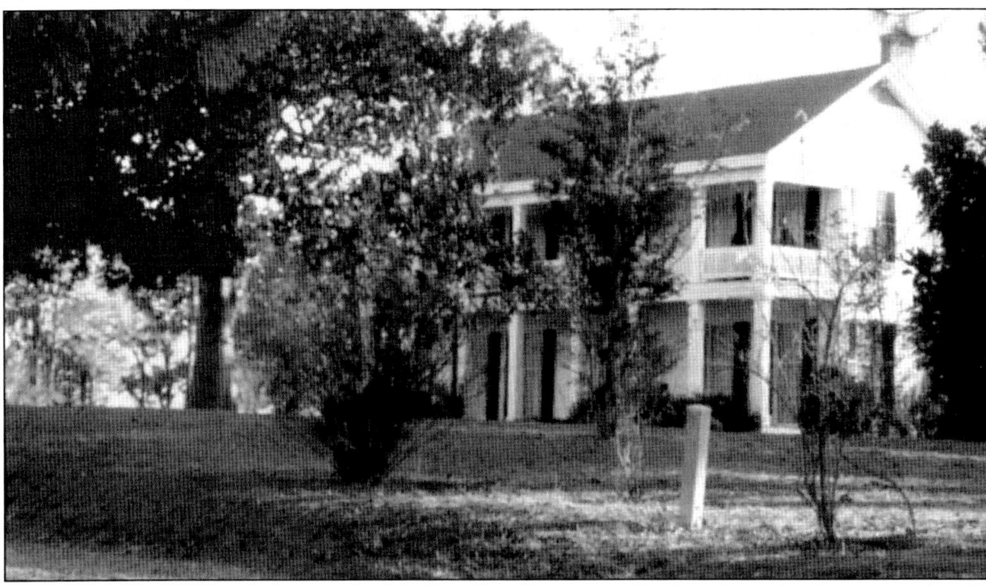

Crescent Plantation. The Crescent Plantation house was built in 1832 by the Barnes family, and was owned by Dr. David Dancy during the Civil War. Mrs. Jost Halter of Zurich, Switzerland currently owns the house, which is one of the three or four buildings in Madison Parish that was not burned to the ground by Union troops. This picture was taken in 1989. (Courtesy of Barbara P. Sevier.)

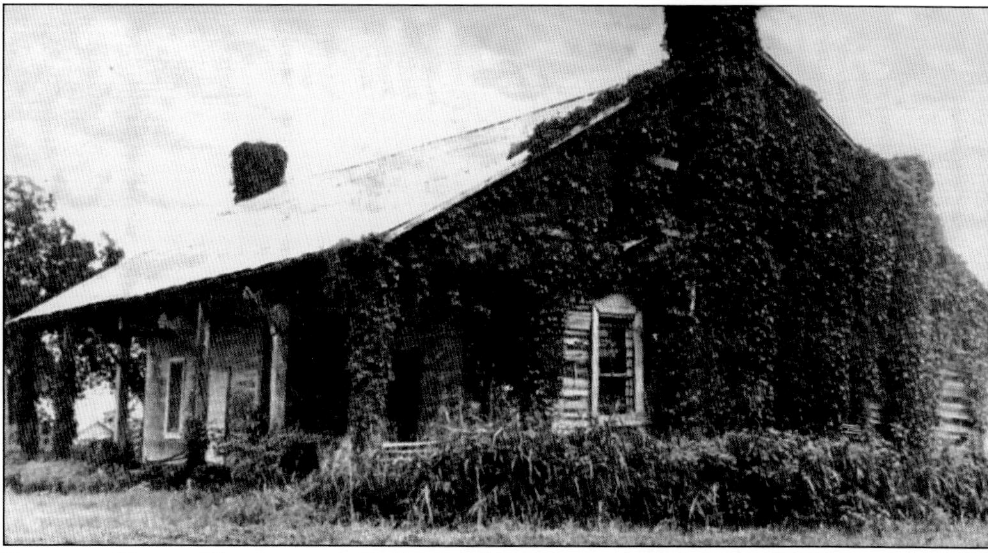

DALKEITH HOUSE. This house on Dalkeith Plantation is another of the few houses to survive the Civil War, during which its attic was a hospital and the ground floor served as a federal prison. The original bars are still on the windows. (Courtesy of Madison Historical Society.)

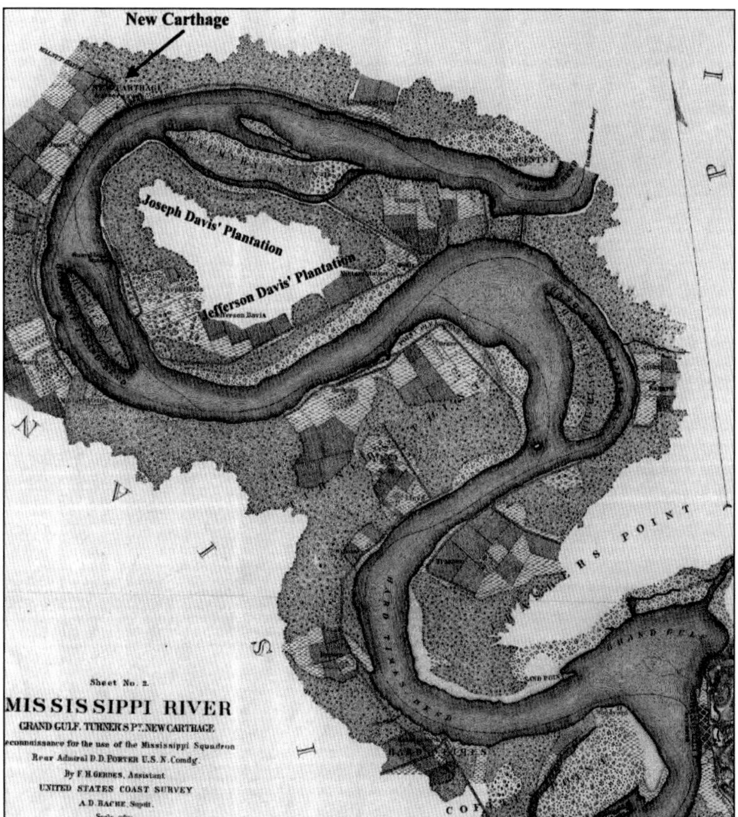

NEW CARTHAGE AREA. A close-up of the New Carthage area shows that it was right across the Mississippi River from Joseph and Jefferson Davis's plantations. Since Jefferson Davis was president of the Confederacy, it is obvious why New Carthage was the primary river crossing point. (From *Library of Congress*.)

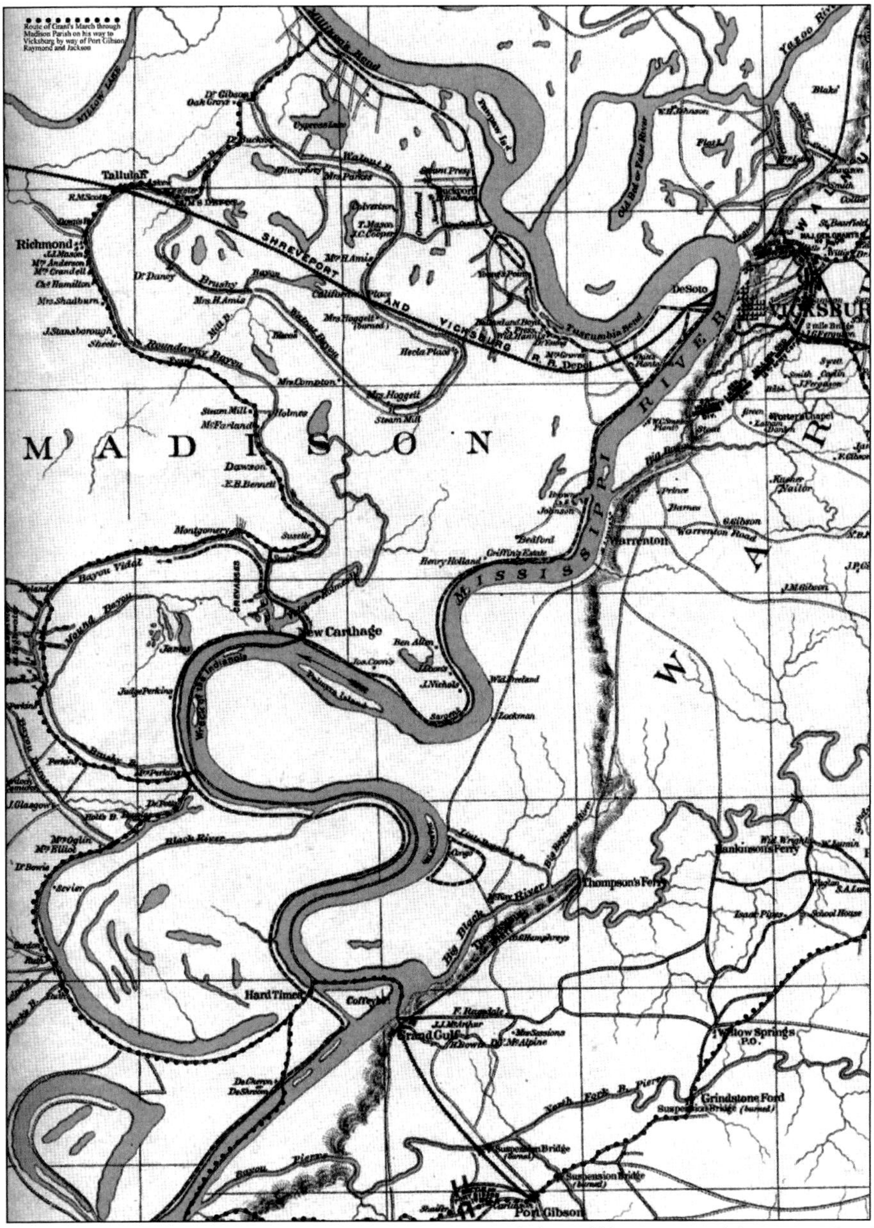

Grant's March. On March 31, 1863, Grant's armies left Milliken's Bend for New Carthage, a distance of 37 miles, where he intended to cross the Mississippi River. After almost a month of marching along muddy roads and mosquito-infested swamps, New Carthage was reached. Floodwaters there made a crossing impossible, however, and Hard Times Landing was chosen as a substitute. On April 29, the troops were put aboard steamers and barges at Hard Times and attempted to land across the river at Grand Gulf. However, Confederate gun batteries there forced the Union troops to retreat. The next day the troops re-boarded the transports and crossed the river six miles below Grand Gulf at Bruinsburg. From there they marched on, northeast towards Port Gibson, Raymond, Jackson, and west towards Vicksburg, which was under siege from May 19 until its surrender on July 4. (Modified from Plate XXXVI, map 1 of the *Atlas to Accompany the Official Records of the Union and Confederate Armies 1861–1865*.)

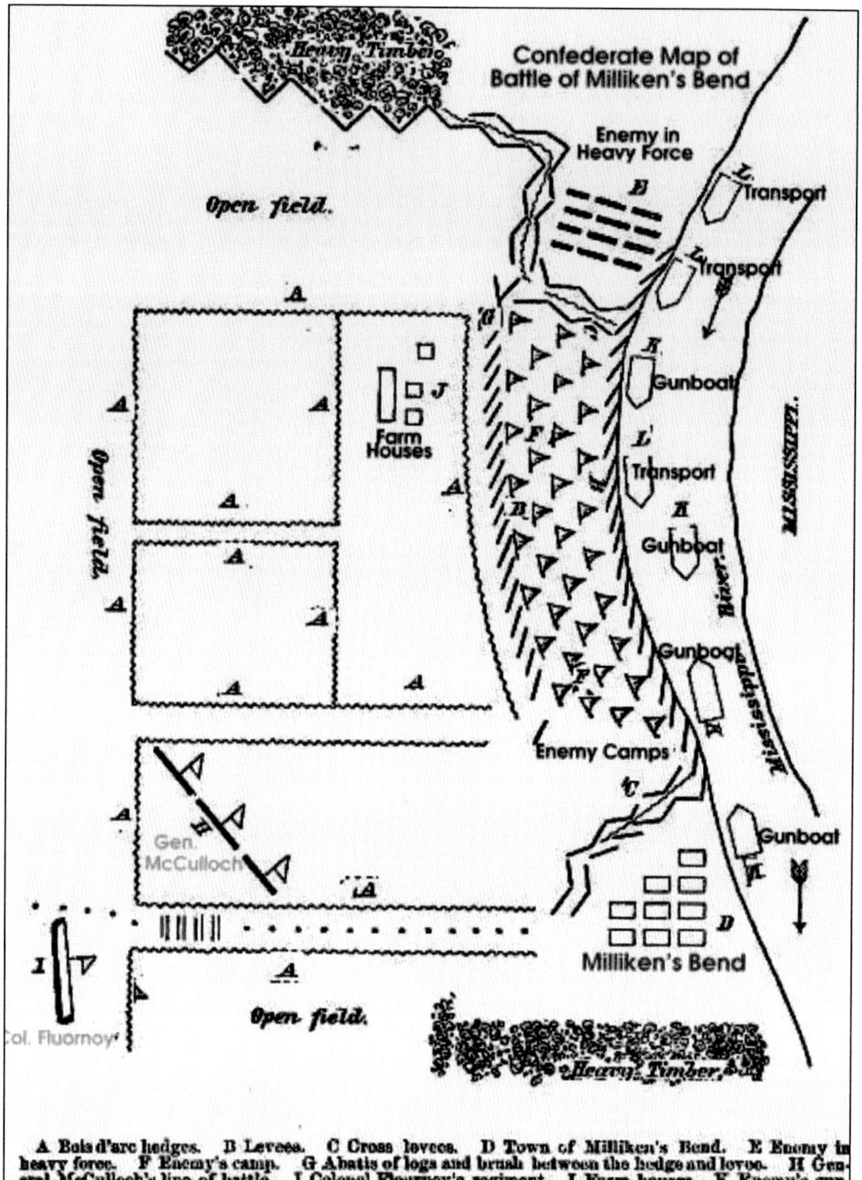

BATTLE OF MILLIKEN'S BEND. The Confederates requested action on the Louisiana side of the river to take some pressure off of Vicksburg. On June 7, 1863, one of the bloodiest, though little publicized, battles of the Civil War—the Battle of Milliken's Bend—occurred. This was the first important battle of the war where black troops fought under fire. Most of the black troops were inexperienced and poorly trained, and some had just joined the Union forces. Although the fighting (which was sometimes hand-to-hand) only lasted a short time, both sides reported a total of almost 1000 casualties. It has been said that if the federal gunboats had not come into action, the entire Union camp at Milliken's Bend would have been pushed into the river. In retribution the Union troops attacked the town of Richmond on June 15 and burned it to the ground. It was never rebuilt. (Modified from *The War of the Rebellion: a Compilation of the Official Records of the Union and Confederate Armies.*)

GEN. W.T. SHERMAN'S 1863 MILITARY MAP OF THE MADISON PARISH–VICKSBURG AREA. (From PLATE XXXVII – map 4 of the *Atlas to Accompany the Official Records of the Union and Confederate Armies 1861–1865.*)

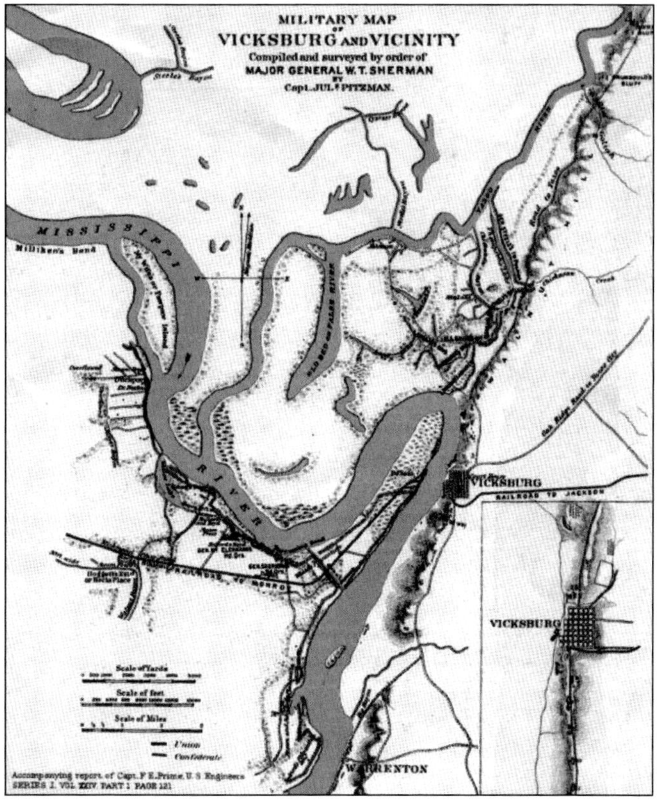

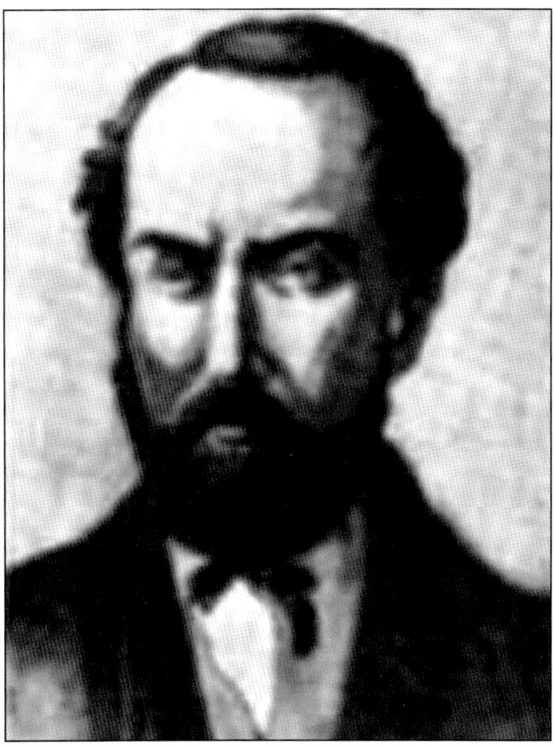

DR. HENRY WIRZ. In 1860, Dr. Henry Wirz was a 35-year-old physician from Switzerland living in Milliken's Bend. During the Civil War he was assigned on March 27, 1864 to be commandant of the Confederate prisoner-of-war camp at Andersonville in South Carolina. (From *Library of Congress.*)

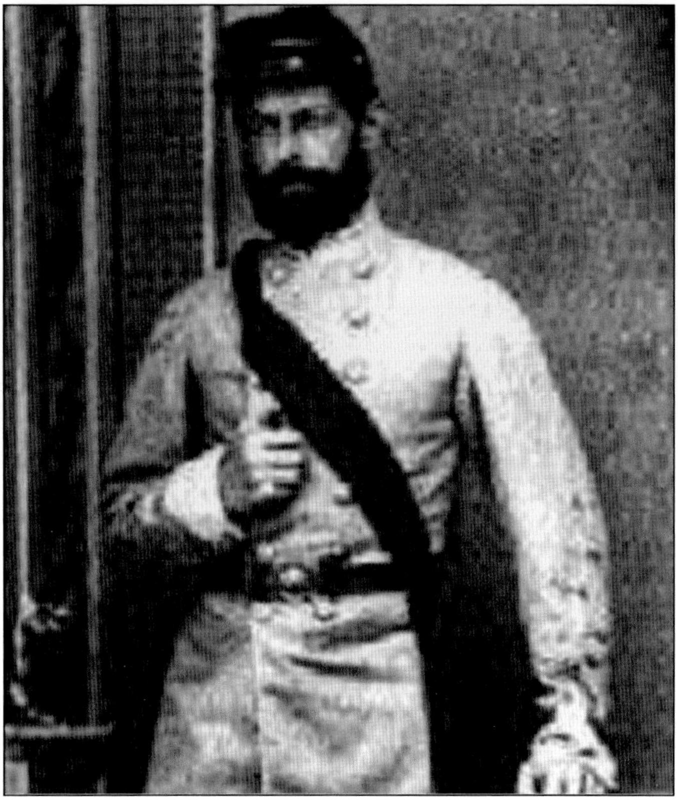

Wirz in Uniform. When arrested on May 7, 1865, Wirz was the only remaining member of the Confederate staff at the prison. Brig. Gen. John Winder, commander of Confederate prisons east of the Mississippi and Wirz's superior at Andersonville, died of a heart attack the previous February. Because of the atrocious conditions at Andersonville (not all the fault of Wirz) he was unfairly sentenced to hang as a war criminal—the only such war criminal put to death by the Union. (From *Library of Congress.*)

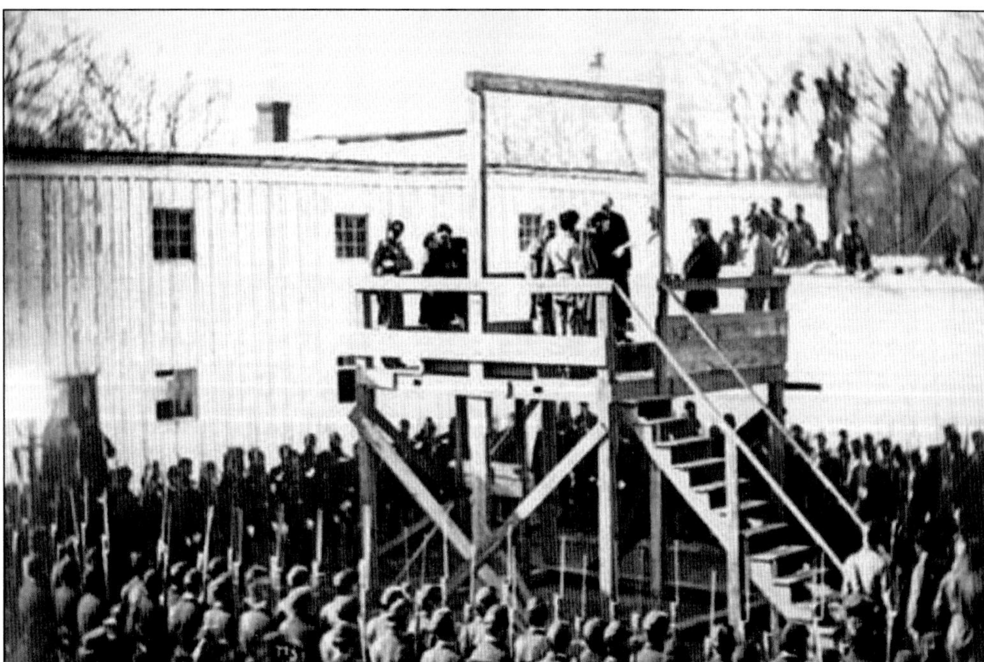

The Hanging of Dr. Wirz. Here Dr. Wirz is read his death warrant just before he was hanged on November 10, 1865. (Alexander Gardner photograph from *Library of Congress.*)

Three

Reconstruction

Following the Civil War, former residents began trickling back from as far away as Texas. Many had buried their most prized possessions, but little was ever found. The houses and barns had been burned, the livestock confiscated, and the plantations were in shambles. Those who had borrowed money to buy land and slaves were forced to default on their loans. Yankee "carpetbaggers," with the consent of the Federal Government, had taken possession of most of the plantations by Federal lease as early as 1864. They had extracted everything they could from the land, and then left it in ruins.

The freed slaves began to gain power even though many of them suffered more during this time than they did before the war. With the second largest pre-war black population in the state (88 percent), Madison Parish was destined for a period of black leadership and rule. An example of this is the Presidential election of 1868 when the Republican Grant, who had treated the white plantation owners shabbily during the war, received 1,453 votes while his Democratic opponent received only 163. During this time practically all of Madison Parish's elected officials were black, much to the consternation of whites who were having a hard time returning their property to full production because of taxation, bollworms, and overflows—partly due to the Union army's destruction of the levees. They were also subject to pillaging bands of former slaves and dishonest carpetbaggers.

In the late 1860s the Ku Klux Klan formed to combat the new social order that had taken hold. By 1874 the Democrats gradually resumed some of the power they had before the war, sometimes by running black candidates of their own. In 1877 president Rutherford B. Hayes withdrew the Federal troops, and racial segregation once again was a way of life. Although by 1884 there were still some blacks running for office, armed whites finally reduced the black vote to the point that there were no registered black voters. This stayed in effect until the 1960s.

One of the most colorful figures of the post-Civil War period was Brig. Gen. Elias Smith Dennis of Illinois, former commanding general of the District of Northeast Louisiana and Commandant of the Union Troops during the Battle of Milliken's Bend, who returned to live on the land he conquered. Elias S. Dennis was born in Newburgh, New York on December 4, 1812 and grew up on Long Island. Around 1836 he migrated to Carlyle, Illinois, and married Mary D. Slade, who was the widow of Charles Slade, founder of Carlyle and U.S. Congressman at time of his death. One of Dennis's stepsons was the legendary Jack Slade, a notorious western gunslinger and self-appointed vigilante whose exploits were described by several authors including Mark Twain in his book Roughing It. From 1842 to 1844, Dennis served in the Illinois House of Representatives. During 1846 to1848 he served as State Senator in Illinois. In 1857 he was appointed by President Buchanan to serve as United States Marshal of Kansas. On August 28, 1861 he was mustered into the service and named Lieutenant Colonel in the 30th Illinois Infantry. In February 1862 he participated in the capture of Fort Donelson, Tennessee. He was later promoted to Colonel on May 1, 1862 and to Brigadier General on November 29, 1862. In April 1863 he fought in the Battle of Port Gibson, Mississippi and in May 1863, the Battle of Raymond, Mississippi. Later in May 1863 he was placed in command of the District of Northeast Louisiana.

Although he must have been hated at first, General Dennis proved to the Madison Parish populace that he was not a carpetbagger and gained their confidence when he was elected Parish Judge in 1874 and Sheriff in 1880. He ultimately became one of the most prominent of Madison Parish's Reconstruction politicians. At some point Dennis became much admired by one of Madison Parish's plantation-owning widows who ultimately willed her plantation to him. Unfortunately, the will proved to be defective and Dennis received nothing from it when she died. On June 7, 1875, without divorcing his wife in Illinois, Elias married Mrs. Mary A. McFarland, another Madison Parish land-owning widow. Madison Parish tax rolls for 1879, 1881, and 1885 show that Mrs. Mary A. Dennis owned 757 acres. In 1879 and 1881 the property was described as "McFarland Place," but in 1885 it was called "Oak Ridge" Plantation. The property, which was located along Roundaway Bayou about seven miles southeast of Tallulah, was not listed in the 1890 tax rolls. Dennis moved back to Carlyle in 1887 and died there of pneumonia, almost in anonymity, at 10 a.m. on December 17, 1894.

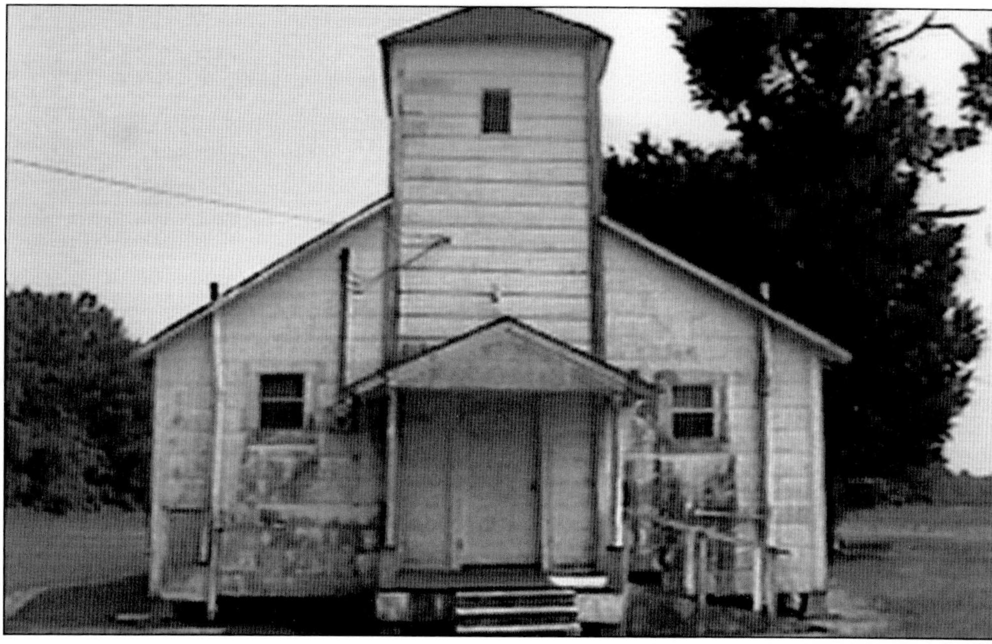

Mount Zion Church. The Mount Zion Church, a black Baptist Church built in 1865, was the oldest church in Madison Parish. Unfortunately vandals burned it to the ground in 1999, along with a white church in the same vicinity. This photograph was taken in 1998. (Courtesy of William R. Sevier.)

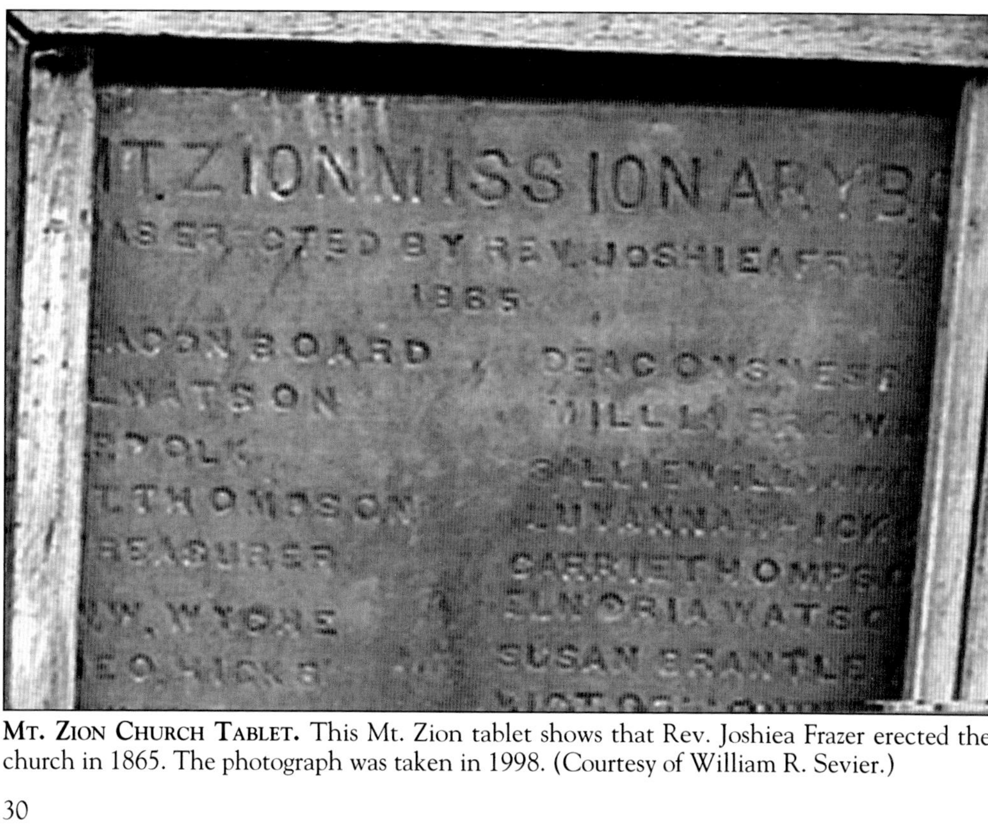

Mt. Zion Church Tablet. This Mt. Zion tablet shows that Rev. Joshiea Frazer erected the church in 1865. The photograph was taken in 1998. (Courtesy of William R. Sevier.)

COL. FRIEND LEMON MAXWELL. Maxwell first came to Madison Parish during the Civil War as the commander of the 59th Indiana Regiment. He was born in Sullivan County, Indiana in 1839. After the Civil War he came back to Louisiana and bought property in Tensas Parish, but lost it all due to flooding. In the 1870s he moved to Madison Parish where he and his brother Edward bought Killarney, Mound, California, and Mexico plantations. Maxwell was a member of the 1898 Louisiana Constitutional Convention and served as first president of the North Louisiana Levee Board, now called the Fifth District Levee Board. By the time of his death in 1915 he owned about 12,000 acres near Mound. (Courtesy of Martha Yerger André.)

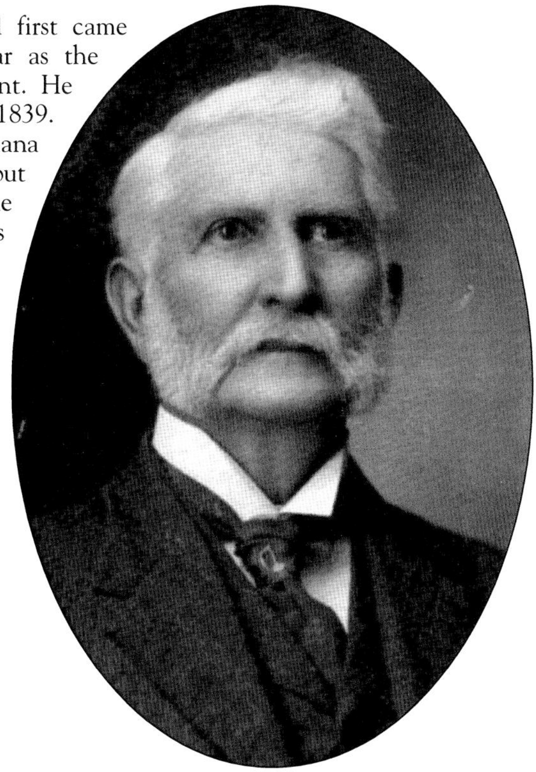

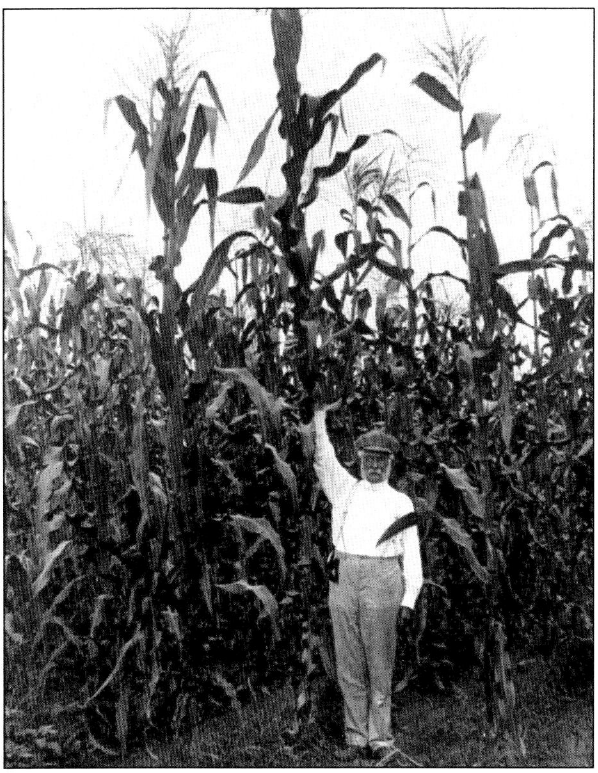

F.L. MAXWELL IN HIS CORN FIELD. Tall corn or tall tale? (Courtesy of Jeanne Yerger.)

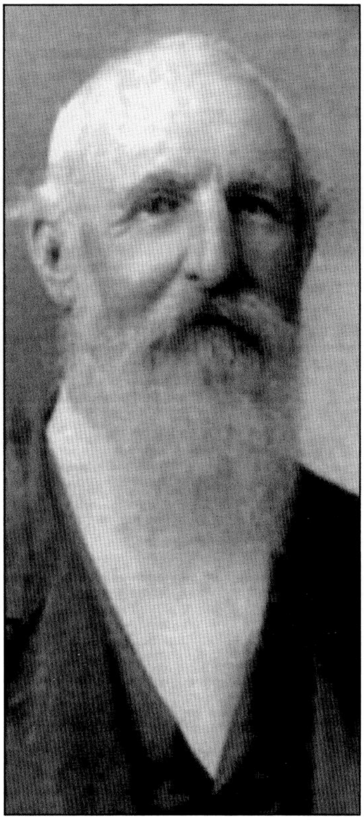

Green Livingston Boney. Boney was born in 1829 in Clarke County, Alabama. He came to Madison Parish in 1858 where he managed the Culverson property near Duckport and was involved in levee contracting. In 1862 he entered the army in Company K of Abbey's Battery of the First Mississippi artillery. He served until the close of the war and was in the battle of Plain's Store and the siege of Port Hudson, Louisiana, where he was captured. He then escaped, was recaptured at Blakely, taken prisoner, and sent to Ship Island, where he was kept prisoner until the close of the war. He was also in the siege of Port Hudson, and was once wounded by a spent minie ball. After the war, Boney, having lost nearly everything, returned to Madison Parish to manage a plantation and ultimately resume his position as a prosperous Madison Parish planter. By January 1870 he had purchased Duckport Plantation and owned several others in the vicinity (including Culverson), together with several thousand acres on Big Black Island in Tensas Parish. By 1881, in addition to the Big Black Island property, he owned almost 4,000 acres in Madison Parish—all rich, alluvial lands along the Mississippi River. In 1877, he was appointed as a police juror of the Third Ward of Madison Parish and served one term. In 1870 he was appointed postmaster at Duckport; he was later police juror of the Second Ward. (Courtesy of Sherrill Sevier Pirone.)

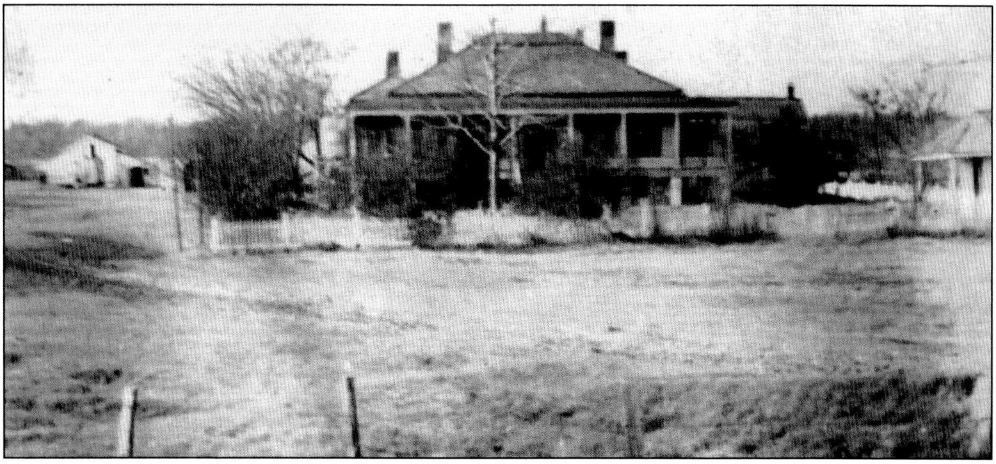

Boney Home at Duckport. G.L. Boney very much admired Jefferson Davis; his home at Duckport, built of cypress timber cut on the plantation, was a copy of Davis's home "Beauvoir" on the Mississippi coast near Biloxi. Since the Mississippi River was only a few hundred yards away, the Boney home was built seven feet off the ground to protect it from flooding. It has been said that steamboats on the river could be seen from the front porch. Unfortunately, the river washed away the home site and most of the land as it eroded its way westward. In fact the original site of the home is now on the east side of the river. It was common practice in the late 19th and early 20th centuries for children of plantation owners to be tutored at home; the Boney home was no exception. The small building to the right was the "school house." There were no high schools in Madison Parish at this time. (Courtesy of Dorothy Sevier Elliott.)

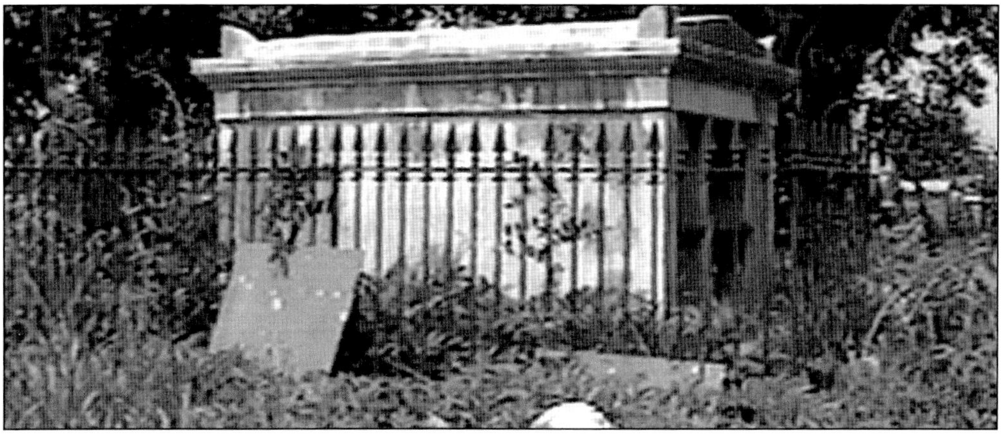

Amis Mausoleum. Henrietta Amis was a wealthy widowed plantation owner. In 1860 the value of Mrs. Amis's property at Fortune's Fork was $350,000. After the Civil War in 1870 the same property was worth only $50,000. Henrietta died in the early 1880s and vandals have since trashed the mausoleum. Mrs. Amis inadvertently played an important part in the naming of Tallulah. In the late 1850s an east-west railroad was to be built through the parish. The story is that Henrietta charmed the railroad engineer into rerouting the railroad through her property and not through Richmond, where it was originally proposed. After the railroad was built and her property value increased, Henrietta supposedly lost interest in the engineer, and he named the watering station (where the railroad crossed Brushy Bayou) Tallulah in honor of a former sweetheart in Georgia. Tallulah has long since become the parish seat and the dominant city in the parish. (Courtesy of William R. Sevier.)

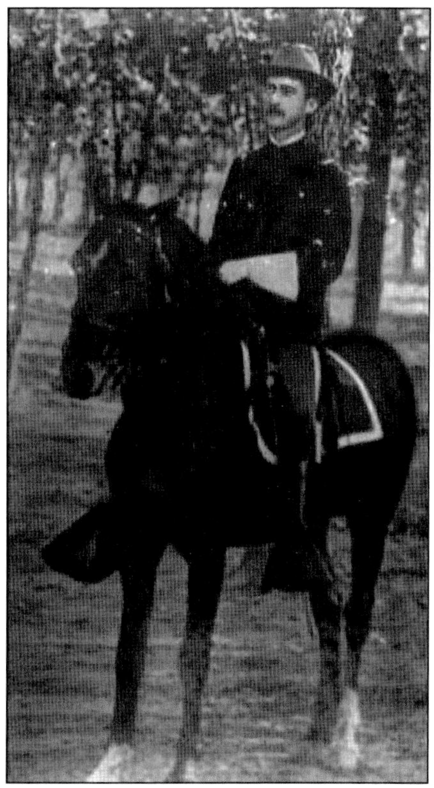

Capt. George S. Yerger Sr. Shown in his Spanish-American War uniform, Yerger was a native of Mississippi. He moved to Madison Parish after the Spanish-American War and became involved in a land partnership with Col. F. L. Maxwell. When Maxwell died in 1915 they each owned about 12,000 acres. Since Yerger had married Maxwell's daughter, Ednah Pearl, in 1901 he now controlled about 24,000 acres—the largest single-owner plantation in the parish. Yerger devoted his entire effort to only cotton, and when the boll weevil and lower prices made the crop uneconomical, he founded the Mound Colony in the late 1920s as an attempt to diversify. He also did this by selling 40 160-acre tracts to farmers from Wisconsin, Iowa, and other midwestern states, and they cultivated crops other than cotton. Unfortunately the Mound Colony was unsuccessful because most farmers planted the same crop, thereby creating a glut. Returning to cotton was also difficult, since many of the farmers were unfamiliar with it. Though many went back north, some stayed and made outstanding citizens. (Courtesy of Martha Yerger André.)

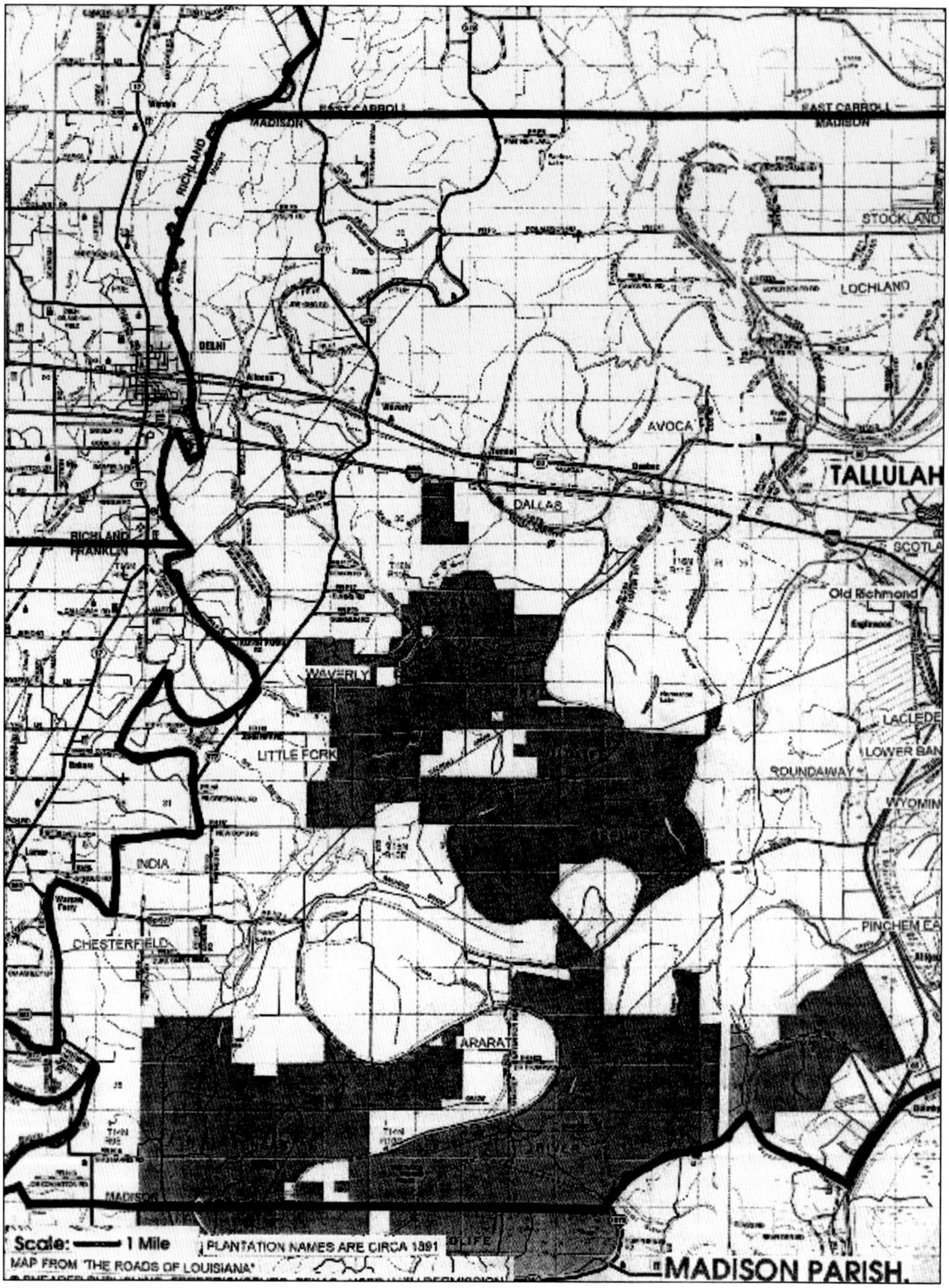

Map of Western Madison Parish with Plantation Names as of 1891. This picture is based on a wall map in the Madison Parish Courthouse. (Modified from *The Roads of Louisiana*, Fredericksburg, Texas: Shearer Publishing.)

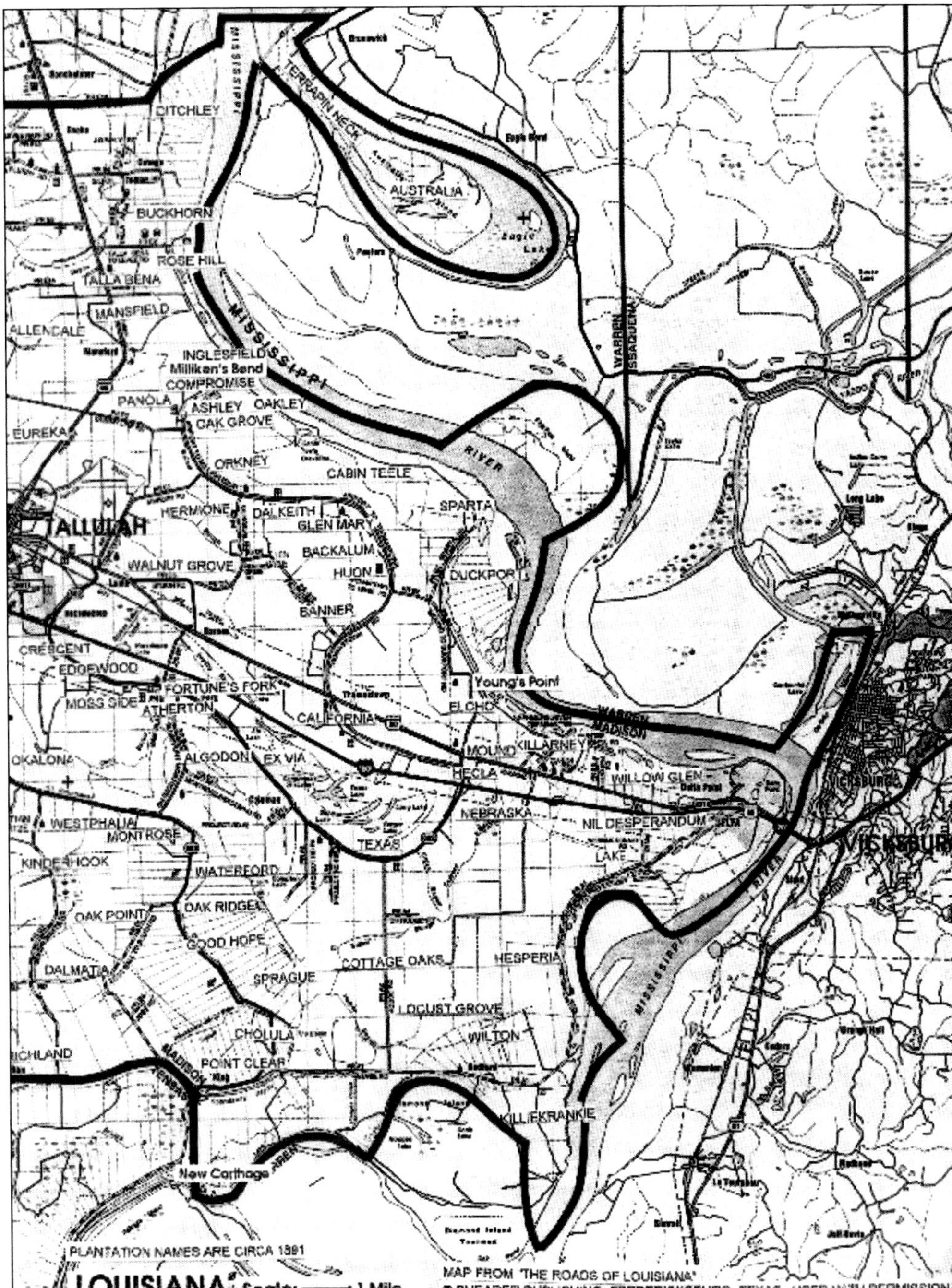

Map of Eastern Madison Parish with Plantation Names as of 1891. This picture is also based on a wall map in the Madison Parish Courthouse. (Modified from *The Roads of Louisiana*, Fredericksburg, Texas: Shearer Publishing.)

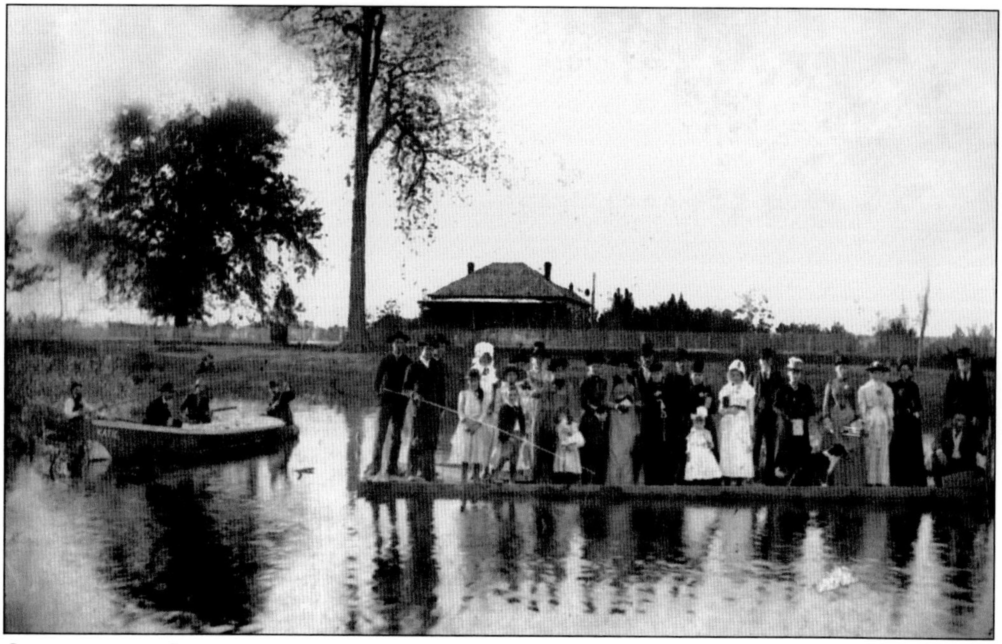

Gathering on Brushy Bayou c. 1890s. This group photograph, taken on the bayou in front of Kate (Kate Stone of *Brokenburn*) and Henry Holmes's house, may or may not be a wedding party. They are certainly too dressed up to be fishing, but nevertheless, that is what they are doing. The boat *Katie* is obviously named for Kate Stone Holmes. Calvin Adams currently owns the house. (Courtesy of the Madison Historical Society.)

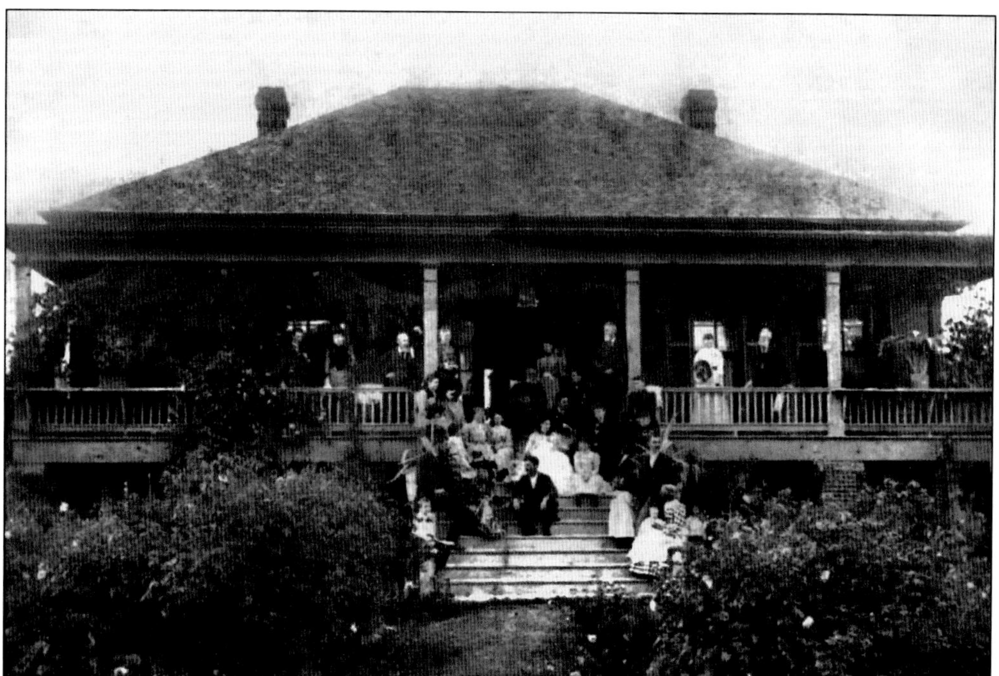

Same Group as Before but Now at the House. Here the group has returned to the homestead. (Courtesy of the Madison Historical Society.)

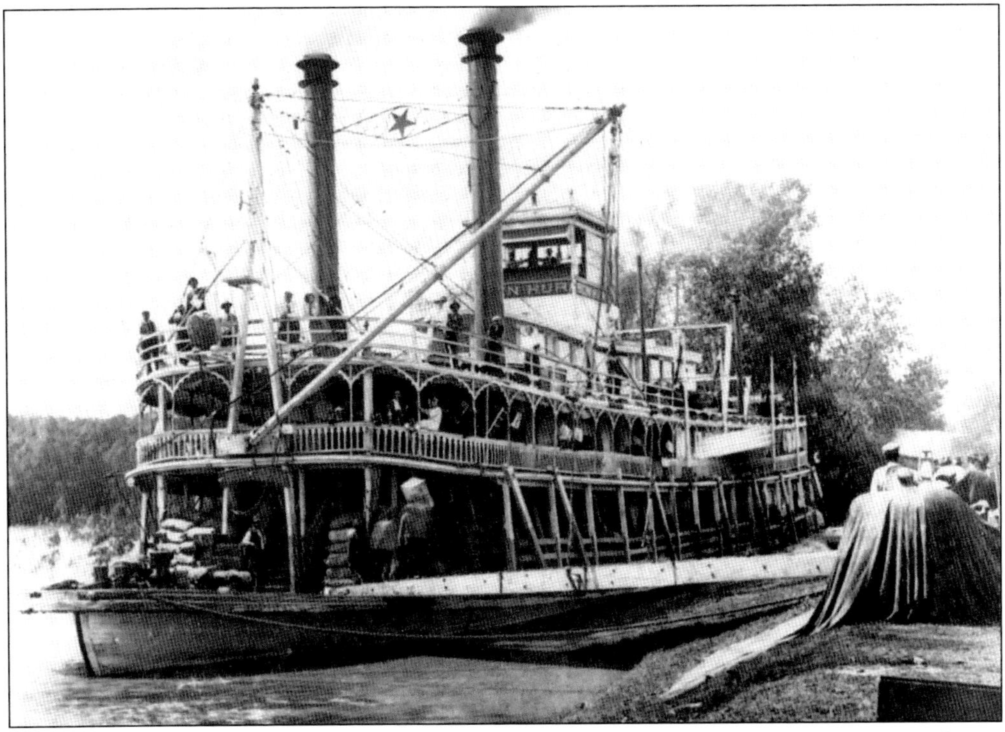

STEAMBOAT *BEN HUR* LOADED WITH PASSENGERS AT AN UNIDENTIFIED MADISON PARISH PORT. During the latter part of the 18th century, practically all transportation was by steamboat. Without it there would have been no economical way to get cotton to market or passengers to their destinations. (Courtesy of the Madison Historical Society.)

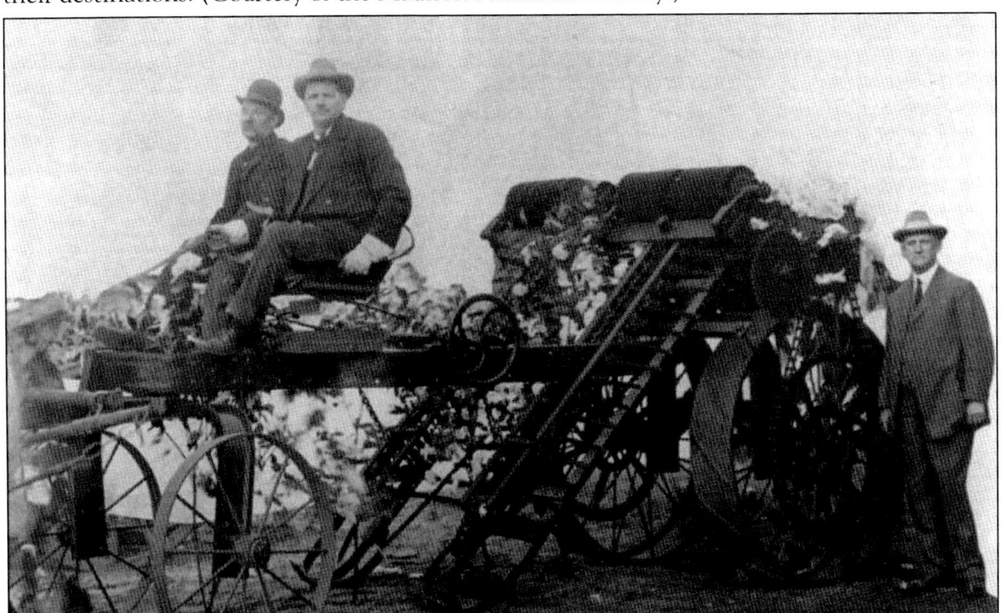

EARLY FARM EQUIPMENT ON MAXWELL FARM. Owner F.L. Maxwell is shown at far right. (Courtesy of Jeanne Yerger.)

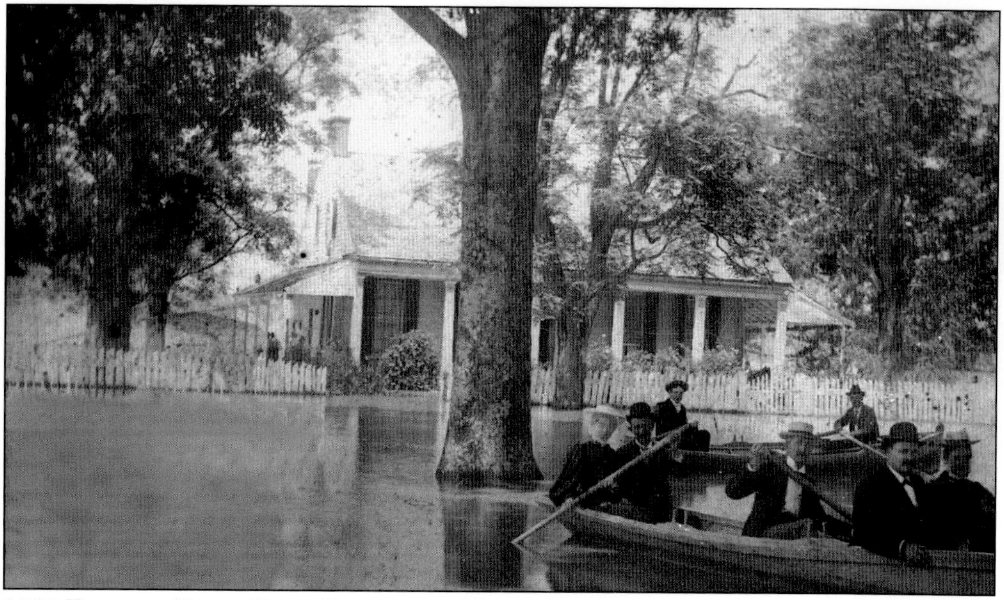

1897 Flood at Point Clear Plantation Near New Carthage. Pictured in the foreground from left to right is Molly Kelley, Dr. Preston Herring (derby), Thomas Phares Kell (white panama hat), Edwin Gladney, and Bessie Kell (sailor hat). Will Evans is one of those in the rear boat. The old house was Grant's headquarters during his march from Milliken's Bend to Bruinsburg and on to Vicksburg. His soldiers scribbled their names in the attic. The house was built in the 1840s but burned in 1907. It was rebuilt but later moved in the mid-1920s, when a levee was scheduled to be built through the site. (Courtesy of Judy Kell Morris.)

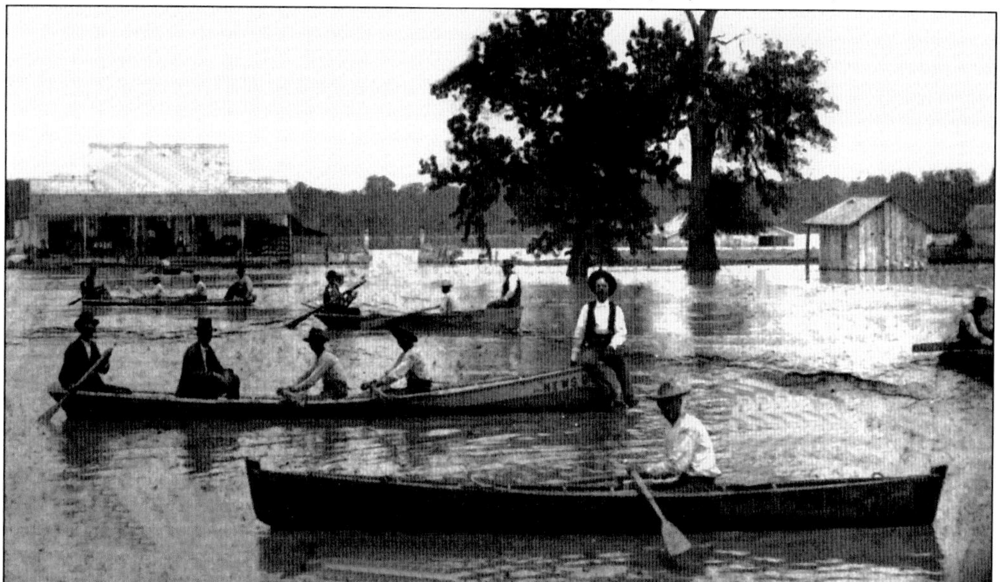

1897 Flood at Point Clear Plantation Near New Carthage. The small building on the right is the plantation doctor's office. The commissary is on the left. Located in extreme southern Madison Parish, New Carthage during the middle and late 1800s was a thriving steamboat landing on the Mississippi River. It was later moved and finally totally abandoned because of river encroachment. (Courtesy of Judy Kell Morris.)

Four

THE EARLY 1900S

The early 1900s was a period of continued improvement on farms. Floods in the late 1880s and again in 1903 and 1912 led to an attempt to rebuild the levees along the Mississippi River. However, funds were not immediately available until 1917 and 1925. But by this time, the levees were not built soon or high enough and in 1927 the "mother of all floods" hit the parish.

The parish was honored in 1907 when President Theodore Roosevelt came on a bear hunt with a large entourage of locally and nationally known people. Ben Lilly, the well-known Southwestern hunter whose daughter would later live in Tallulah for many years, came, as did Holt Collins, a famed black bear hunter from Mississippi. This event did not command nearly the amount of attention that accompanied Roosevelt's 1902 bear hunt in Mississippi, where he refused to shoot a tied-up bear and thus the name "Teddy Bear" was coined. However, several pictures taken on the 1907 Madison Parish hunt were erroneously credited to the 1902 hunt.

Yellow fever was not a newcomer to Madison Parish, having caused epidemics in 1866, 1874, and 1878. However, in 1905 the worst outbreak of that disease ever recorded occurred. The epidemic, confined to Tallulah and its vicinity, became so contagious that the town was evacuated by train for a time.

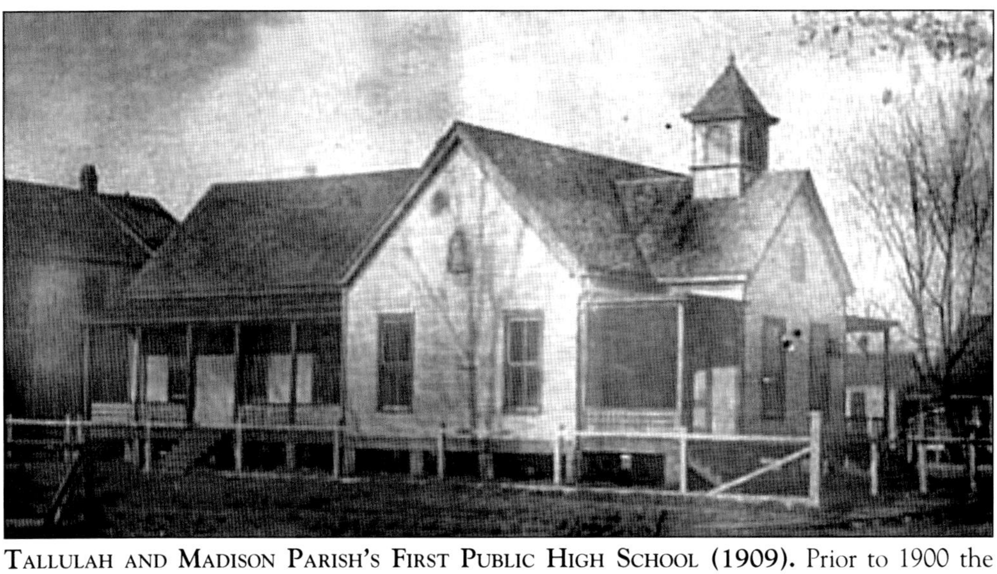

TALLULAH AND MADISON PARISH'S FIRST PUBLIC HIGH SCHOOL (1909). Prior to 1900 the only schools in Madison Parish were one-room buildings, mostly on the outlying plantations. There was no high school at all. Early in the 1900s a high school was built in Tallulah, and in 1927 construction was underway on a new high school, although the flood that year delayed its completion. (Courtesy of Mary Gregg.)

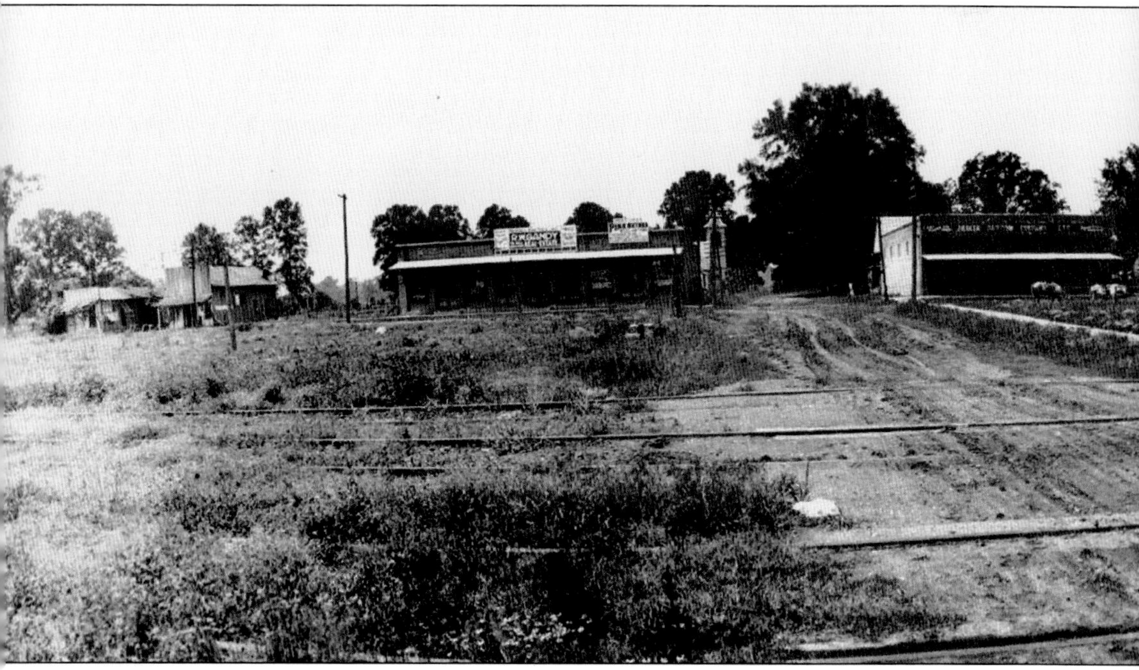

Tallulah Panorama Taken in Late 1890s or Early 1900s. The top photograph is looking south. The road is now the northbound lane of U.S. Highway 65, and the building to

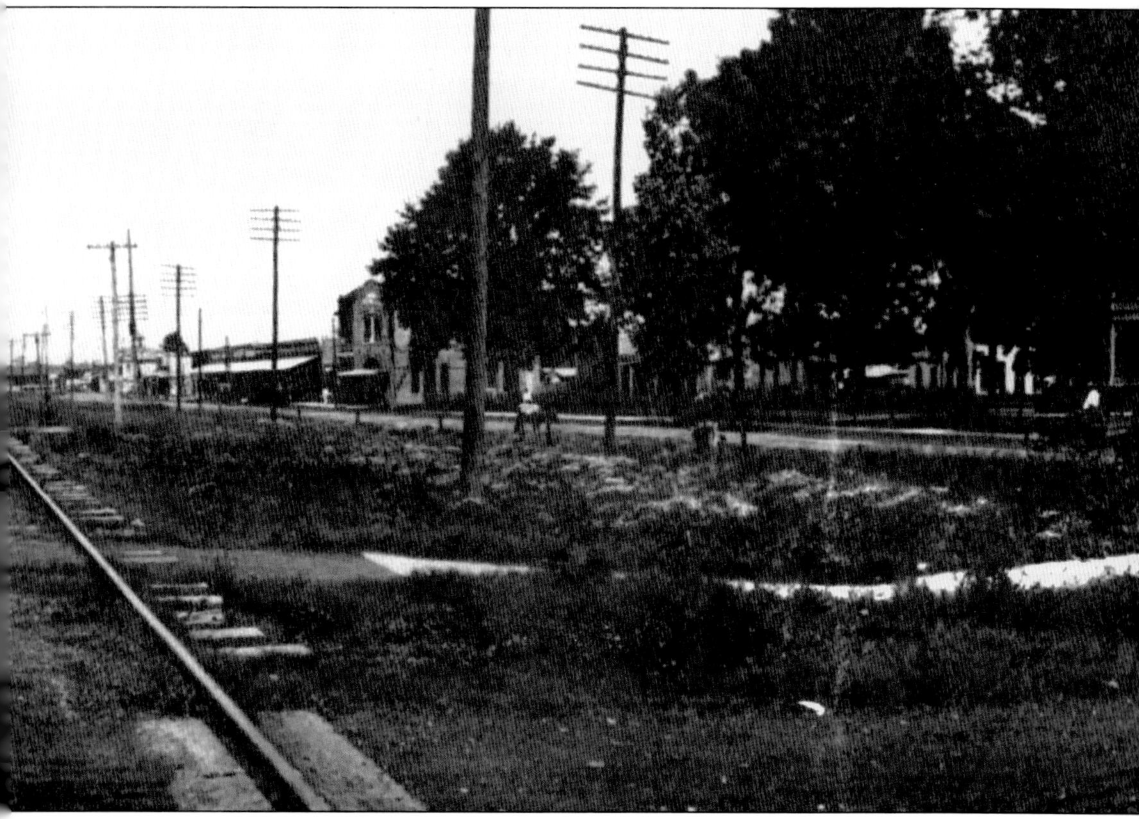

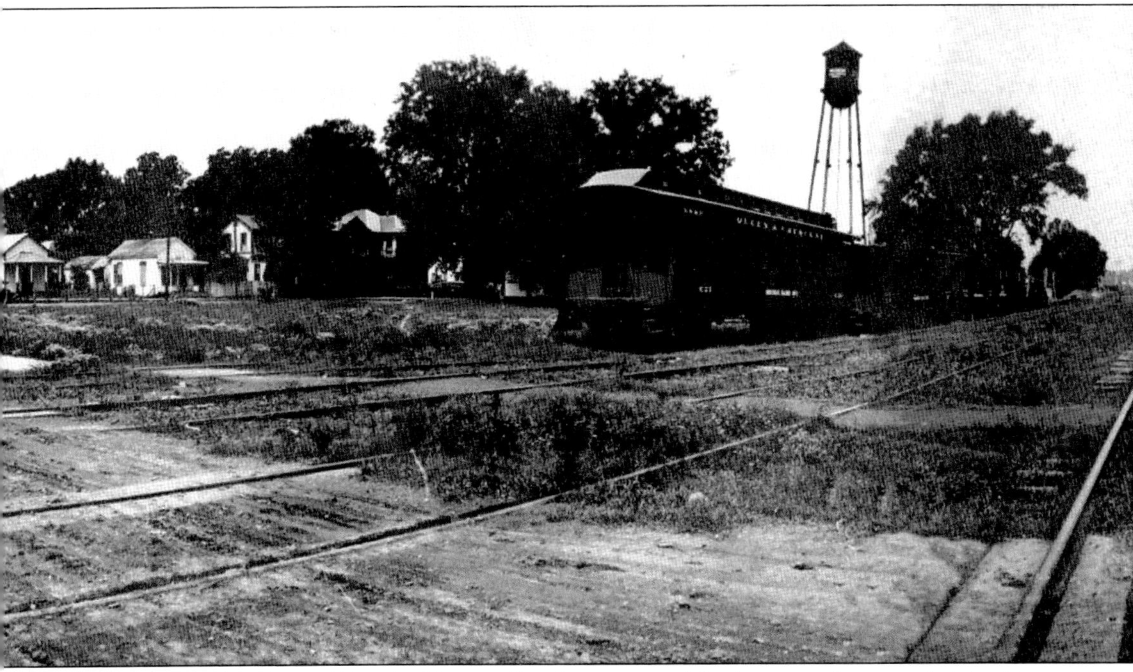

right of the road is the old Ziegler-Darrow Hardware store. The bottom photograph is looking north toward the courthouse. (Courtesy of Henry C. Sevier Jr.)

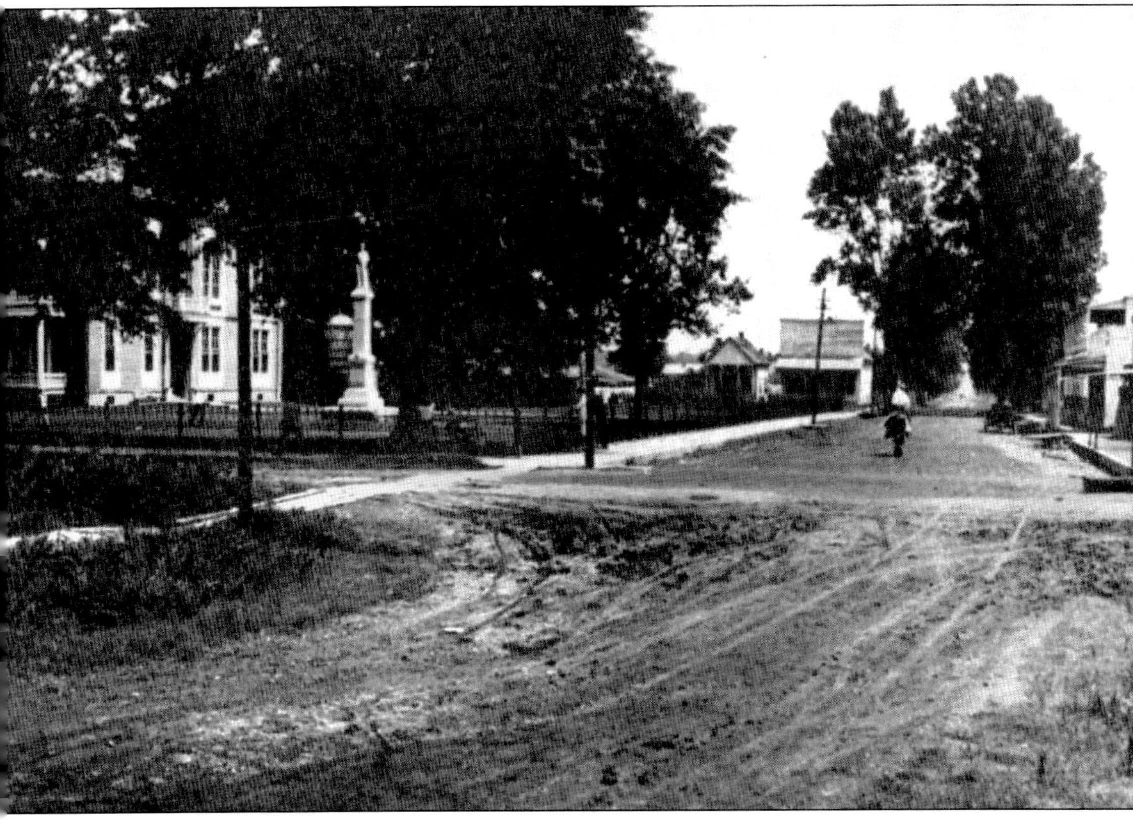

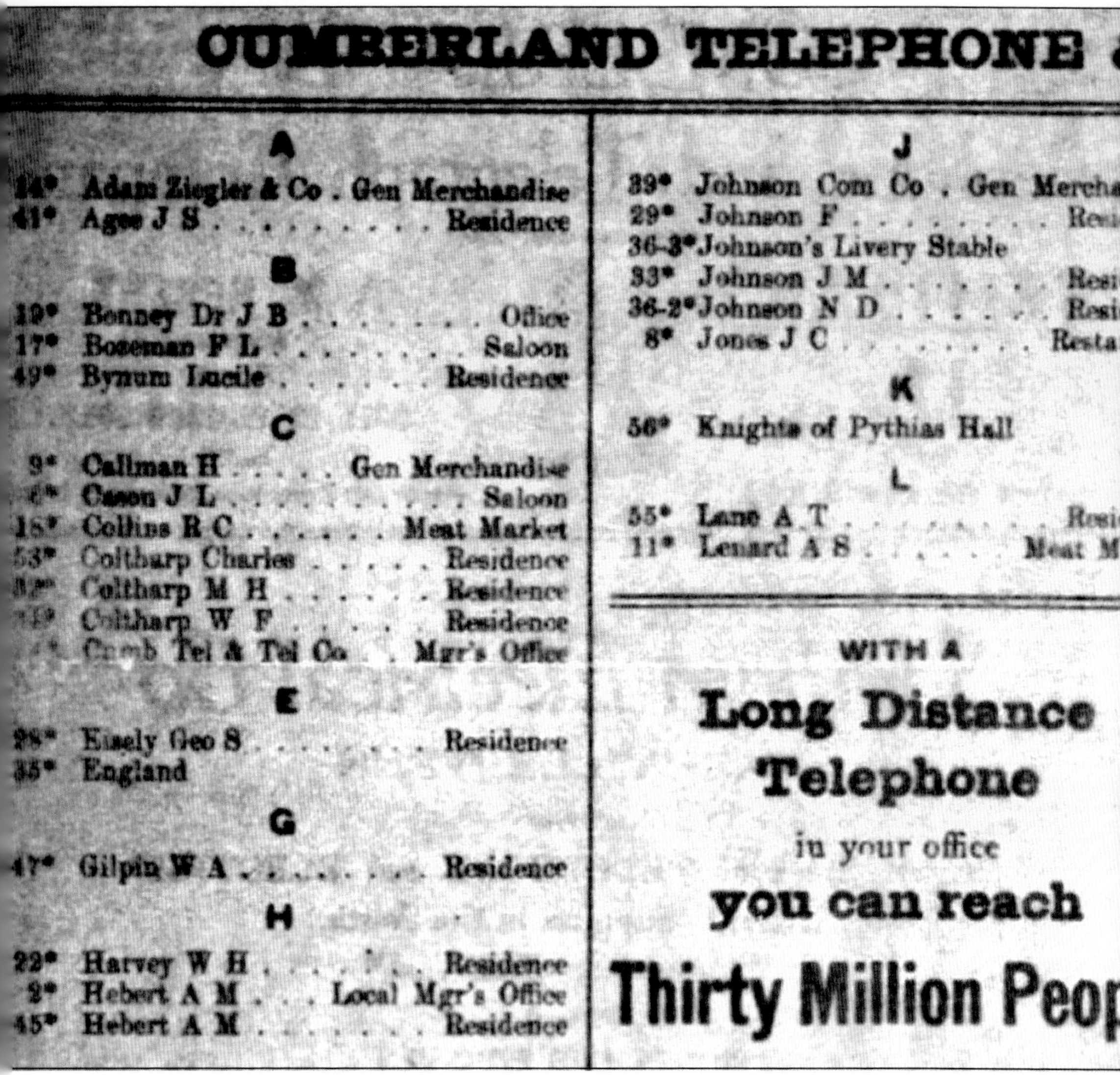

CUMBERLAND TELEPHONE &

A

14* Adam Ziegler & Co . Gen Merchandise
41* Agee J S . . . . Residence

B

19* Bonney Dr J B . . . . Office
17* Boseman F L . . . . Saloon
49* Bynum Lucile . . . . . . Residence

C

9* Callman H . . . . . Gen Merchandise
6* Cason J L . . . . Saloon
18* Collins R C . . . . Meat Market
53* Colthard Charles . . . . . Residence
32* Coltharp M H . . . . . . Residence
19* Coltharp W F . . . . . . Residence
1* Cumb Tel & Tel Co . . Mgr's Office

E

28* Eisely Geo S . . . . Residence
35* England

G

47* Gilpin W A . . . . Residence

H

22* Harvey W H . . . . Residence
2* Hebert A M . . . Local Mgr's Office
45* Hebert A M . . . . Residence

J

39* Johnson Com Co . Gen Mercha
29* Johnson F . . . . Resi
36-3*Johnson's Livery Stable
33* Johnson J M . . . . Resi
36-2*Johnson N D . . . . Resi
8* Jones J C . . . . Resta

K

56* Knights of Pythias Hall

L

55* Lane A T . . . . Resi
11* Lenard A S . . . . Meat M

WITH A
Long Distance
Telephone
in your office
you can reach
Thirty Million Peop

1903 Tallulah Telephone Book. This may be the first telephone book in Tallulah's history. The Cumberland Telephone and Telegraph Co. of Nashville, Tennessee has long since

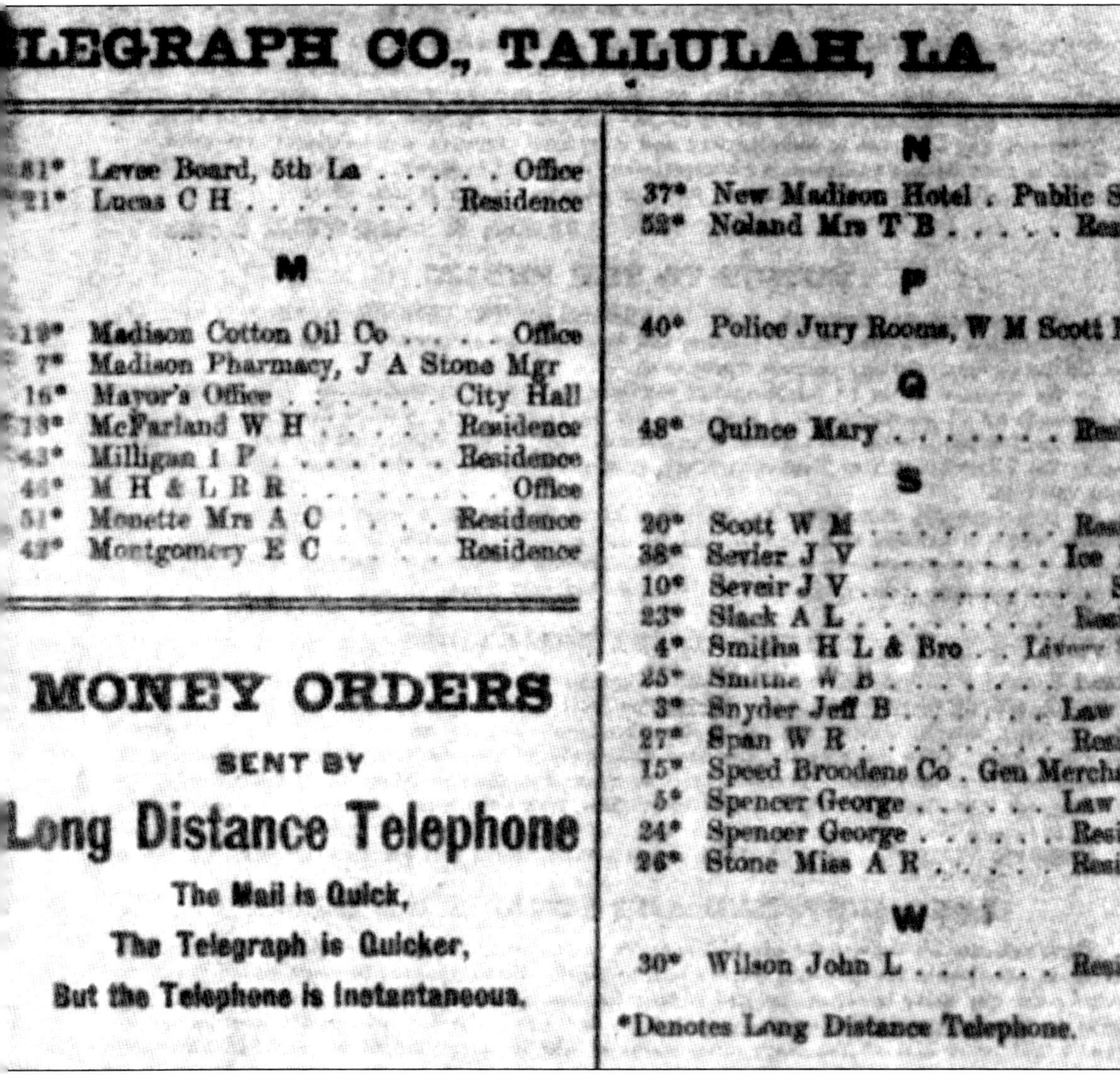

LEGRAPH CO., TALLULAH, LA

81* Levee Board, 5th La . . . . . . Office
21* Lucas C H . . . . Residence

M

19* Madison Cotton Oil Co . . . . . . Office
7* Madison Pharmacy, J A Stone Mgr
16* Mayor's Office . . . . City Hall
13* McFarland W H . . . . . . Residence
43* Milligan I P . . . . Residence
46* M H & L R R . . . . Office
51* Monette Mrs A C . . . . . . Residence
42* Montgomery E C . . . . . . Residence

MONEY ORDERS

SENT BY

Long Distance Telephone

The Mail is Quick,

The Telegraph is Quicker,

But the Telephone is Instantaneous.

N

37* New Madison Hotel . Public S
52* Noland Mrs T B . . . . . . Resi

P

40* Police Jury Rooms, W M Scott P

Q

48* Quince Mary . . . . Resi

S

20* Scott W M . . . . Resi
38* Sevier J V . . . . Ice
10* Seveir J V . . . . S
23* Slack A L . . . . Resi
4* Smiths H L & Bro . . . Livery
25* Smiths W B . . . . Resi
3* Snyder Jeff B . . . . Law
27* Span W R . . . . Resi
15* Speed Broodens Co . Gen Mercha
5* Spencer George . . . . Law
24* Spencer George . . . . Resi
26* Stone Miss A R . . . . Resi

W

30* Wilson John L . . . . Resi

*Denotes Long Distance Telephone.

disappeared from Tallulah. Of the 52 entries over half were residences, the remainder being offices and businesses. (Courtesy of the Madison Historical Society.)

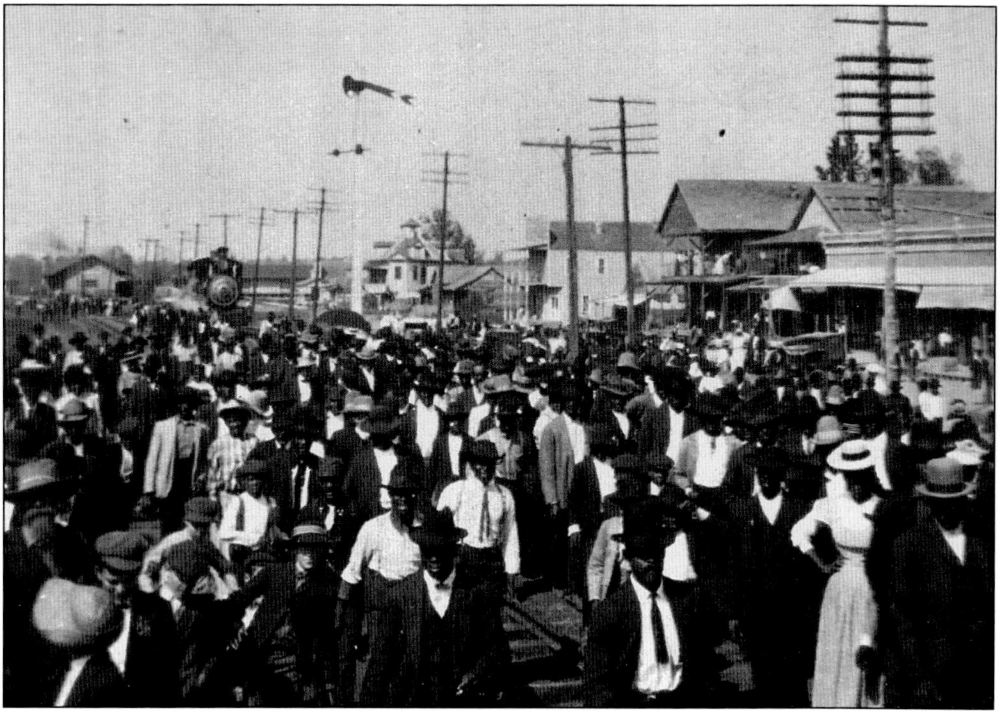

DEPOT STREET IN TALLULAH WITH PRESIDENT THEODORE ROOSEVELT'S TRAIN ARRIVING. In 1907 President Theodore Roosevelt came to Madison Parish on a bear hunt. He came first on a steamboat to Vicksburg; from there he took the train to Tallulah. This is the welcoming committee. (Courtesy of Marion Lawrence Walker Lott.)

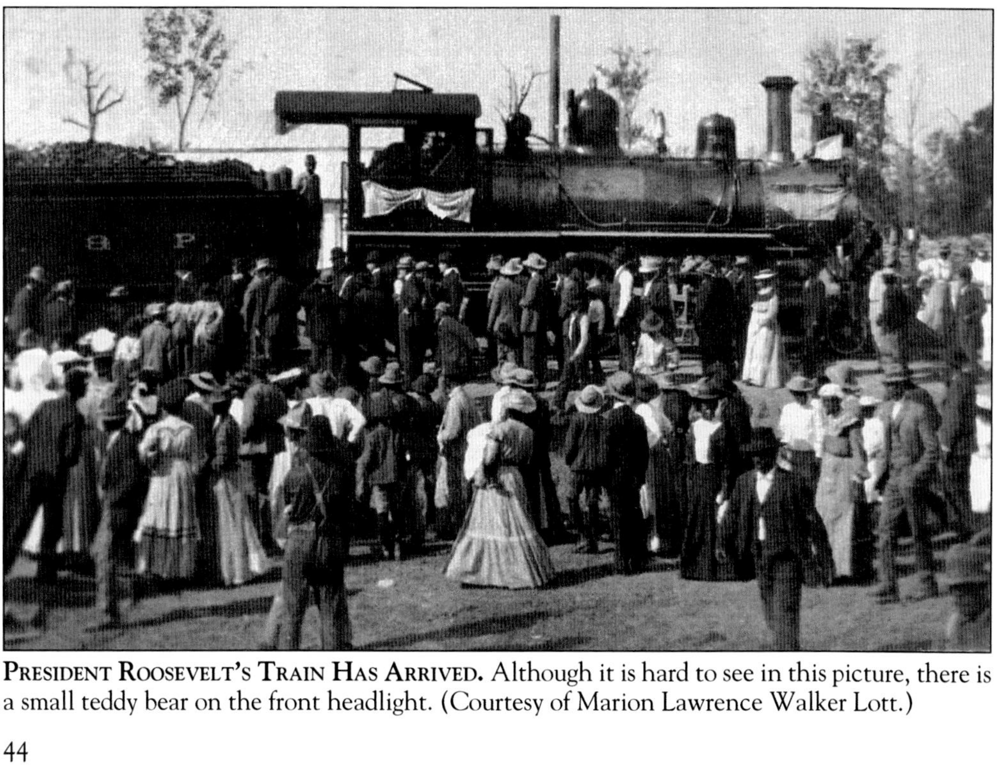

PRESIDENT ROOSEVELT'S TRAIN HAS ARRIVED. Although it is hard to see in this picture, there is a small teddy bear on the front headlight. (Courtesy of Marion Lawrence Walker Lott.)

CLOSE-UP OF ENGINE SHOWING SMALL TEDDY BEAR. The Teddy Bear became Roosevelt's symbol in 1902 after he refused to shoot a tethered bear on a similar bear-hunting trip in Mississippi. (Courtesy of Marion Lawrence Walker Lott.)

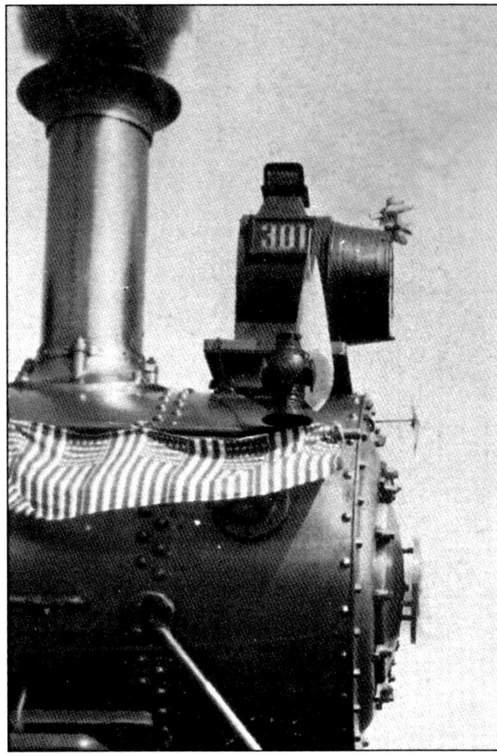

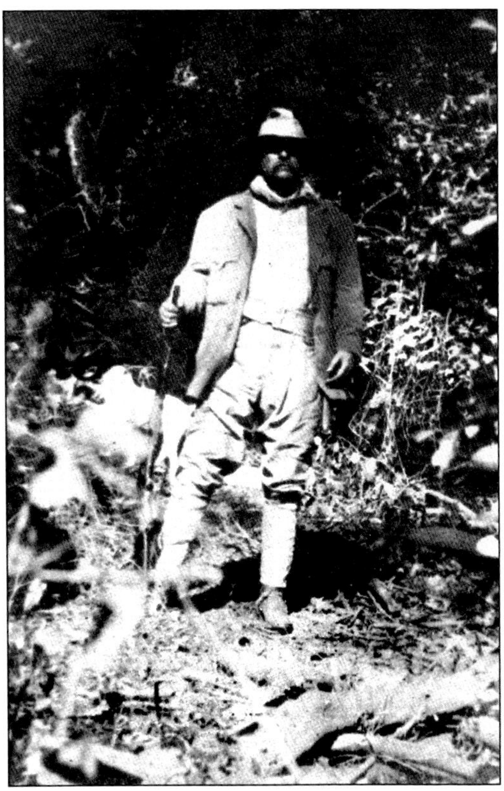

ROOSEVELT LISTENING FOR THE PACK. This is a photograph of the 1907 Roosevelt bear hunt. During this event the hunters harvested three bear, six deer, a turkey, a possum, a dozen squirrels, and a wildcat. According to Roosevelt's account of this trip in his article *In the Louisiana Canebrakes* (*Scribner's Magazine*, January 1908), "we ate everything except the wild-cat." (Courtesy of Marion Lawrence Walker Lott.)

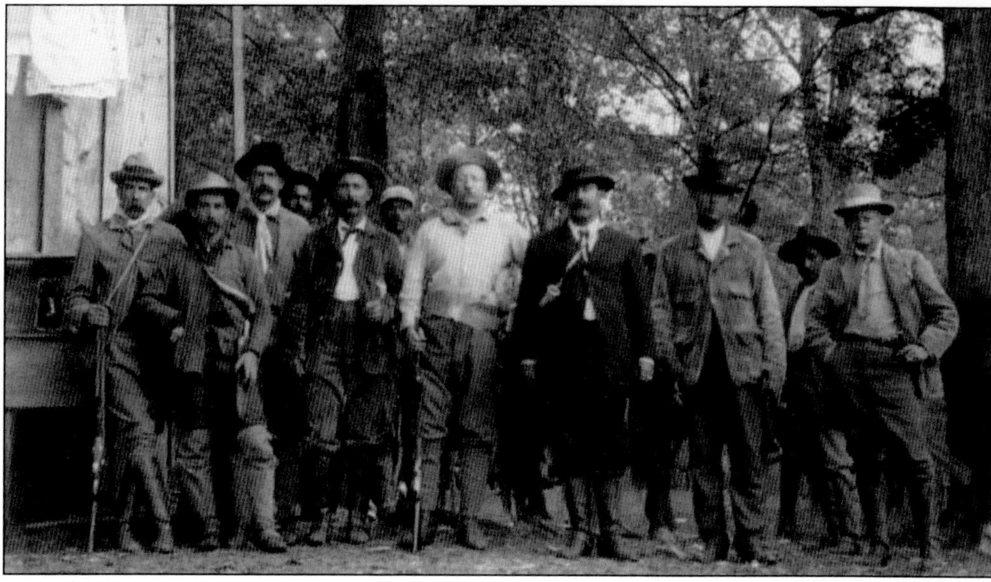

TEDDY ROOSEVELT'S ENTOURAGE. This photograph was taken in northern Madison Parish just north of Bear Lake. Many publications have credited the photograph to Roosevelt's 1902 hunt in Sharkey County, Mississippi. This simply is not true, as there is ample documentation to show that it was taken on the 1907 hunt in Madison Parish. Among those pictured are the following: (in the front row from left to right) Surgeon-General Rixey of the United States Navy, John Osborn, Harley Metcalfe, President Roosevelt, Clive Metcalf, Jack Vesey, and Major Amacker. (Courtesy of Marilyn Bedgood.)

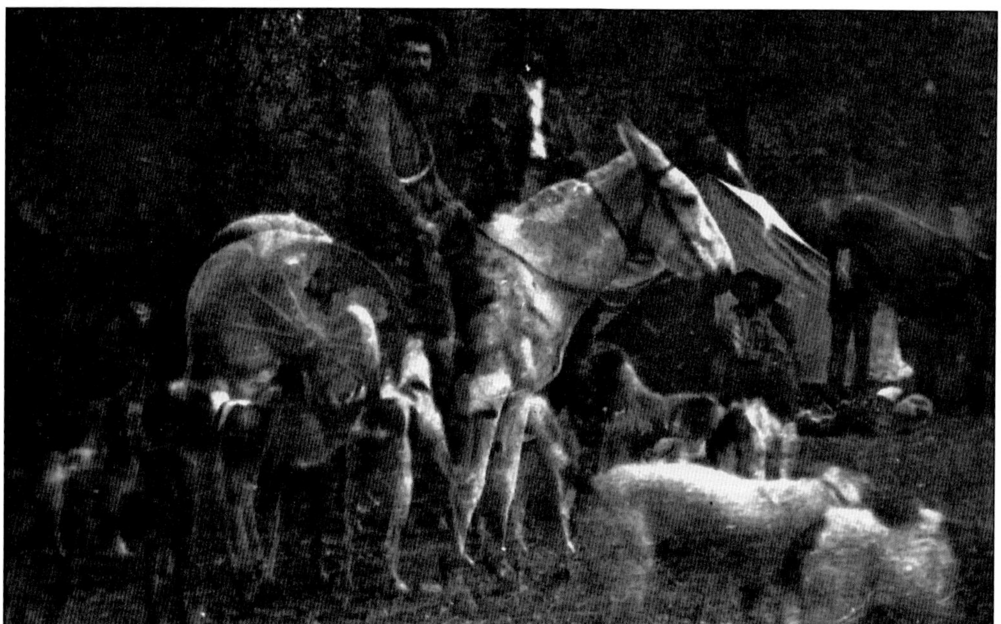

BEN LILLY. This was taken during the 1907 Roosevelt bear hunt. Lilly was well known from Louisiana to New Mexico for his hunting ability. He traveled the entire area with his Bible, dog, and mule. Lilly's daughter, Mrs. Ada Mae Eisley, was Madison Parish School Supervisor for almost 40 years. (Courtesy of Marion Lawrence Walker Lott.)

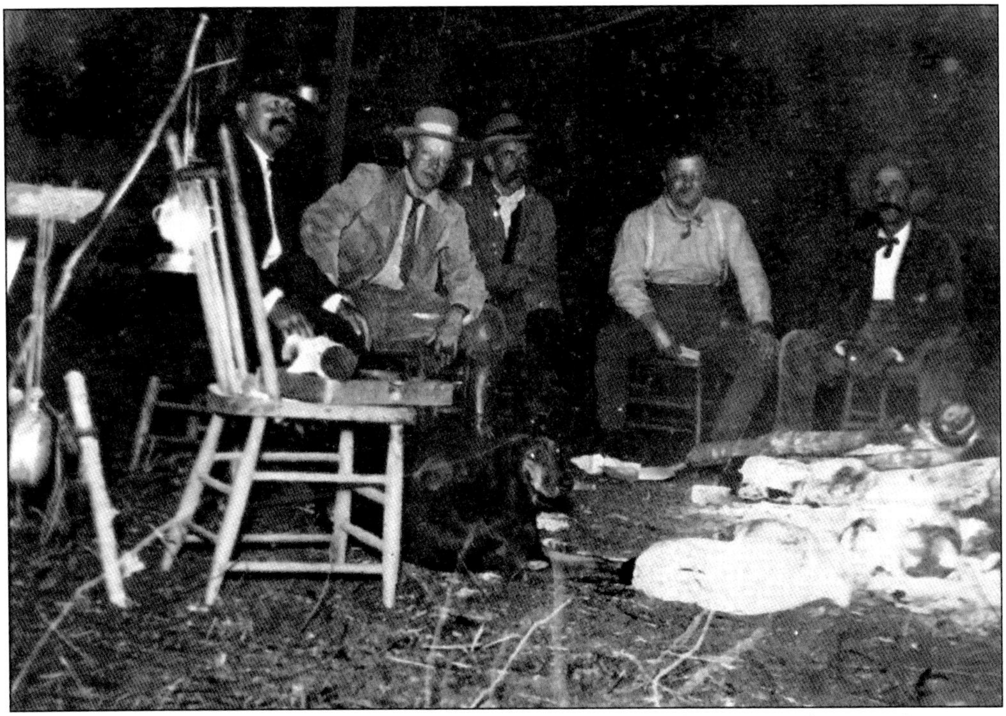

Campfire. This picture is from the 1907 Roosevelt bear hunt. (Courtesy of Marion Lawrence Walker Lott.)

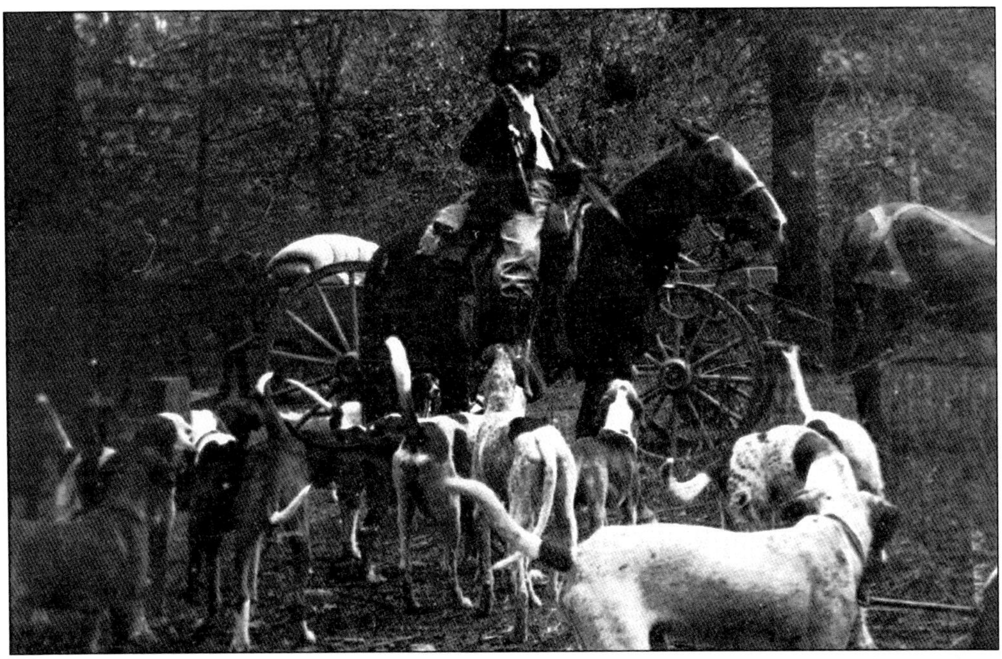

Holt Collier. Also on the hunt was the renowned African-American bear hunter from Mississippi, Holt Collier, about whom a book has recently been written: *Holt Collier: His Life, His Roosevelt Hunts, and the Origin of the Teddy Bear* by Minor Ferris Buchanan, 2002. (Courtesy of Marion Lawrence Walker Lott.)

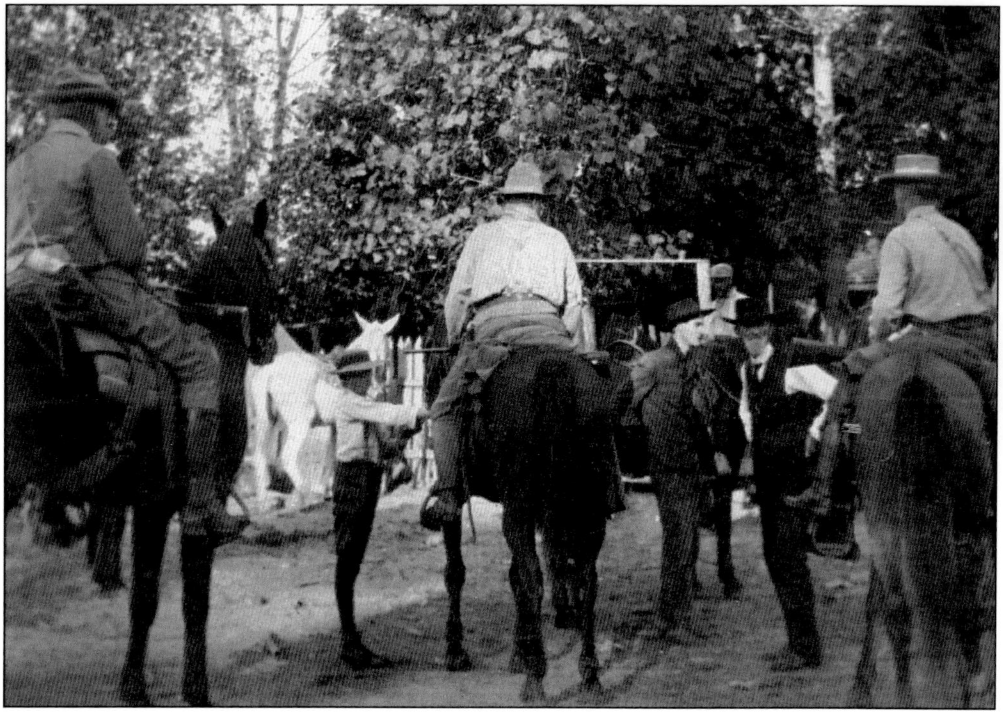

Roosevelt Mounted up and Ready to Go. Roosevelt is shown here during the 1907 Roosevelt bear hunt. (Courtesy of Marion Lawrence Walker Lott.)

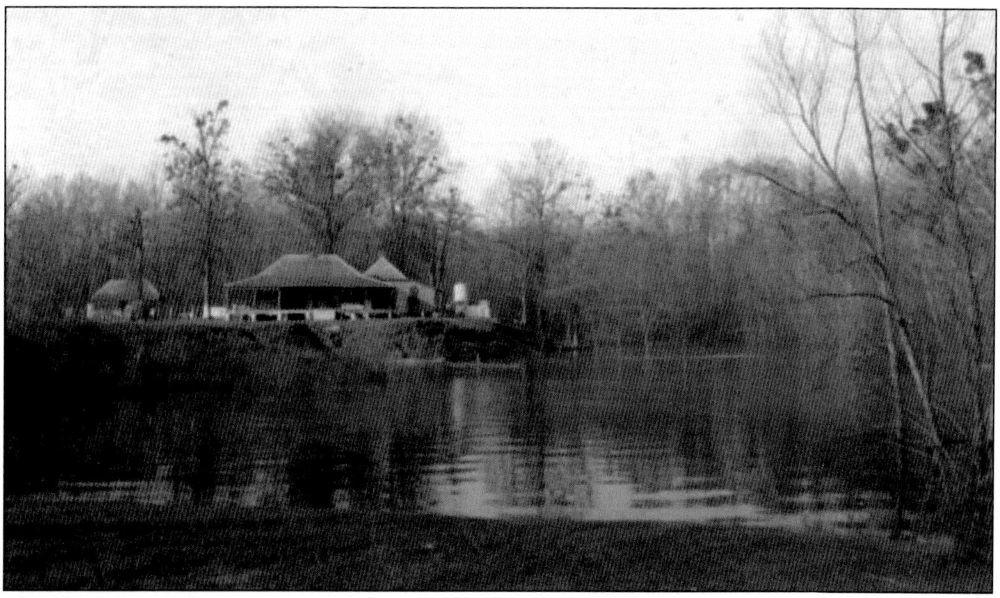

The Bear Lake Hunting Club. This is the first such club in Louisiana and was established in 1899 with 100 shares issued at $50 each. According to local historians, Theodore Roosevelt and his party pitched their tents here during the 1907 bear hunt. The first directors were W.A. Montgomery (Captain), W.S. Holmes (Lieutenant), J.B. Snyder (Secretary), R.A. Inge, T.A. Chichester, M.W. Curry, Dr. J.F. Hodge, and George Spencer. This photograph was taken in the 1920s. (Courtesy of Marilyn Bedgood.)

MADISON PARISH BLACK BEAR. This photograph, taken somewhere in Madison Parish, is an example of what President Roosevelt and his party were hunting. (Courtesy of Judy Kell Morris.)

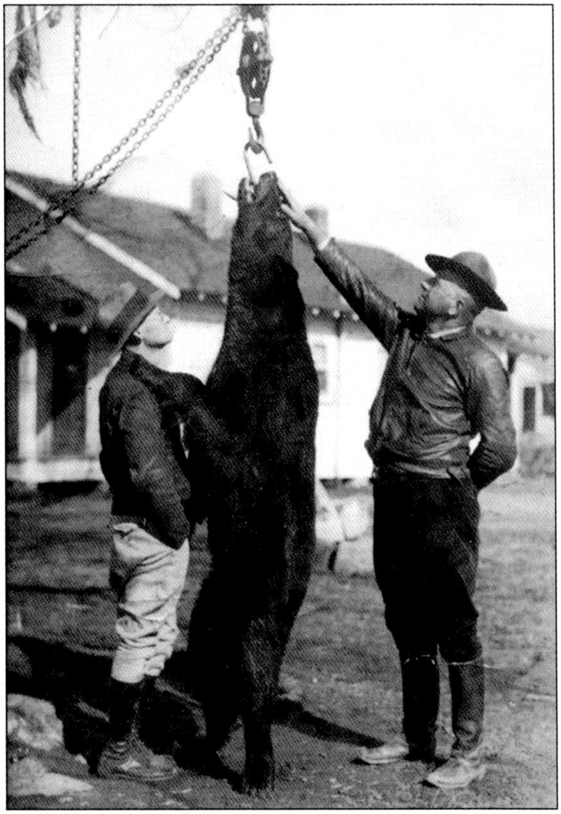

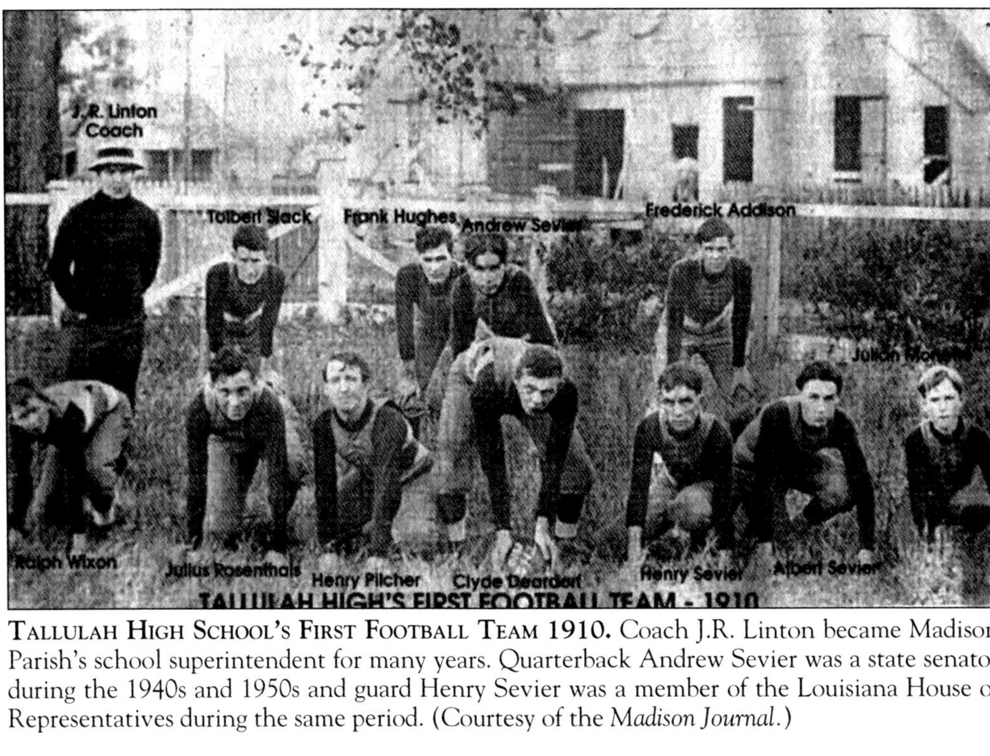

TALLULAH HIGH SCHOOL'S FIRST FOOTBALL TEAM 1910. Coach J.R. Linton became Madison Parish's school superintendent for many years. Quarterback Andrew Sevier was a state senator during the 1940s and 1950s and guard Henry Sevier was a member of the Louisiana House of Representatives during the same period. (Courtesy of the *Madison Journal*.)

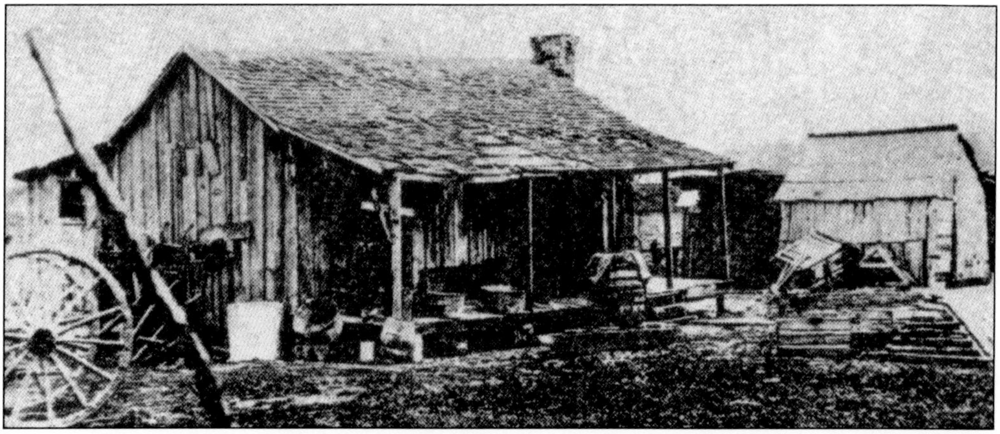

MADAM WALKER'S BIRTHPLACE. On December 23, 1867, Sarah Breedlove was born in this one-room cabin on a Madison Parish cotton plantation near the town of Delta. She was the first member of her family to be born free. After spending 20 years as a laundress and enduring innumerable hardships in her early life, Sarah invented a hair-care product that made her the first black female millionaire, and perhaps the first female millionaire of any race. By 1916 Madam C.J. Walker, as she came to be known, was recognized throughout the United States as a talented entrepreneur. (Courtesy of A'Lelia Bundles/Walker Family Collection.)

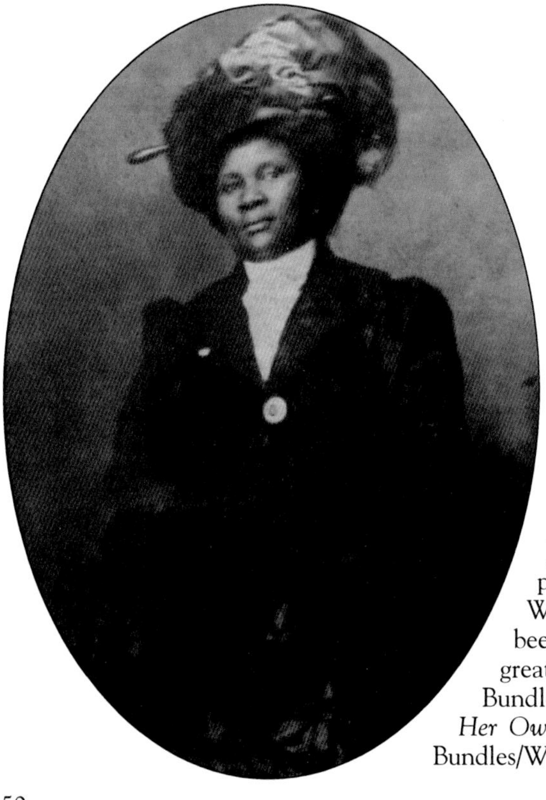

MADAM WALKER. In June 1918 Madam Walker moved into her newly built mansion, Villa Lewaro, on the Hudson River. Unfortunately she was destined to live less than a year more and died at the age of 51 on May 25, 1919. On January 29, 1998, 45 million United States postage stamps were issued in Madam Walker's honor. Two books have recently been written about Madam Walker by her great-great-great-granddaughter, A'Lelia Perry Bundles: *Madam C.J. Walker* in 1991 and *On Her Own Ground* in 2001. (Courtesy of A'Lelia Bundles/Walker Family Collection.)

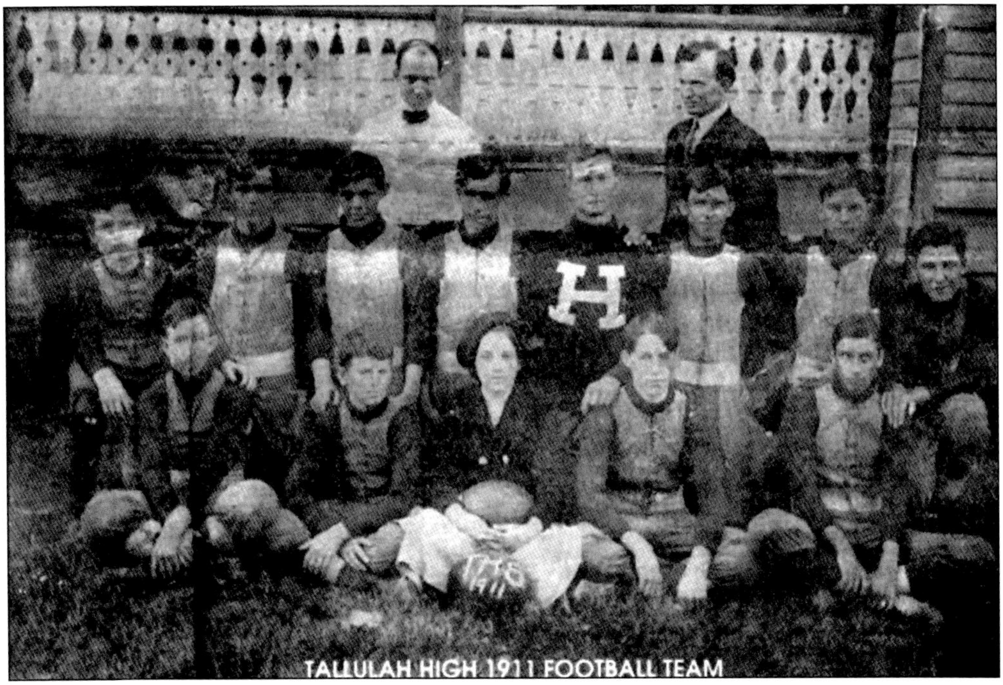

1911 TALLULAH HIGH FOOTBALL TEAM. These are unidentified members of the 1911 Tallulah High School football team. (Courtesy of the *Madison Journal*.)

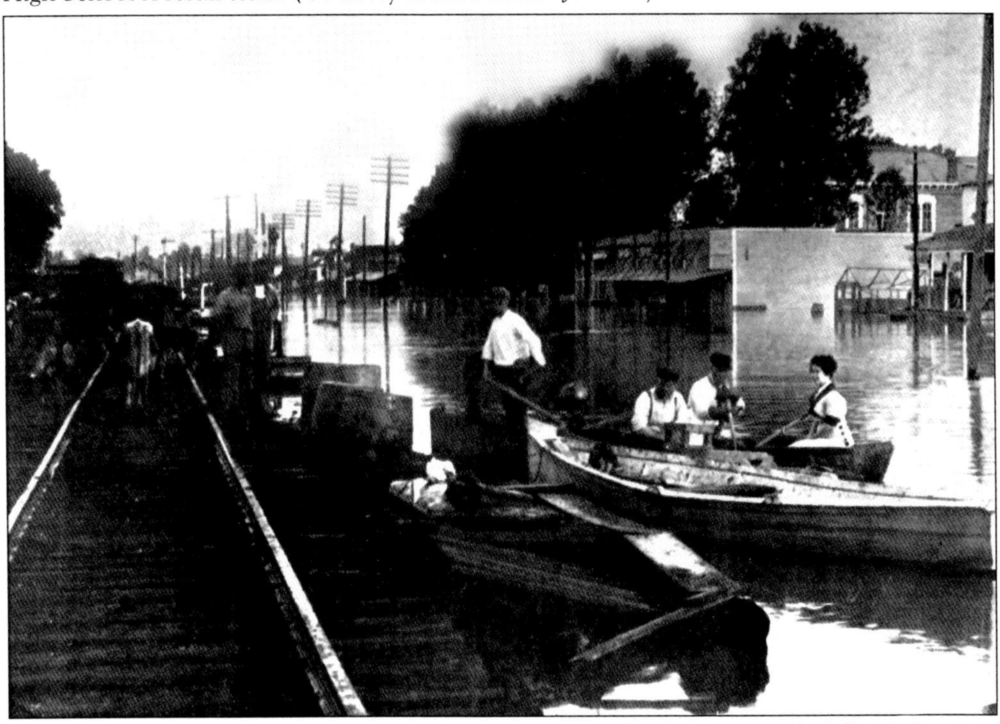

1912 FLOOD IN TALLULAH. Second only in destruction to the devastating 1927 flood, the 1912 flood caused much damage. The Madison Parish Courthouse can be seen in the upper right. (Courtesy of the Madison Historical Society.)

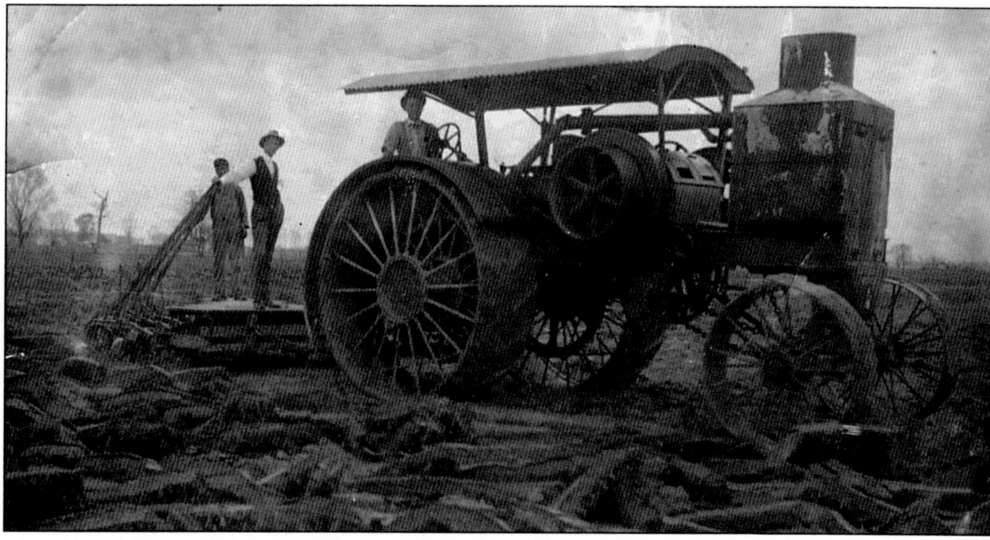

Madison's First Tractor. This early 1900s Fairbanks-Morse tractor, the first tractor in Madison Parish, was so heavy that it was bogged down in the mud almost continually. Seated at the tractor is an engineer from New Orleans who had to come up often to fix it. Standing beside him is the unfortunate owner of the monstrous machine, Richard K. Boney, son of G.L. Boney. (Courtesy of Sherrill Sevier Pirone.)

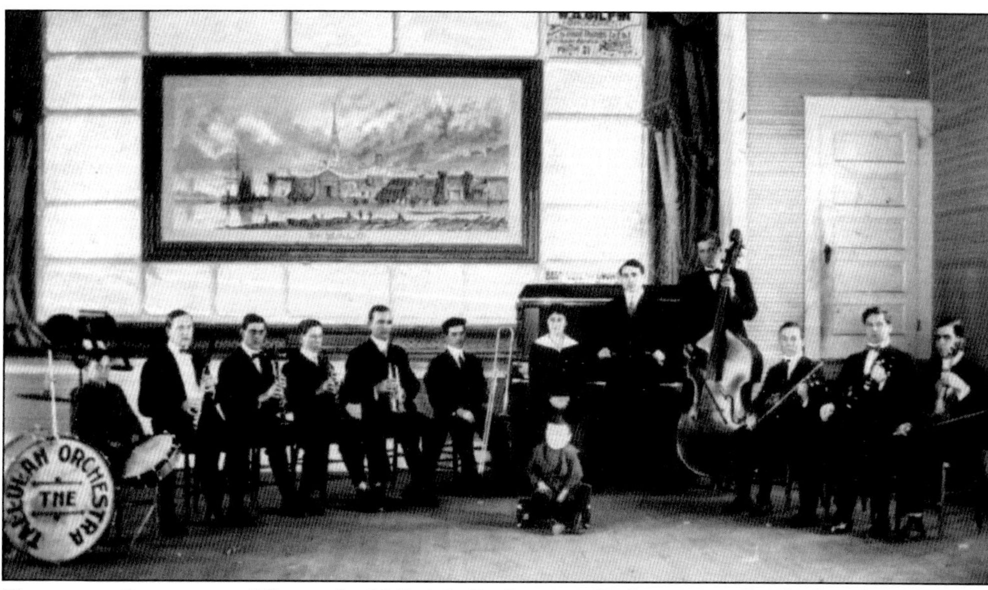

Tallulah Orchestra. This is the Tallulah Orchestra of February 1915. The big drum appears to be the same as that in the 1927 picture of the three-piece "orchestra." (Courtesy of Charles Michael Finlayson.)

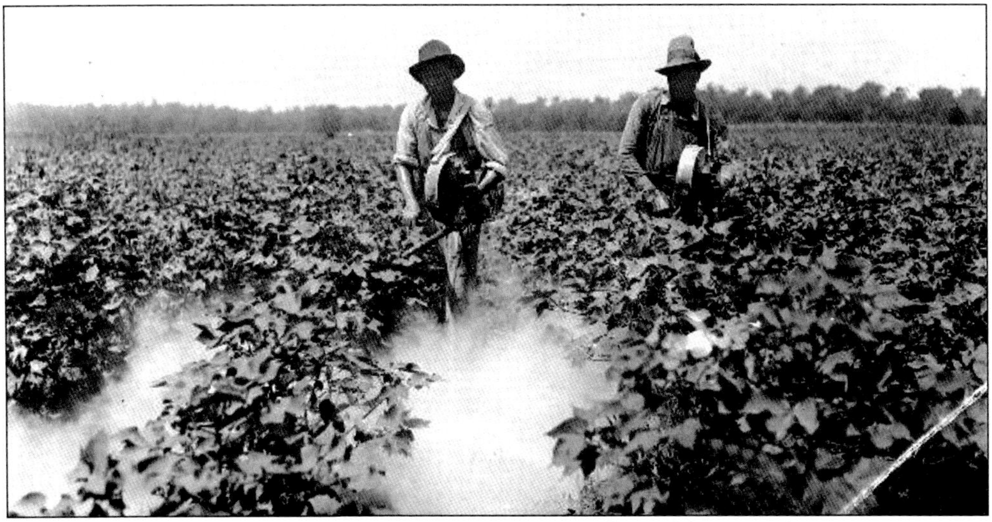

Dusting Cotton by Hand. In 1914 the Bureau of Entomology of the United States Department of Agriculture established laboratories at Tallulah to combat the boll weevil, which had been devastating cotton crops. Dusting the cotton fields with a chemical insecticide such as calcium arsenate was the primary result of the USDA studies. This is a photograph of hand dusting on Duckport Plantation in the early 1920s. (Courtesy of Dorothy Sevier Elliott.)

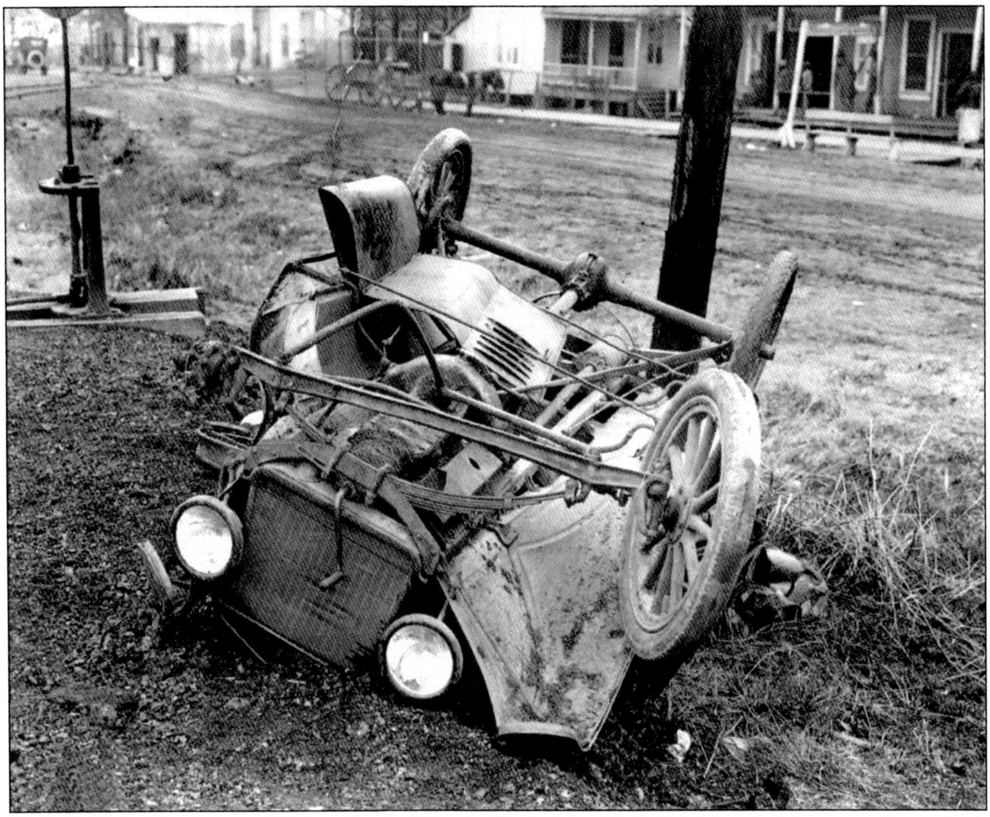

Train and Car Wreck. This is the result of a downtown Tallulah train and car wreck in 1921. The train won. (Courtesy of Charles Michael Finlayson.)

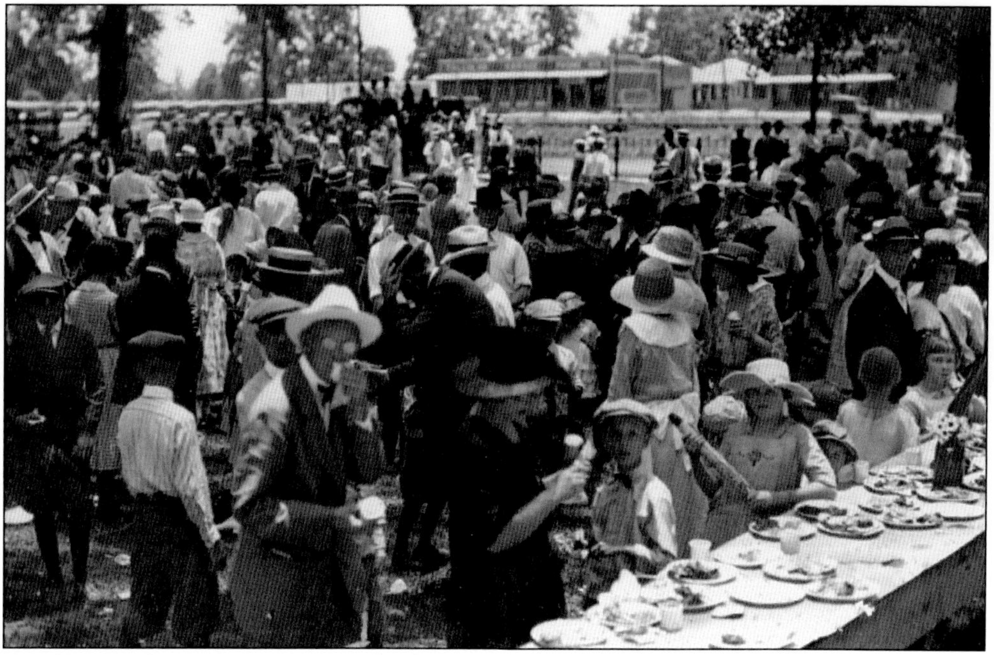

"No Flood" Celebration, 1922. Floods seemed to be coming in 10-year cycles, so a celebration was held in Tallulah when no flood occurred 10 years after the 1912 flood. Little did people realize that five years hence would bring the most disastrous flood in Madison Parish's history. (Courtesy of the Madison Historical Society.)

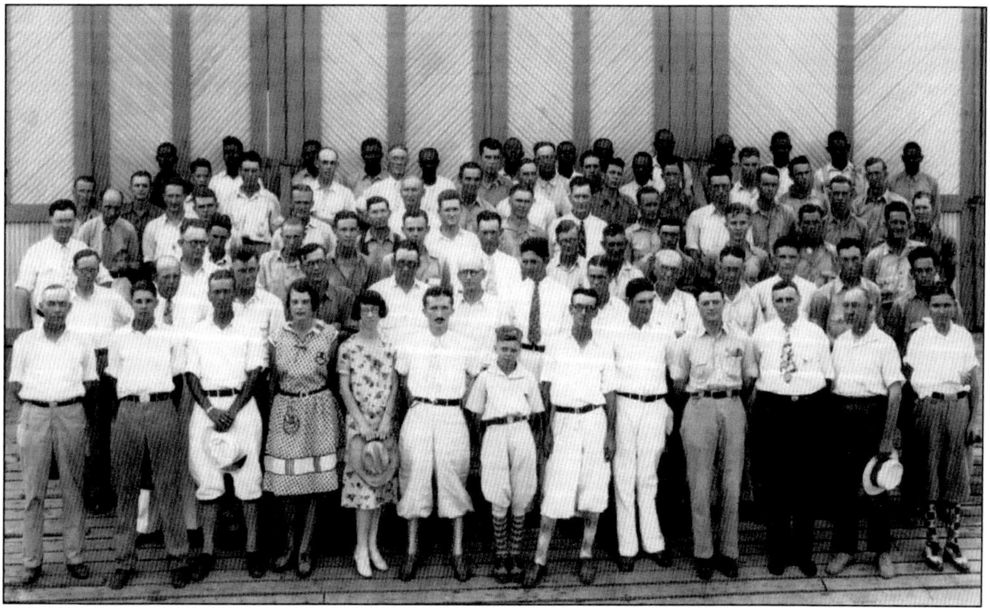

1925 Agricultural Experiment Station Staff. All of these people are deceased today, but many continued to make Tallulah their home even after the "lab" closed. (Courtesy of Louis Buckner.)

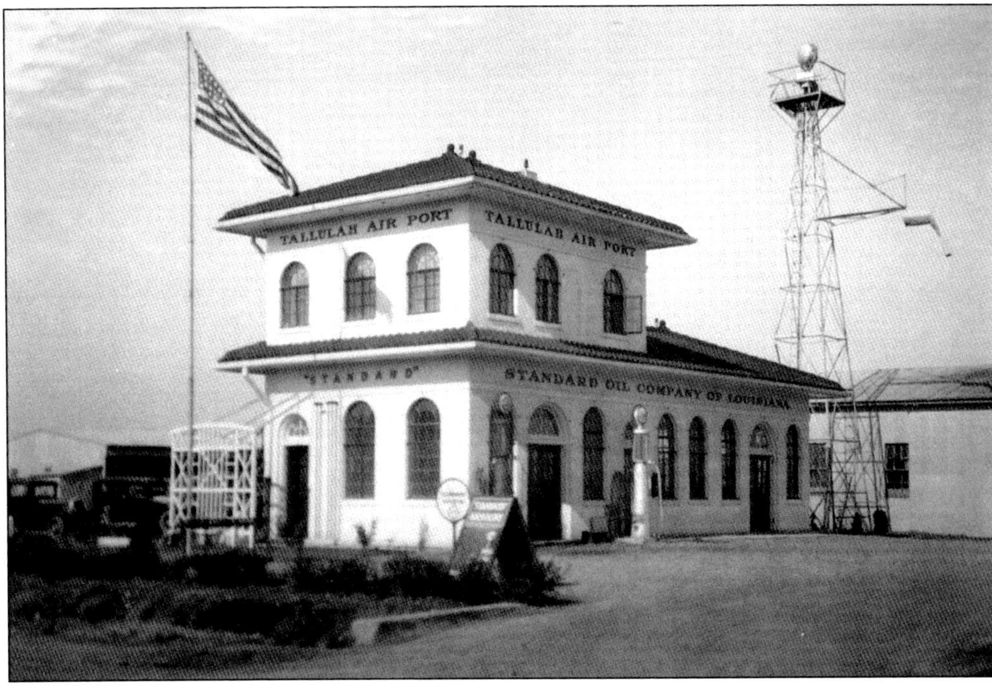

TALLULAH AIRPORT. Crop dusting from airplanes originated in the mid-1920s at Tallulah due to the efforts of Dr. B.R. Coad, head of the Agricultural Experiment Laboratory. The "lab" became the center for designing, building, and testing airborne dusting equipment. From the Tallulah airport hundreds of flights tested dusting equipment on both sides of the Mississippi River. From this work emerged Delta Dusters, a company that later became Delta Airlines. The Tallulah airport, pictured above, is reportedly the first in Louisiana. (Courtesy of Charles Michael Finlayson.)

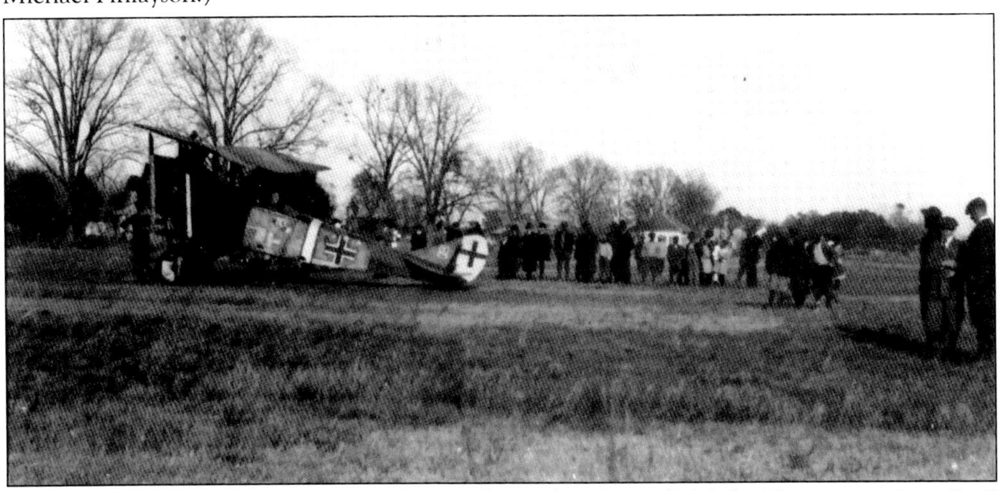

GERMAN AIRPLANES LAND IN TALLULAH. By the mid-1920s Tallulah had become such an "air" center that German air force fighters visited the city. However, instead of landing at the airport, they landed on the southeast side of Brushy Bayou, across from what is now Tallulah High School. Supposedly they did this so they would not have to walk far to town. The house in the center of the picture was the Boney-Sevier house at 402 South Lincoln Street. (Courtesy of Charles Michael Finlayson.)

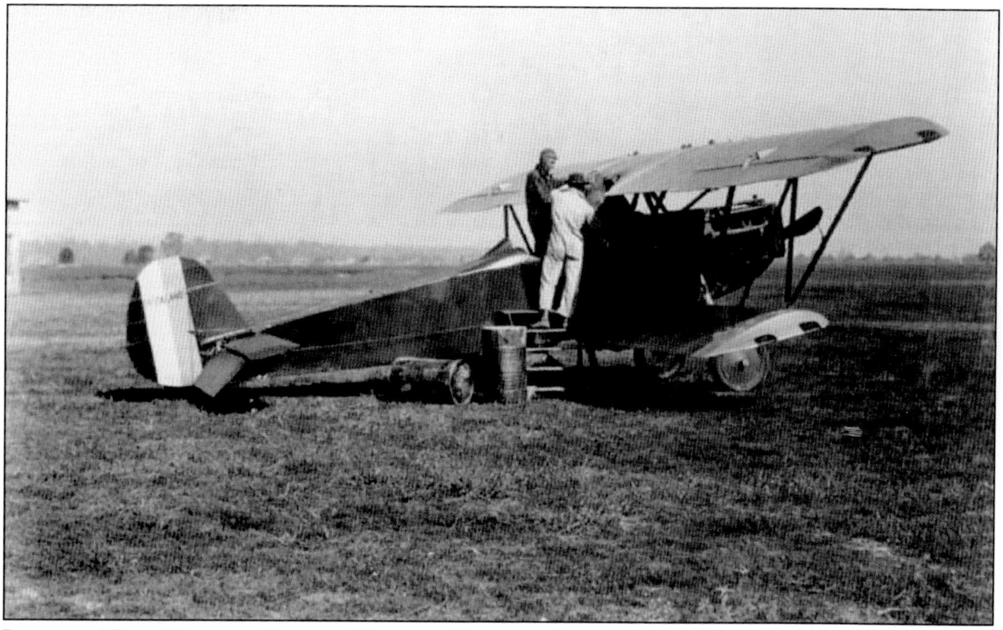

LOADING HUFF-DALAND COTTON DUSTER. Using airplanes to spread cotton dust could cover the greatest area by far. Here a Huff-Daland plane gets loaded for a test flight. The USDA bought the first Huff-Daland in May 1924, and this picture must have been taken shortly thereafter. (Courtesy of Ken Smith.)

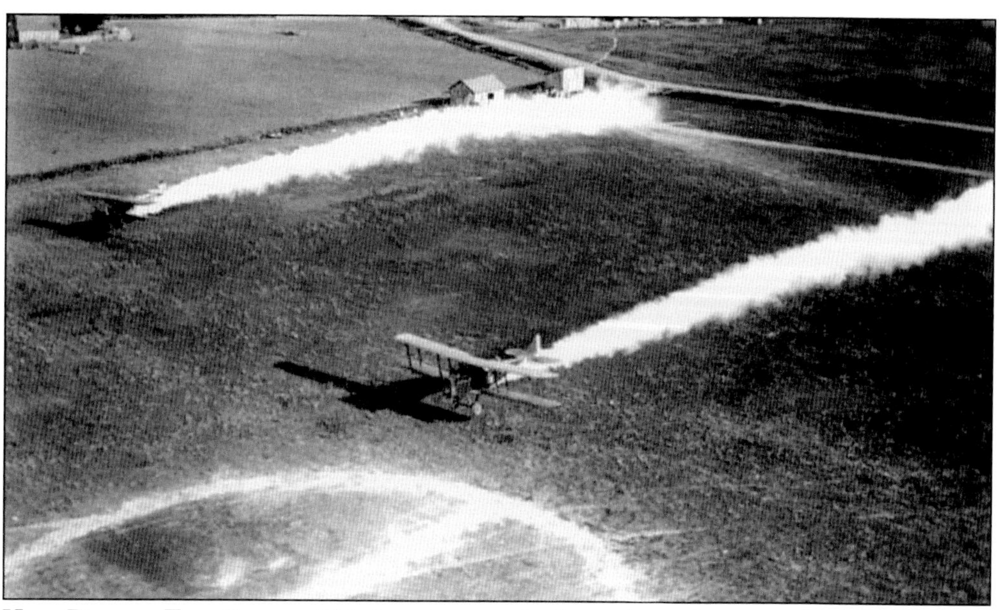

HUFF-DALAND TEST FLIGHT. This is a photograph of one the early cotton dusting test flights involving the Huff-Daland in Madison Parish. (Courtesy of Ken Smith.)

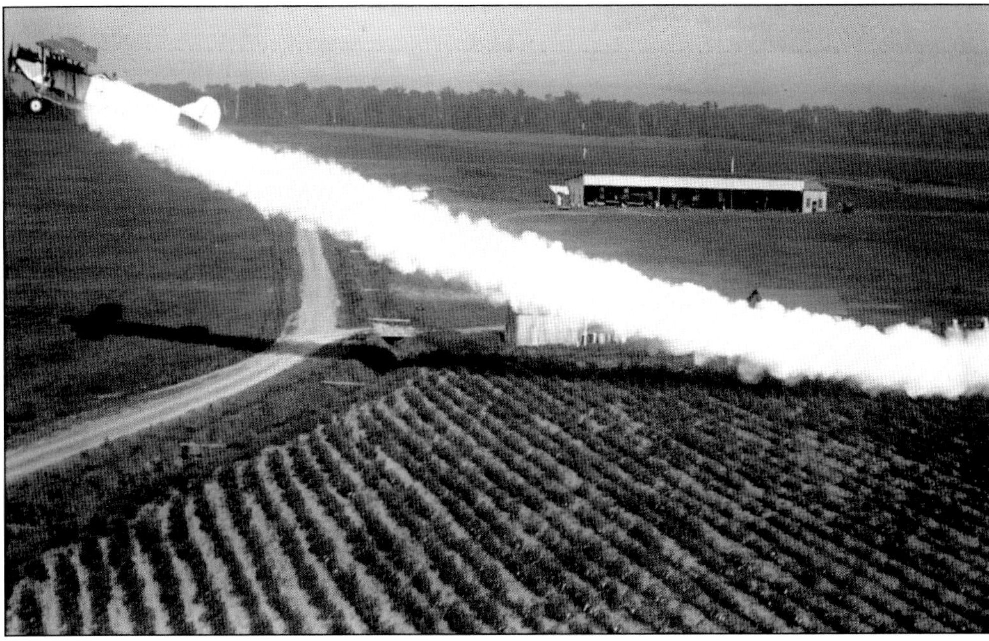

ANOTHER HUFF-DALAND DUSTER IN ACTION. The area depicted is Shirley Plantation just east of Tallulah. The buildings in the background were part of the Tallulah Airport where the dusters were based. (Courtesy of Charles Michael Finlayson.)

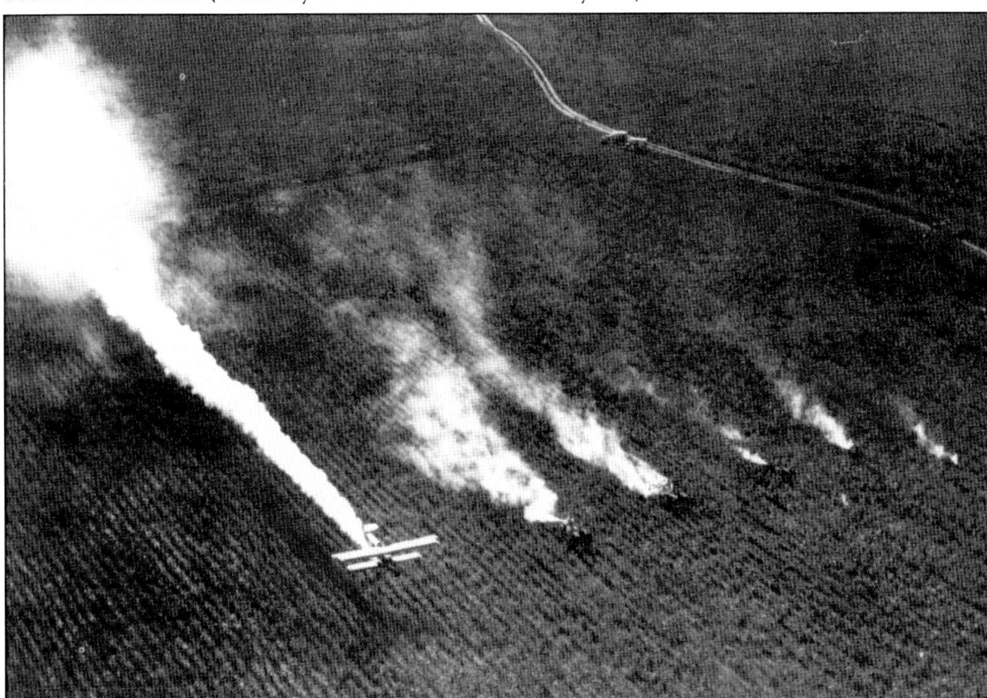

ALL TYPES OF COTTON DUSTING. This photograph, taken about 1925, shows several types of dusting being performed simultaneously. This effectively demonstrates the efficiency of dusting by air. (Courtesy of Charles Michael Finlayson.)

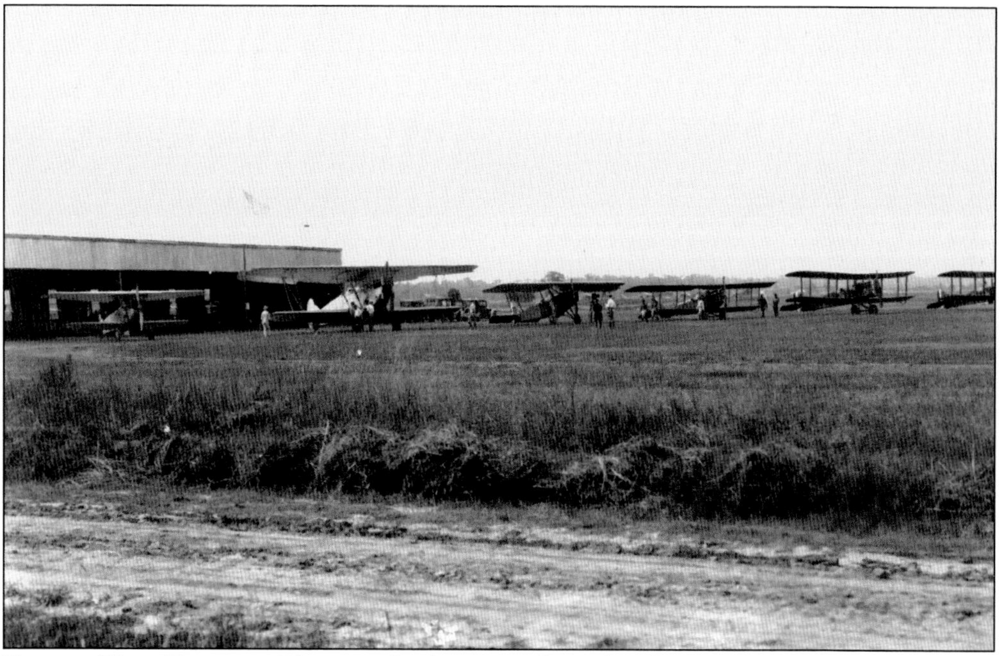

FLEET OF HUFF-DALANDS. This must be the entire fleet of Huff-Dalands. However, the United States Army Air Force insignia can be seen on the wings and bodies of some. (Courtesy of Charles Michael Finlayson.)

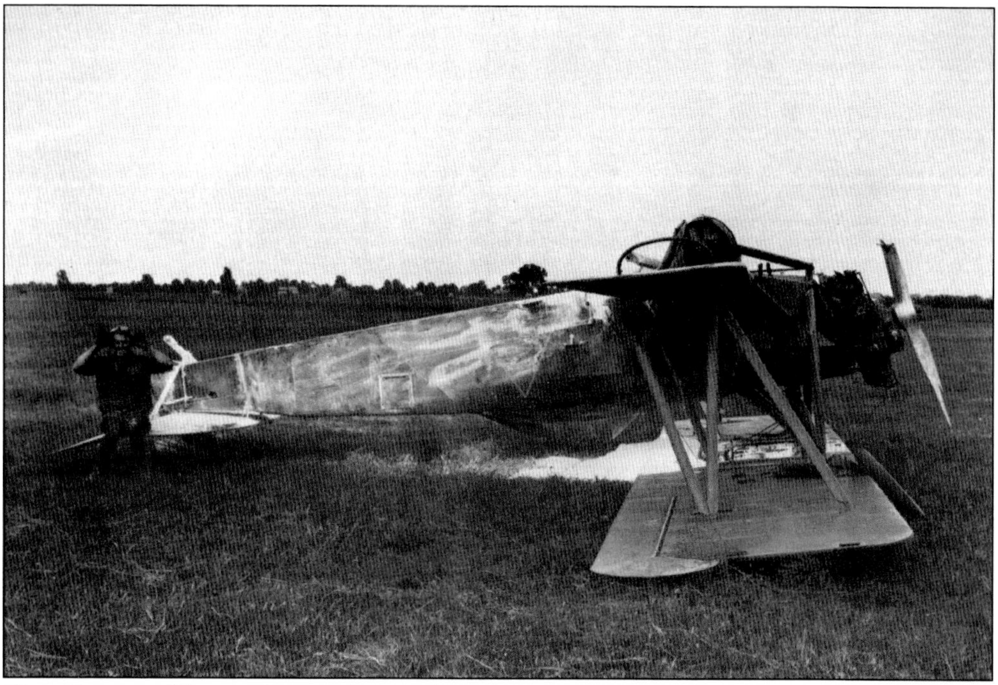

HUFF-DALAND WRECK. Cotton dusting from the air was a very dangerous business, although the pilot does not seem too unhappy. (Courtesy of Charles Michael Finlayson.)

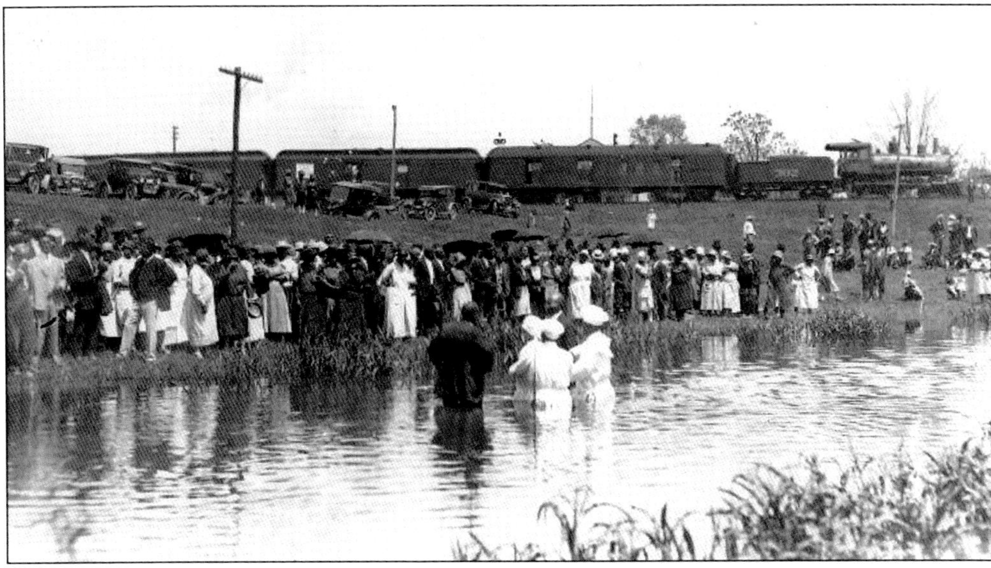

Brushy Bayou Baptizing. In the 1920s, 1930s, and 1940s, baptisms at Tallulah in Brushy Bayou, between the Johnson Street Bridge and the Illinois Central Railroad, occurred throughout the summer months and were always well attended. The candidates marched from their church dressed in fine white vestments and lined up to be immersed in the waters of Brushy Bayou. Much chanting and singing of beautiful black gospels occurred during the baptizing ceremony. This photograph was apparently taken in the 1920s. (Courtesy of Sherrill Sevier Pirone.)

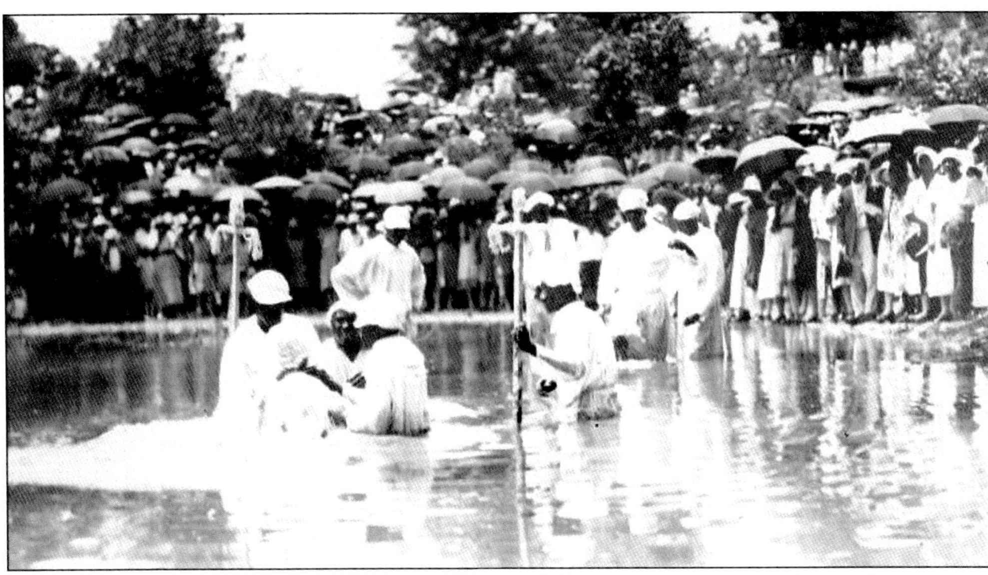

Brushy Bayou Baptizing—Immersion. The candidate is being immersed into the waters of Brushy Bayou. (Courtesy of Mary Jo Provine Briggs.)

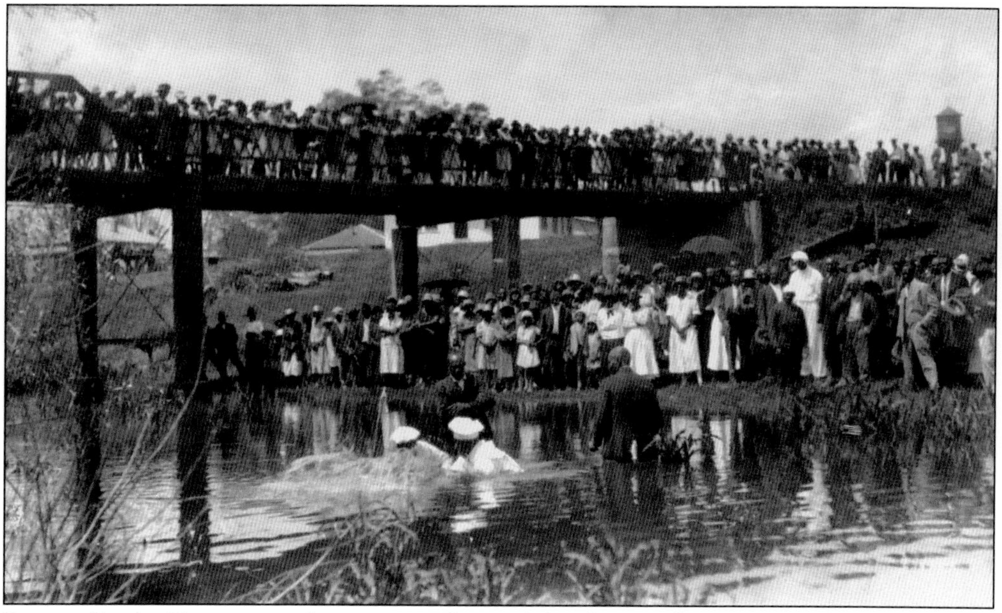

Brushy Bayou Baptizing—Immersion. The candidate has just been immersed into the waters of Brushy Bayou. Note the old Johnson Street Bridge, which was replaced in the early 1930s. A later picture of this bridge will show it below water level during the 1927 flood. (Courtesy of Sherrill Sevier Pirone.)

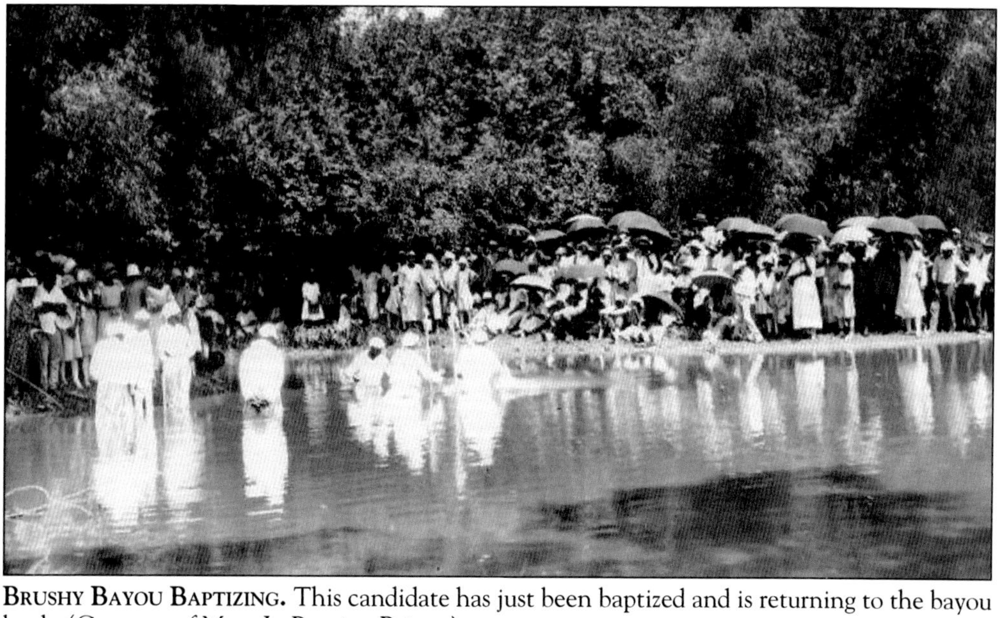

Brushy Bayou Baptizing. This candidate has just been baptized and is returning to the bayou bank. (Courtesy of Mary Jo Provine Briggs.)

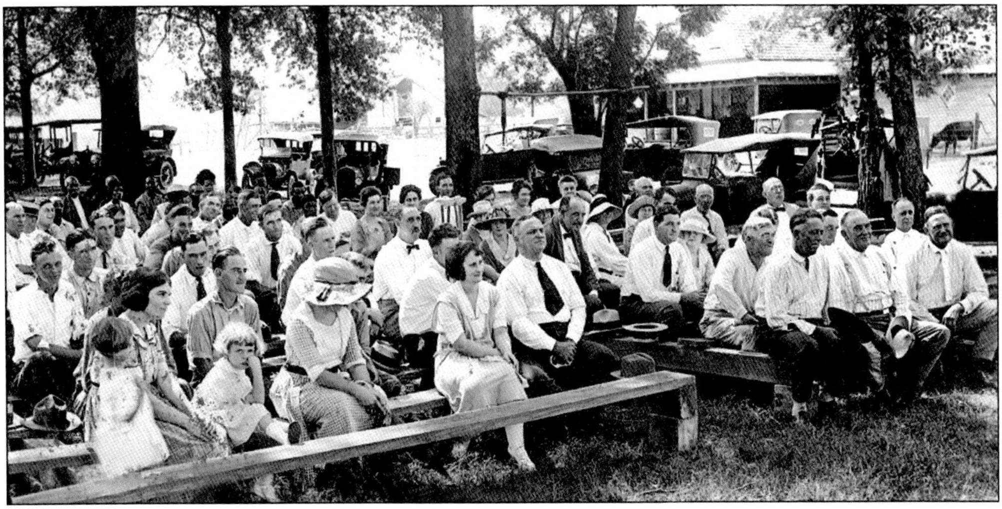

1920s Public Gathering. This 1920s get-together was reportedly a meeting to discuss the eradication of the boll weevil. The house in the background is that of the Moberleys on Laclede Plantation. (Courtesy of Henry C. Sevier Jr.)

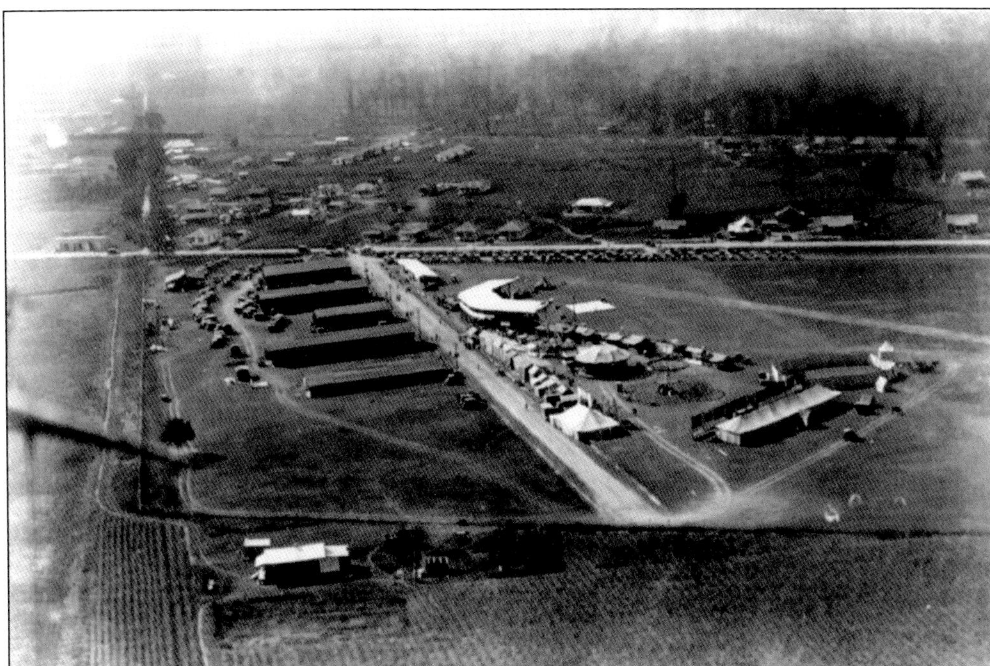

Aerial View of Louisiana Delta Fair in Tallulah. During the first part of the 20th century, the Louisiana Delta Fair was held each October and included exhibits from Madison, East Carroll, and Tensas Parishes. The fair was phased out during the latter part of the century and has not been held in many years. (Courtesy of the USDA.)

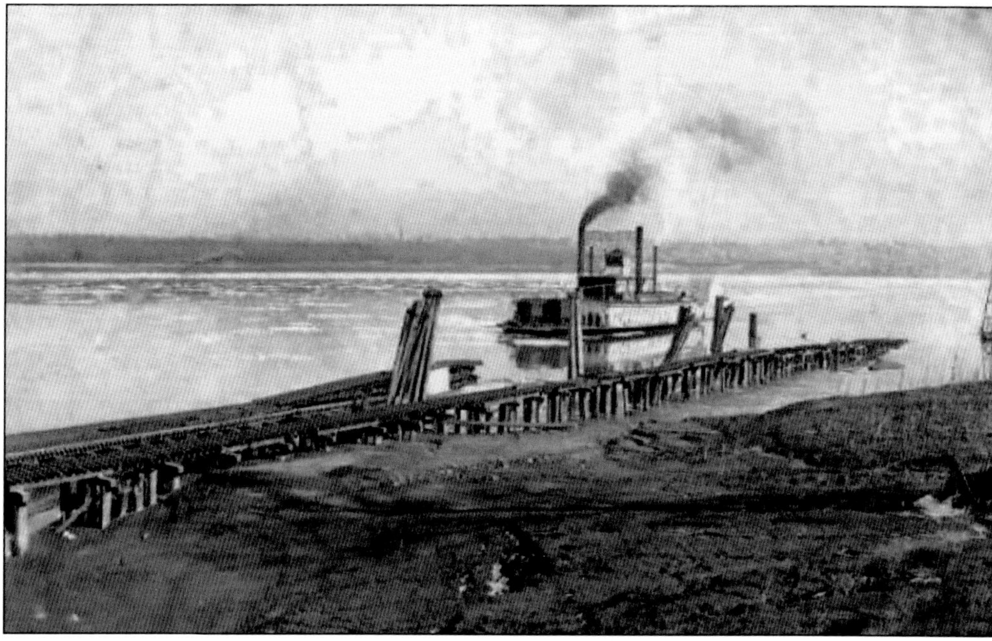

DELTA TO VICKSBURG FERRY. In the 1920s and earlier there was no bridge across the Mississippi River to Vicksburg. This ferry operated for many years, even after the Vicksburg Bridge on U.S. Highway 80 was built. (Courtesy of Sally Jo Foster Gibson.)

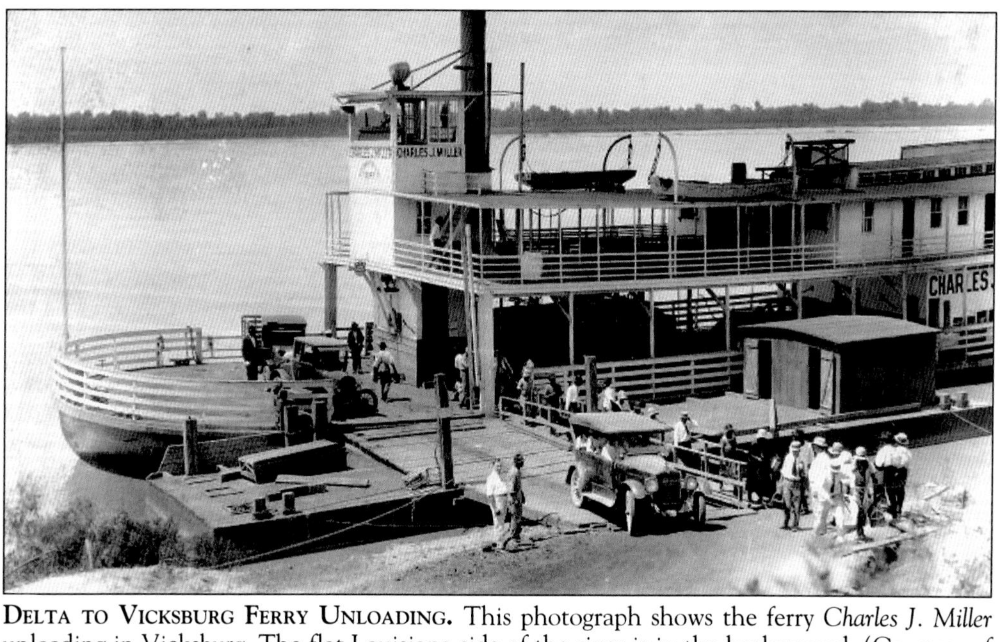

DELTA TO VICKSBURG FERRY UNLOADING. This photograph shows the ferry *Charles J. Miller* unloading in Vicksburg. The flat Louisiana side of the river is in the background. (Courtesy of Mary Jo Provine Briggs.)

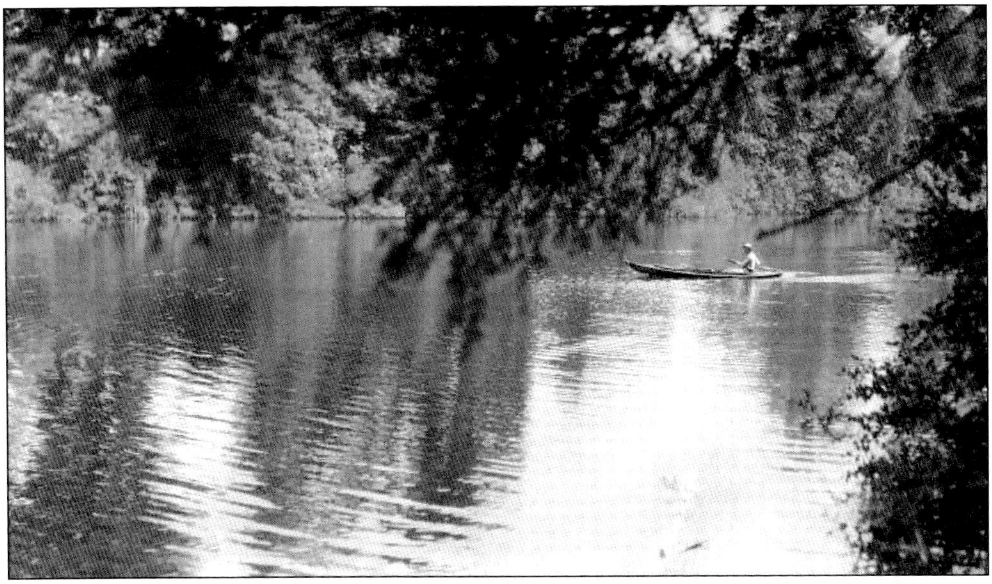

Bear Lake. In addition to being the home of the Bear Lake Hunting Club, during the 1920s until the 1940s, Bear Lake was the most popular swimming hole in the area and was also a popular fishing lake. (Courtesy of Mary Jo Provine Briggs.)

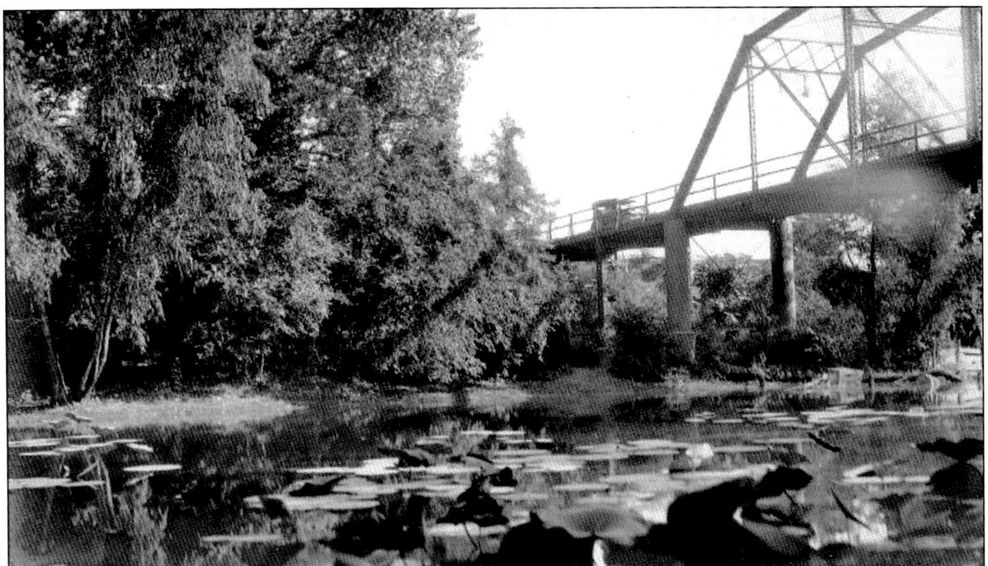

Bear Lake Bridge. This old bridge over the southern end of Bear Lake was abandoned during the 1930s. (Courtesy of Mary Jo Provine Briggs.)

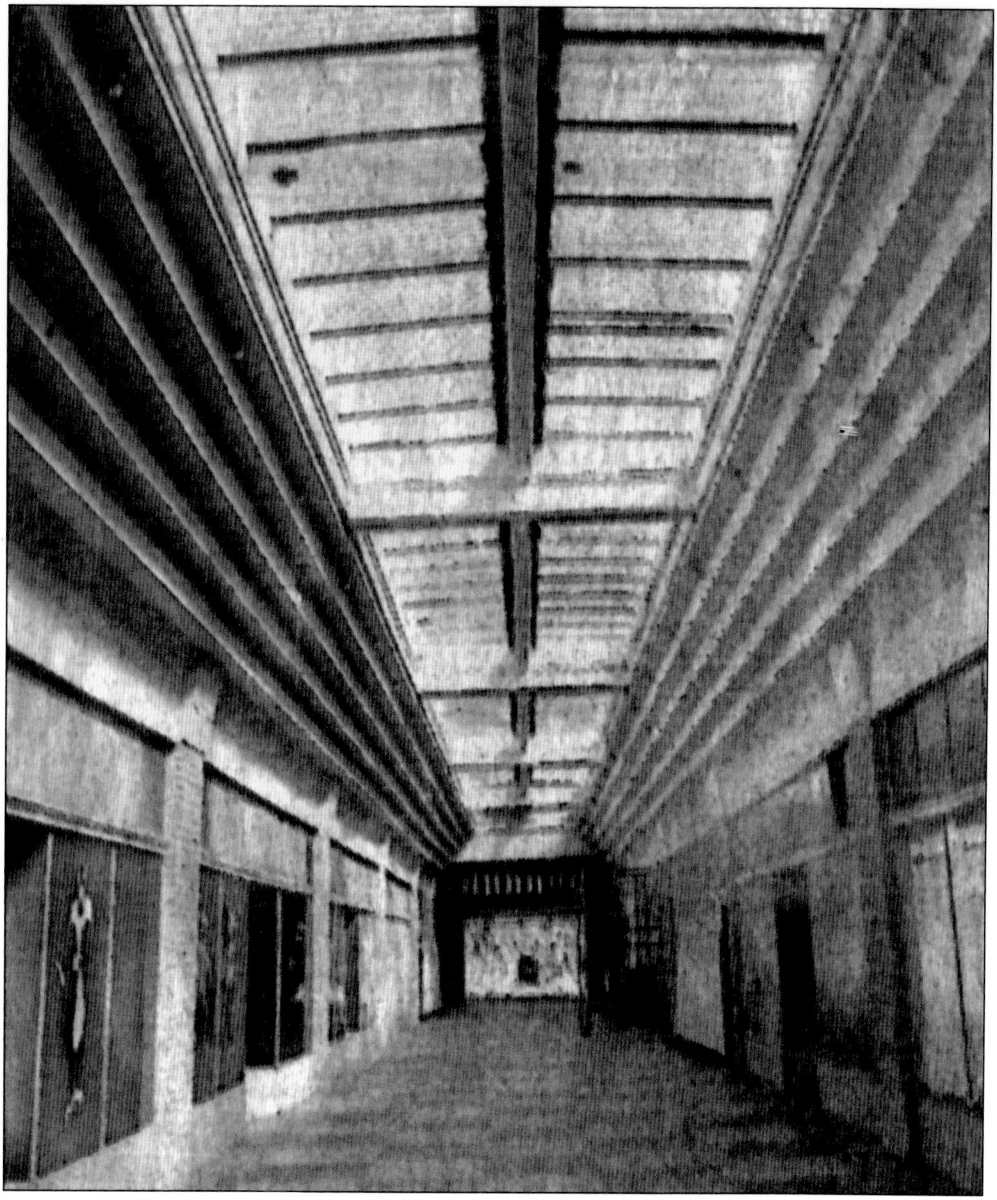

INTERIOR OF BLOOM'S ARCADE. In 1927 Mertie M. and Abe Bloom built the first covered mall in the United States in Tallulah. The mall, built by famed architect A. Hays Town, is the only European-style arcade mall in Louisiana. Now practically abandoned, in its heyday the mall featured a series of exclusive specialty shops. (Courtesy of the Madison Historical Society.)

Five

The 1927 Flood

Due to its flat, low-lying position and its proximity to the Mississippi River, the lands making up Madison Parish have been subject to flooding throughout historic times. Prior to the colossal 1927 flood, devastating floods occurred in 1849, 1850, 1867, 1871, 1882, 1892, 1897, 1903, and 1912.

Natural levees are built on the banks of flooding streams due to the coarser and heavier sediments first laid down during an overflow. However, these levees are only a few feet higher than the surrounding territory and will not hold even a moderate rise in the stream level. When people came to raise crops on the rich, alluvial soil next to the rivers it became apparent that a system of artificial levees had to be devised. By 1844 levees had been built along the Mississippi River all the way to the Arkansas line. These levees were about four feet higher than the highest ridges and had a base of about 20 feet. By 1852 the levees had risen to 10 feet with a base of 50 to 80 feet. During the Civil War the levees were destroyed for military reasons, and afterwards there was no money to rebuild them. During the 1880s Madison's levees were increased eight feet in height, about the same elevation as the 1882 flood. The levees were broken again in 1903, and again they were made higher and stronger. After the disastrous flood of 1912, a devastating event second only to that of 1927, the levees were refurbished again.

During the heavy rains of 1926–1927, the area soils were soaked and the streams were full. Levees began to break all along the river, and at 2 p.m. on May 3, 1927 the levee broke at Cabin Teele Plantation near Milliken's Bend. Water from this crevasse ultimately covered the entire parish to a depth of six inches to ten feet and caused some $2,000,000 in damage. This flood did not recede in some places until late July.

Madison Parish history is indebted to Haw Kirkpatrick and Perry Glick of the USDA for most of the following pictures, which are presented in as chronological an order as possible.

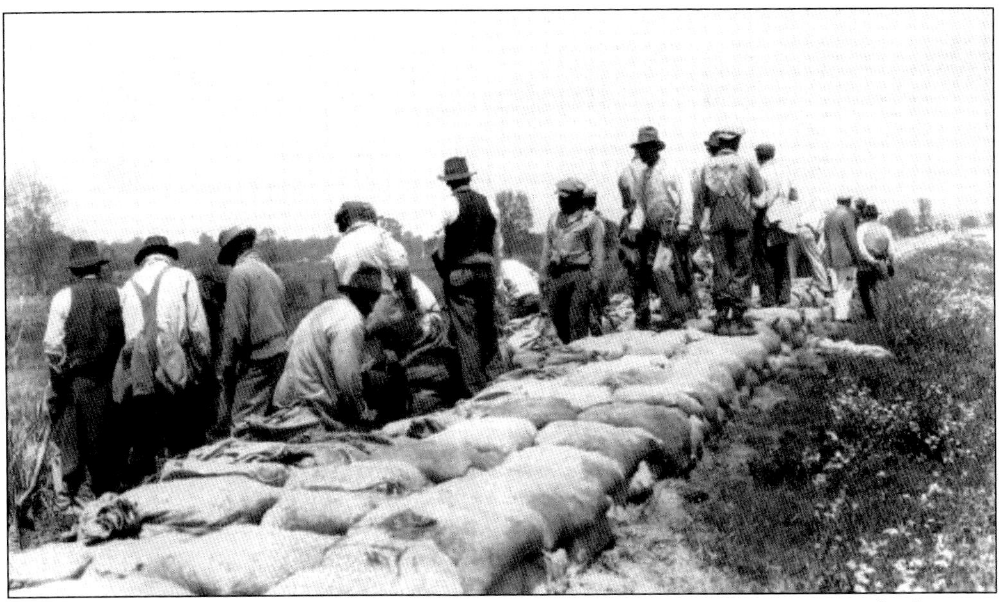

April 28, Duckport—Filling sandbags. Preparations began in April to raise the levee to prevent a possible flood. This picture at Duckport shows workmen filling the sandbags with material six days before the levee broke. (Courtesy of the USDA.)

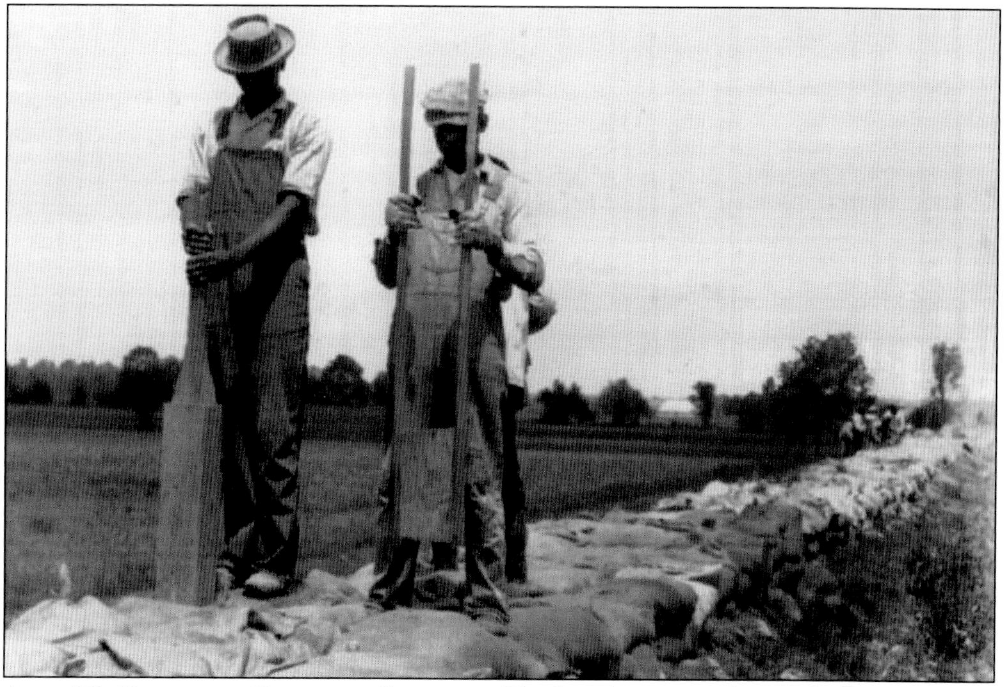

April 28, Duckport—Preparing Sandbags. The boards were used to pack the bags tightly and evenly. (Courtesy of the USDA.)

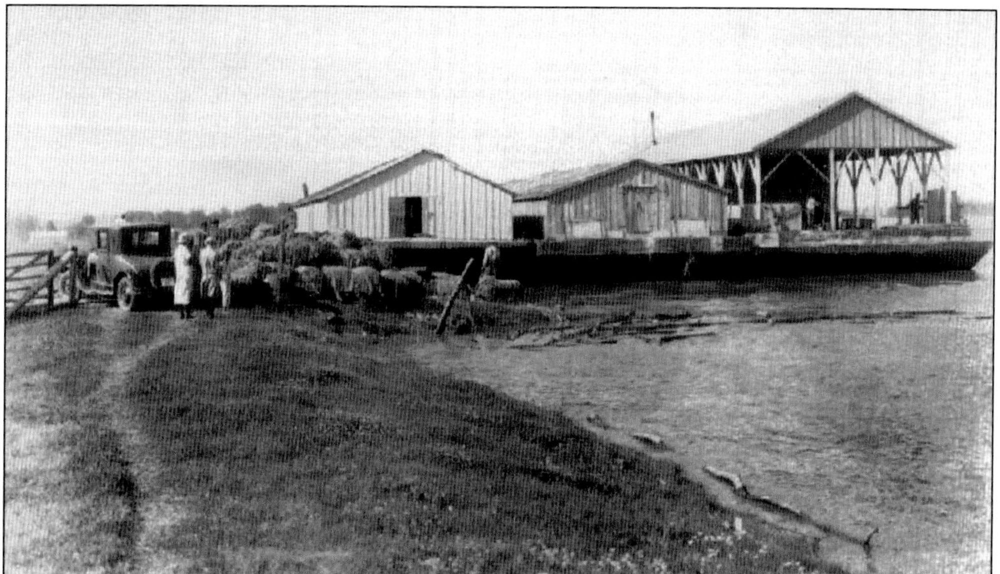

April 28, Duckport—Quarterboats. These boats housed the men and material used to strengthen the levees. Note how close the water level is to the top of the levee. (Courtesy of the USDA.)

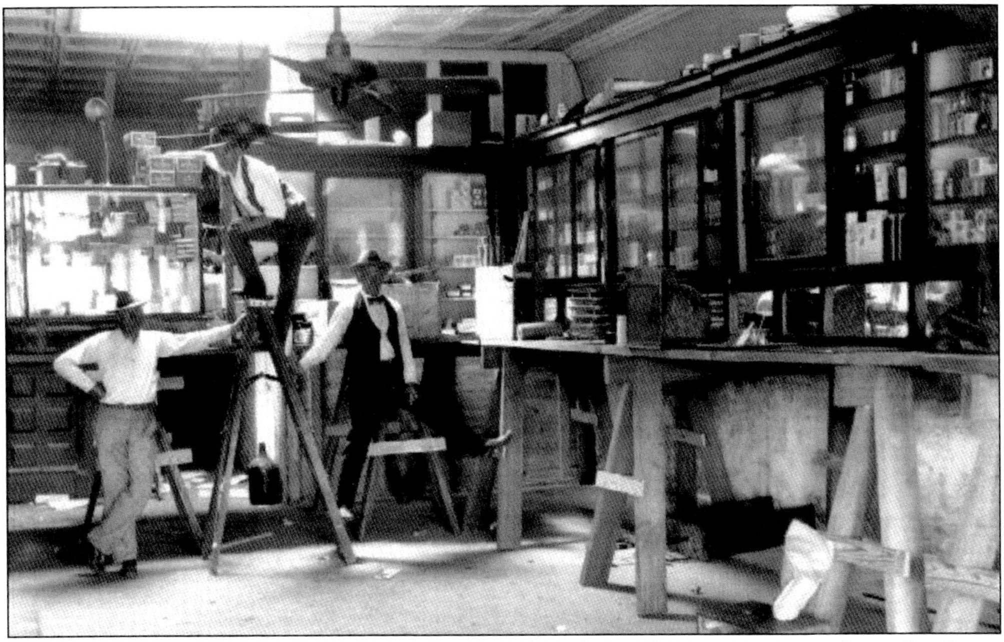

MAY 5, TALLULAH—BLOOM DRUG COMPANY. This shows the situation two days after levee broke. Pictured are Mertie Bloom (on the ladder) and two unidentified men just hours before the water arrived. (Courtesy of the USDA.)

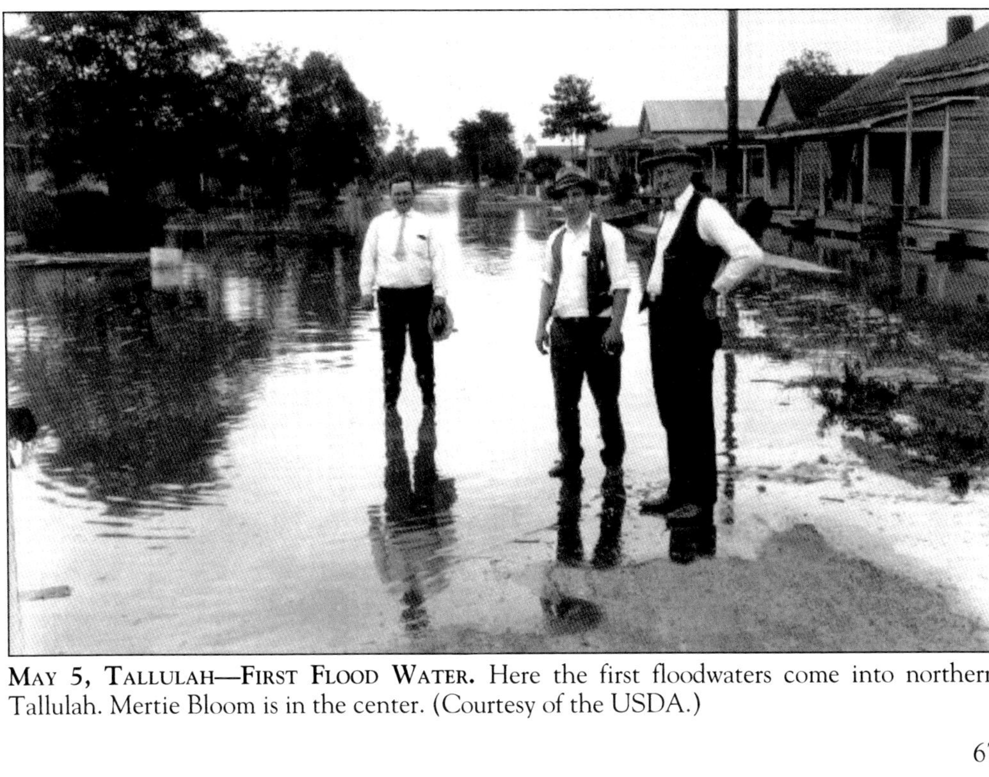

MAY 5, TALLULAH—FIRST FLOOD WATER. Here the first floodwaters come into northern Tallulah. Mertie Bloom is in the center. (Courtesy of the USDA.)

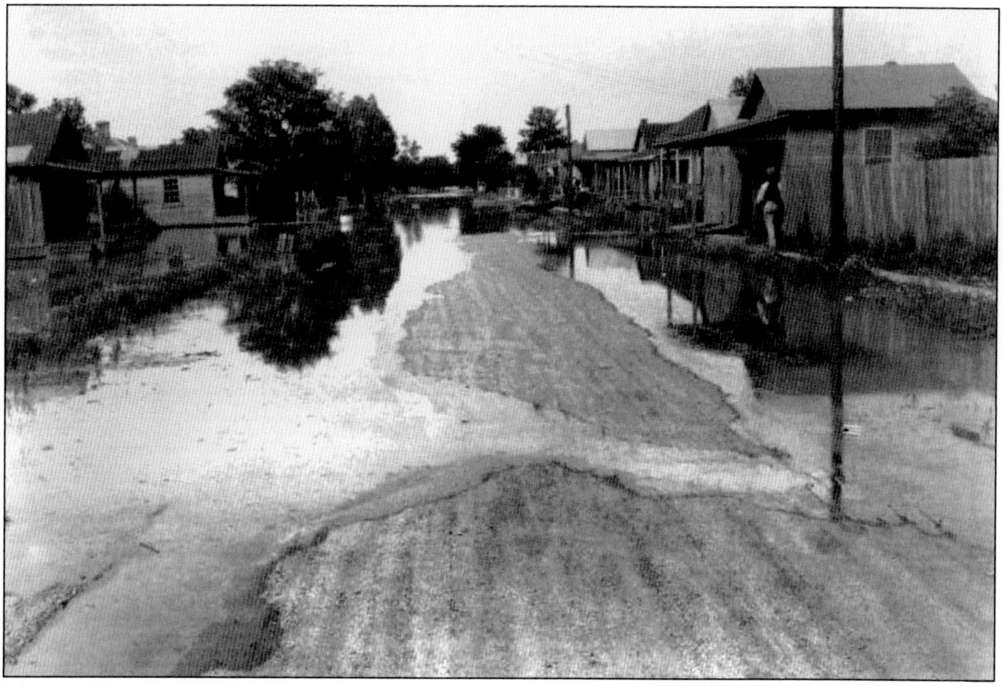

MAY 5, TALLULAH—FIRST FLOOD WATER. This shows waters coming into northern Tallulah much faster. (Courtesy of the USDA.)

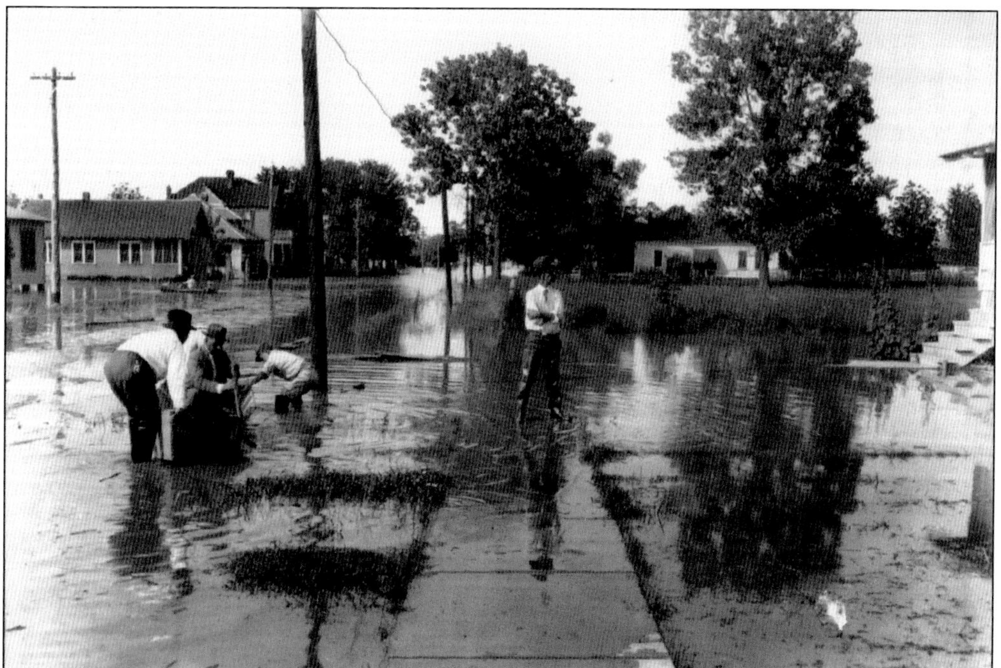

MAY 5, TALLULAH—FIRST FLOOD WATER. This photograph is looking north on North Cedar (U.S. Highway 65). Water now has reached almost downtown. Houses at center left belonged to the Claughtons and Sheriff A.J. Sevier. (Courtesy of the USDA.)

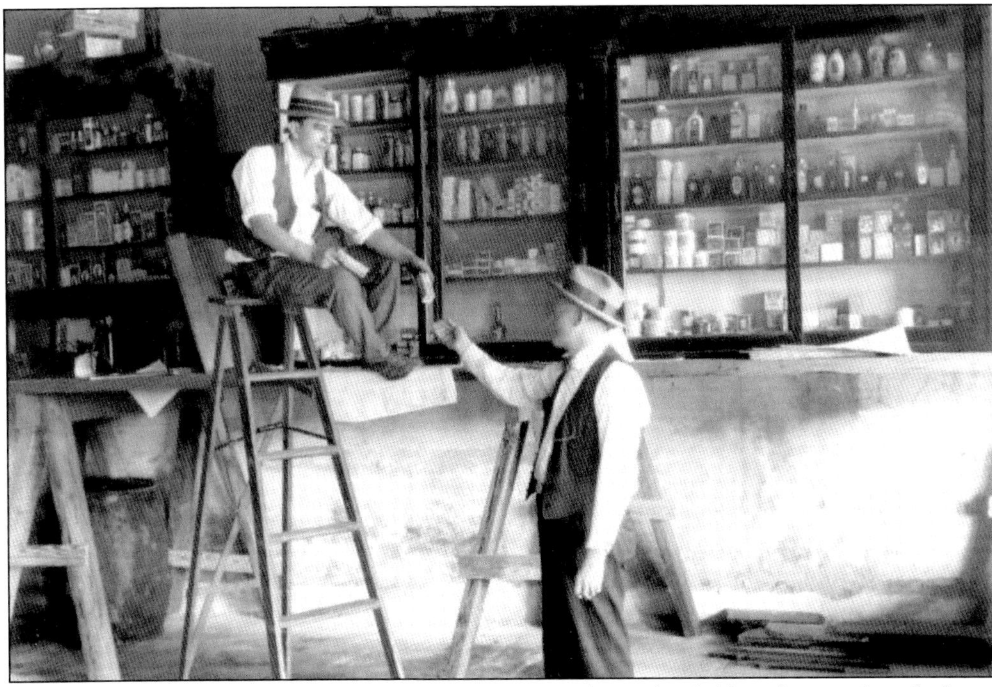

MAY 5, TALLULAH—BLOOM DRUG COMPANY. Mertie Bloom (on left) and an unidentified man celebrate with a beer after they raised their goods above the expected flood level. (Courtesy of the USDA.)

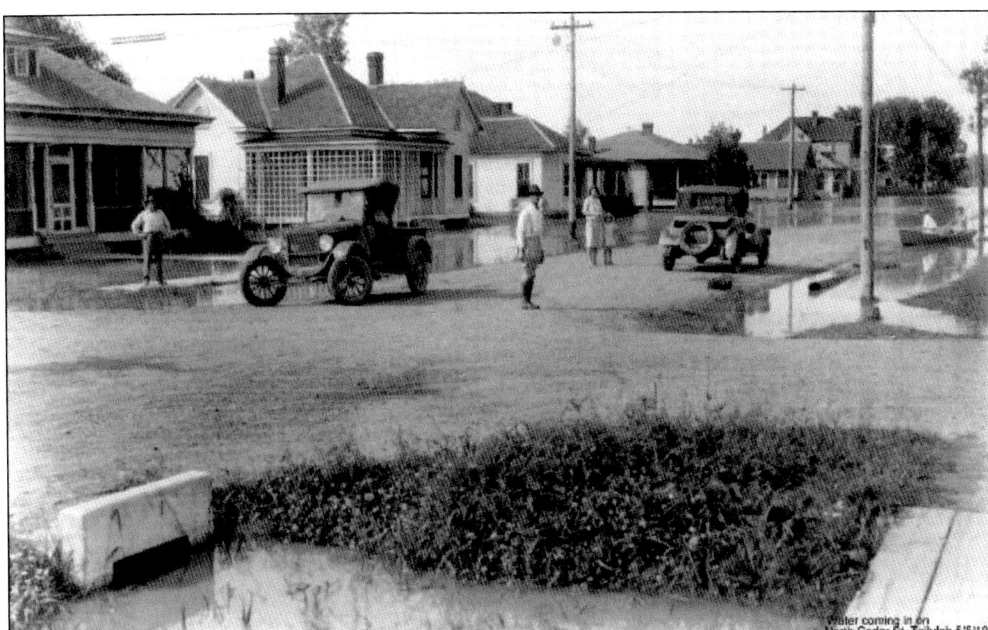

MAY 5, TALLULAH—FIRST FLOOD WATER. Here is another view looking north on North Cedar (U.S. Highway 65). (Courtesy of the USDA.)

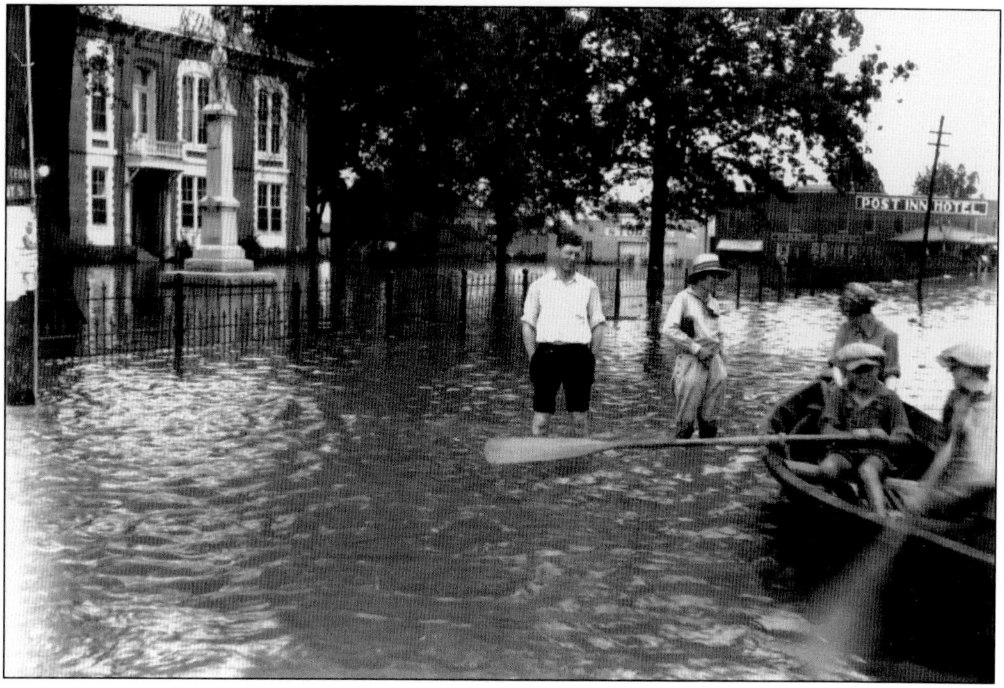

MAY 7, TALLULAH—DOWNTOWN. This was taken four days since the break in the levee, on the east side of the courthouse. Two days later the floodwaters had covered all of Tallulah. The people are standing in what is now the northbound lane of U.S. Highway 65. (Courtesy of the USDA.)

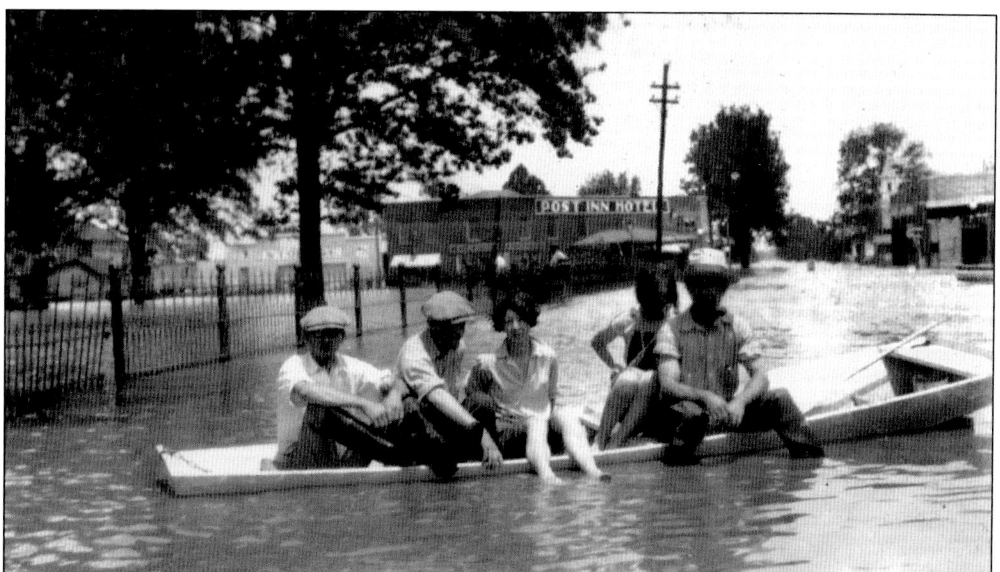

MAY 7, TALLULAH—DOWNTOWN. Here is another photograph on east side of courthouse. Martha Boney (facing forward) and Liz Kell are with three unidentified gentlemen, all employees of the USDA. (Courtesy of Judy Kell Morris.)

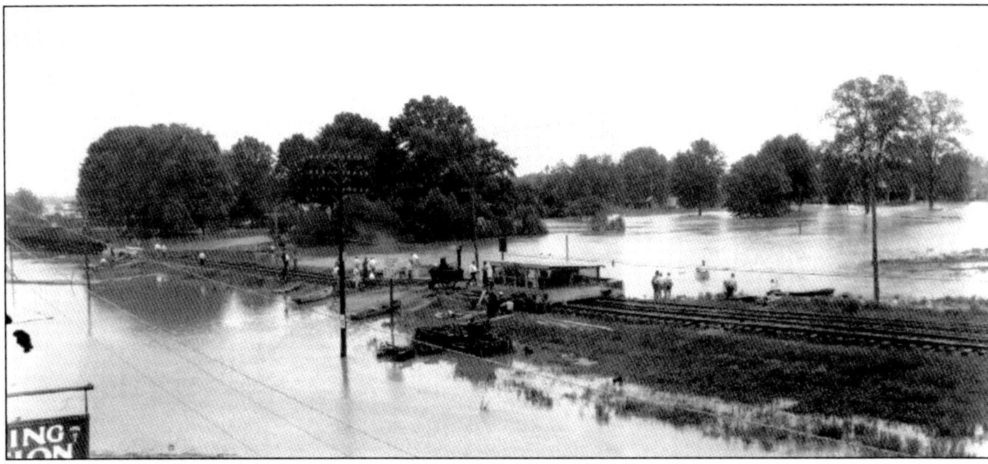

May 7, Tallulah—Red Cross Kitchen. Shown here is a Red Cross kitchen on the Illinois Central Railroad. This panoramic view is to the southeast across Brushy Bayou. (Courtesy of the USDA.)

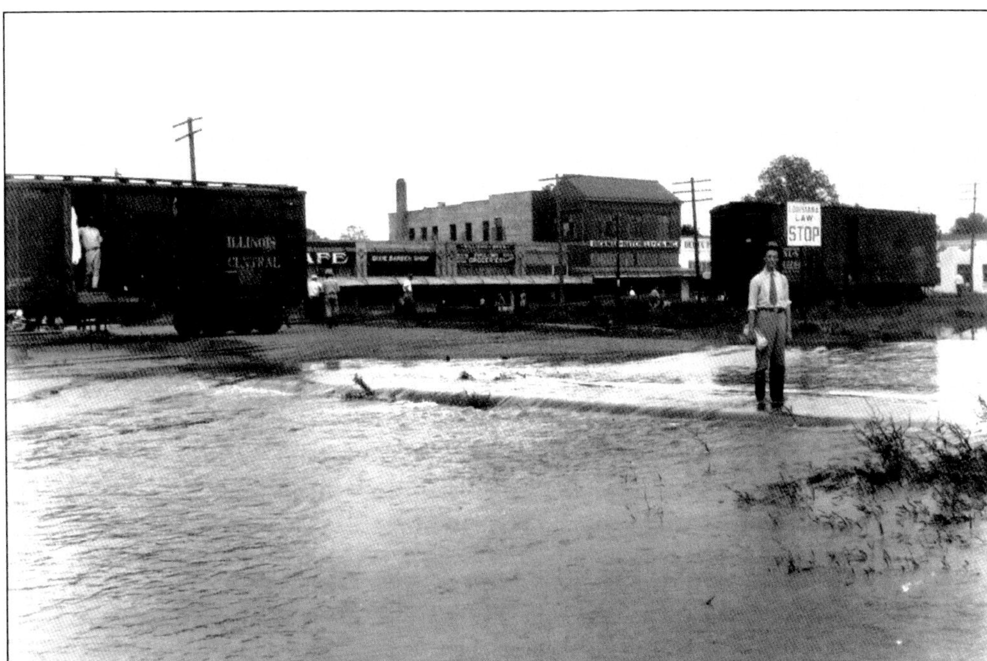

May 7, Tallulah—Wader. A wader walks on the south side of the Illinois Central Railroad. The railroad bed now is the highest part of town and the railroad cars became home to many refugees. (Courtesy of the USDA.)

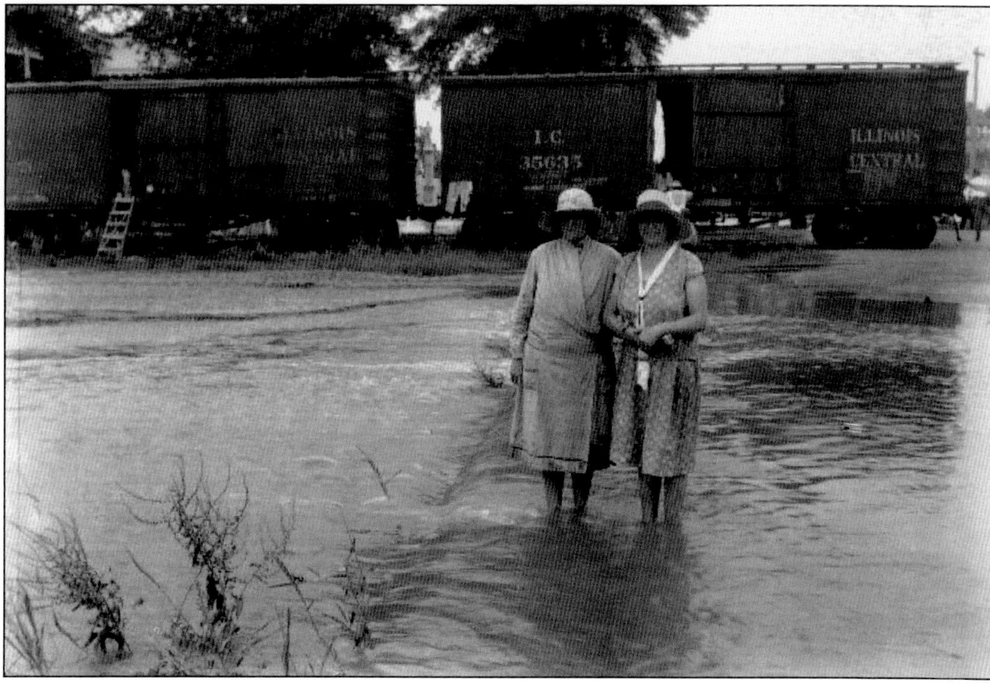

MAY 7, TALLULAH—MORE WADERS. Two ladies are seen here wading on the south side of the railroad track. (Courtesy of the USDA.)

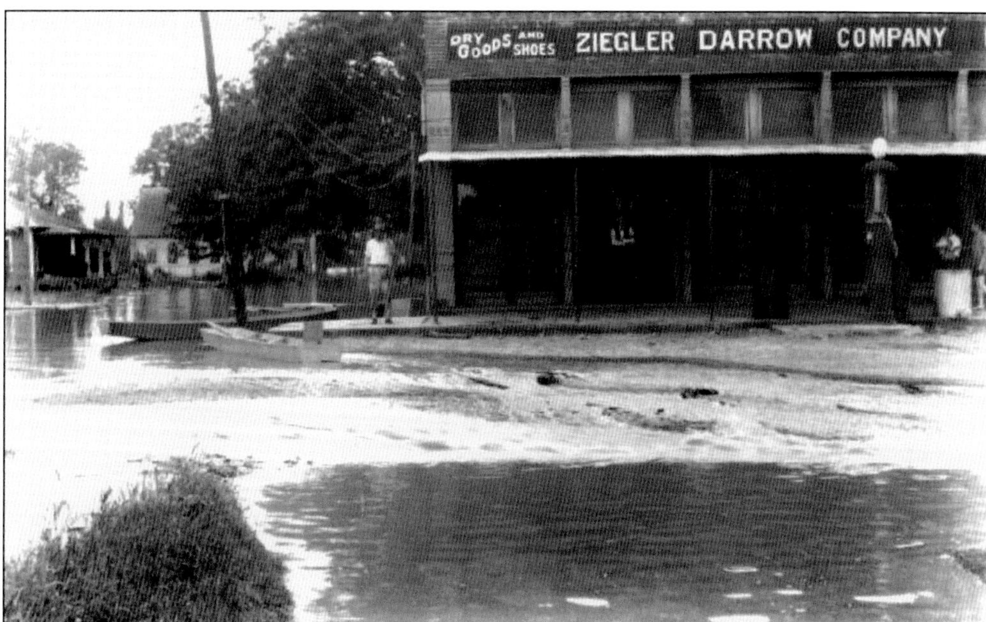

MAY 7, TALLULAH—ZIEGLER-DARROW HARDWARE. Ziegler-Darrow Hardware is seen on the south side of the railroad track. (Courtesy of the USDA.)

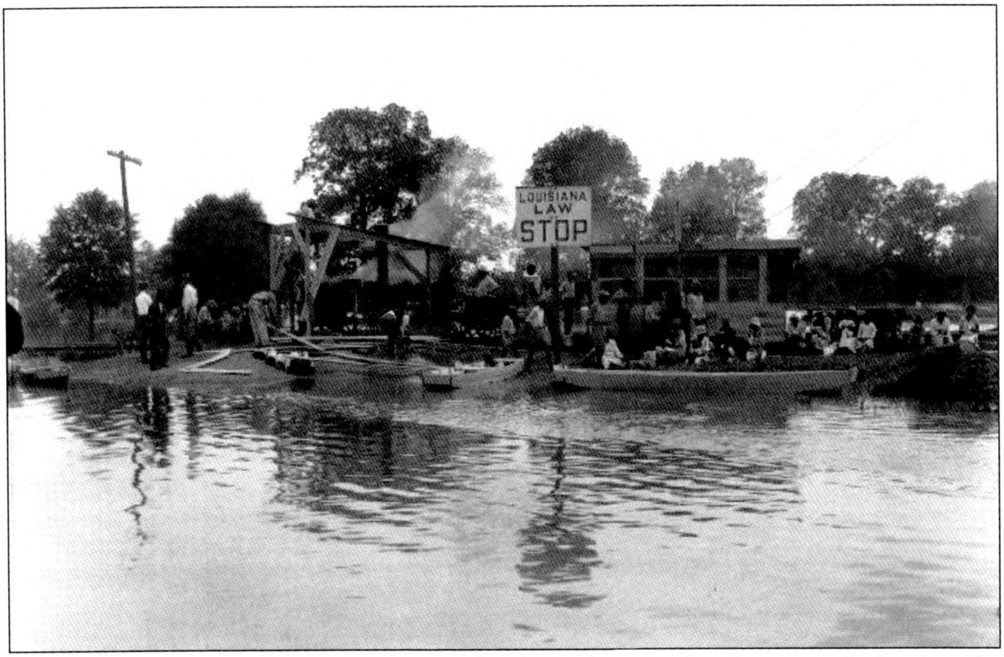

MAY 8, TALLULAH—RED CROSS KITCHEN. This shows the scene five days since the break in the levee. A Red Cross kitchen on the Illinois Central Railroad is shown as a close-up of a previous picture. (Courtesy of the USDA.)

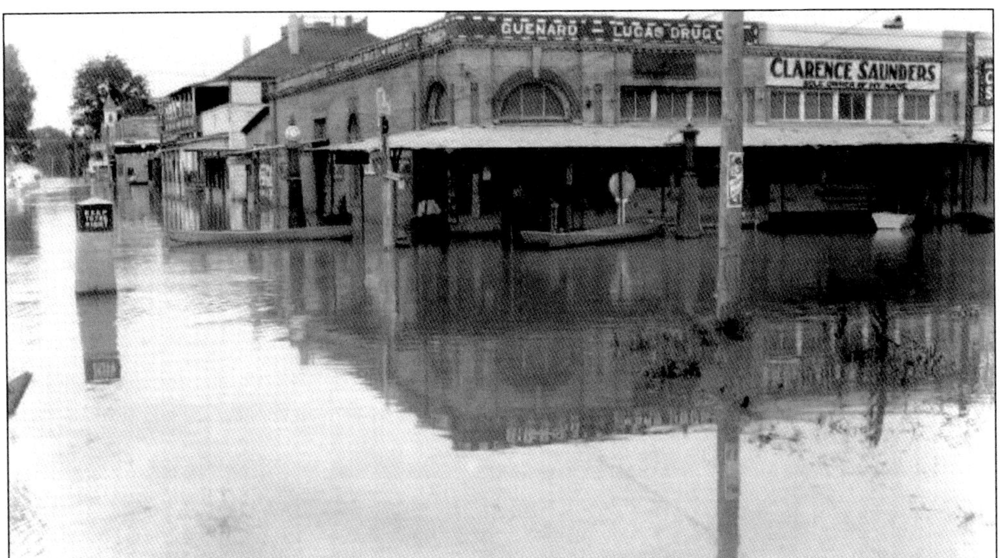

MAY 8, TALLULAH—CORNER OF DEPOT (NOW SNYDER) AND NORTH CEDAR. The Guenard-Lucas Drug Store is on the right. (Courtesy of the USDA.)

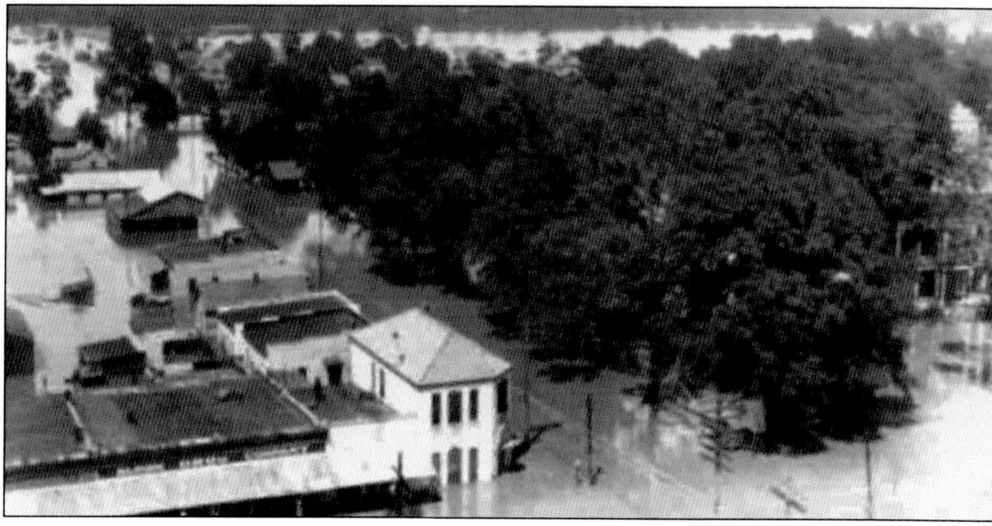

MAY 8, TALLULAH—CORNER OF DEPOT (NOW SNYDER) AND NORTH CHESTNUT. The Old Tallulah State Bank is in the left foreground and the courthouse is on the right. The street between them is now southbound U.S. Highway 65. (Courtesy of Reid Foster.)

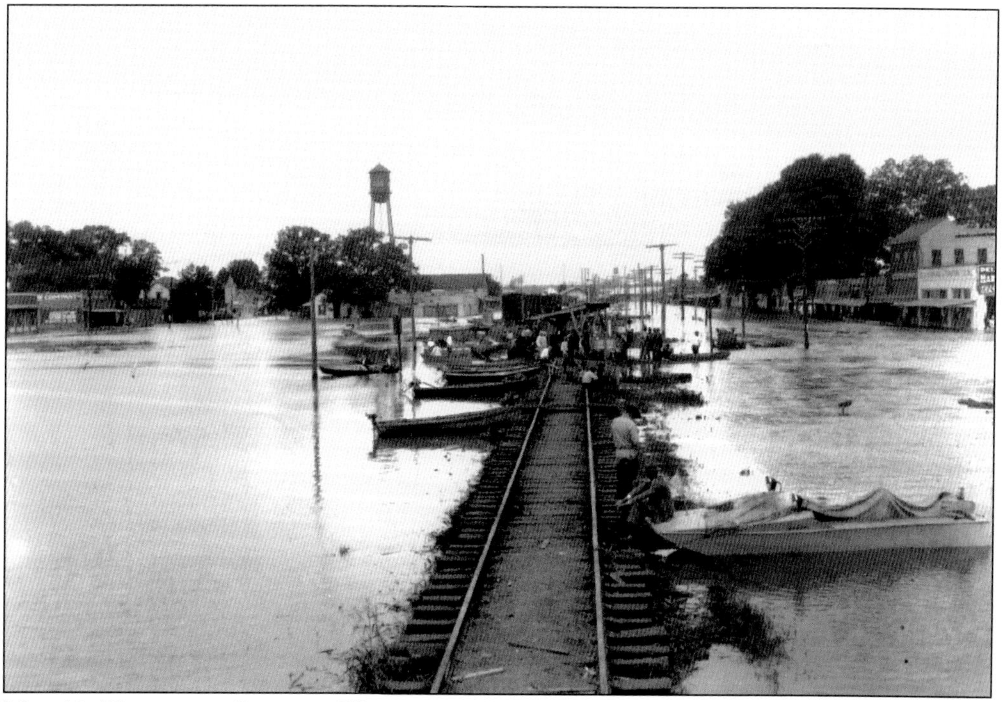

MAY 10, TALLULAH—LOOKING WEST ALONG ILLINOIS CENTRAL RAILROAD. It has been seven days since the break in the levee in this photograph. (Courtesy of the USDA.)

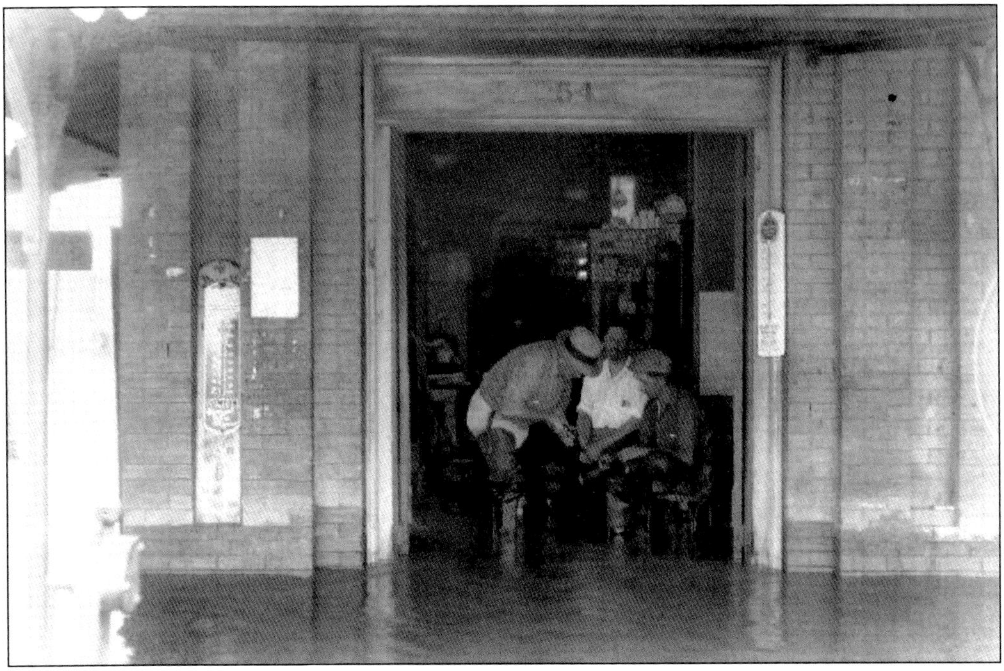

May 10, Tallulah—Shooting Dice at Guenard-Lucas Drug. Johnson, Agee, and Long are seen from left to right. (Courtesy of the USDA.)

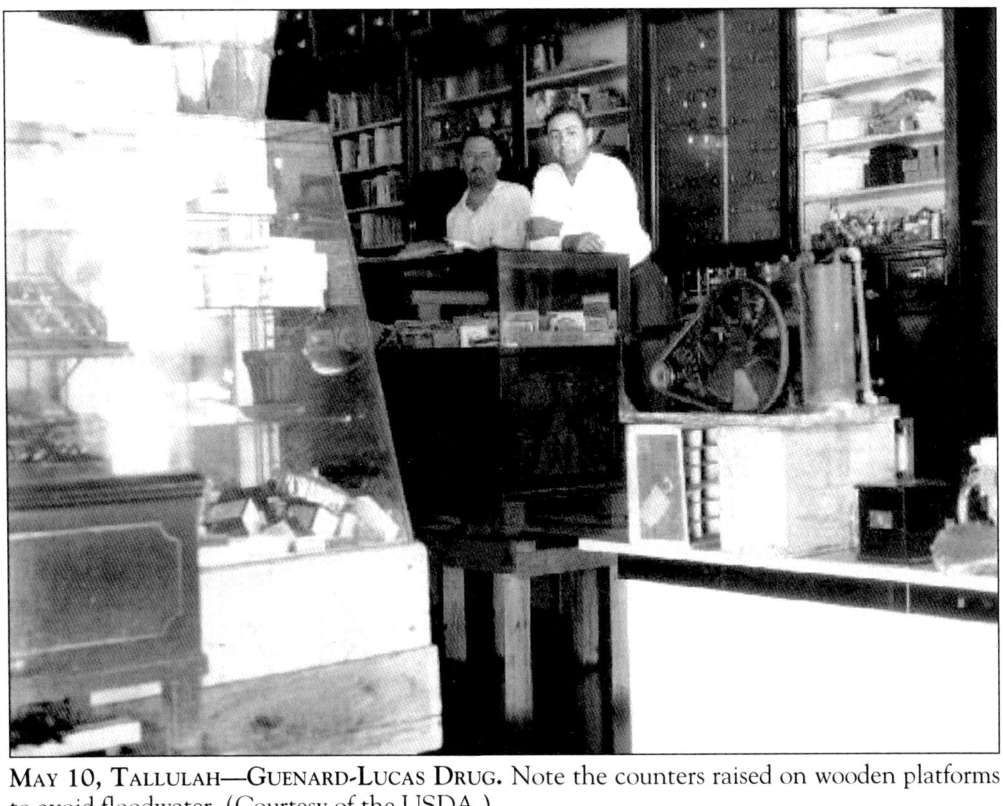

May 10, Tallulah—Guenard-Lucas Drug. Note the counters raised on wooden platforms to avoid floodwater. (Courtesy of the USDA.)

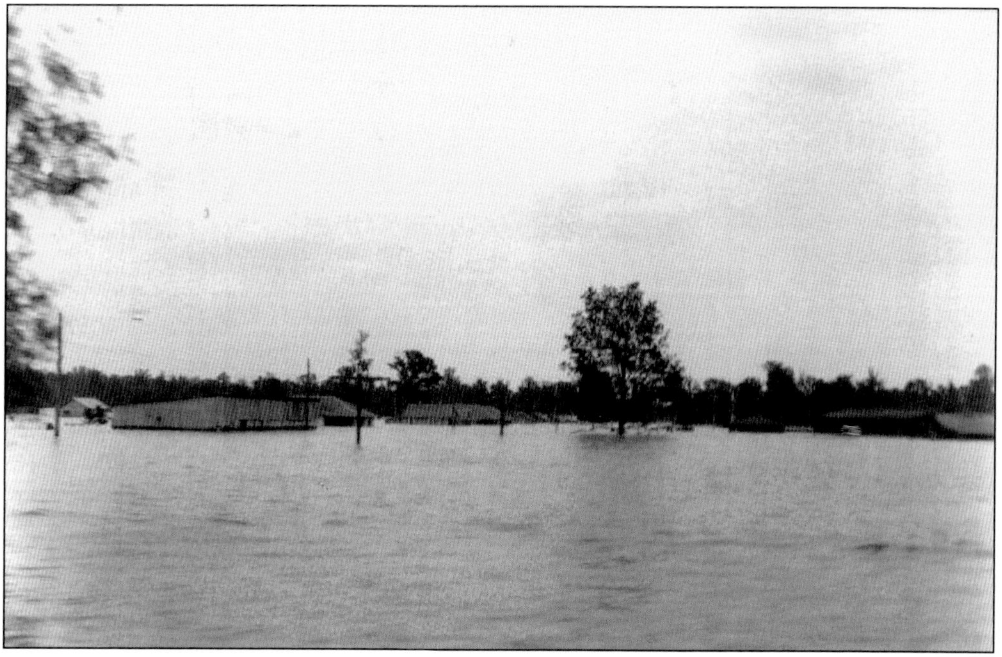

MAY 10, TALLULAH—U.S. HIGHWAY 65 NORTH. The water is much deeper now and about to reach the roofs of some of the houses in the background. (Courtesy of the USDA.)

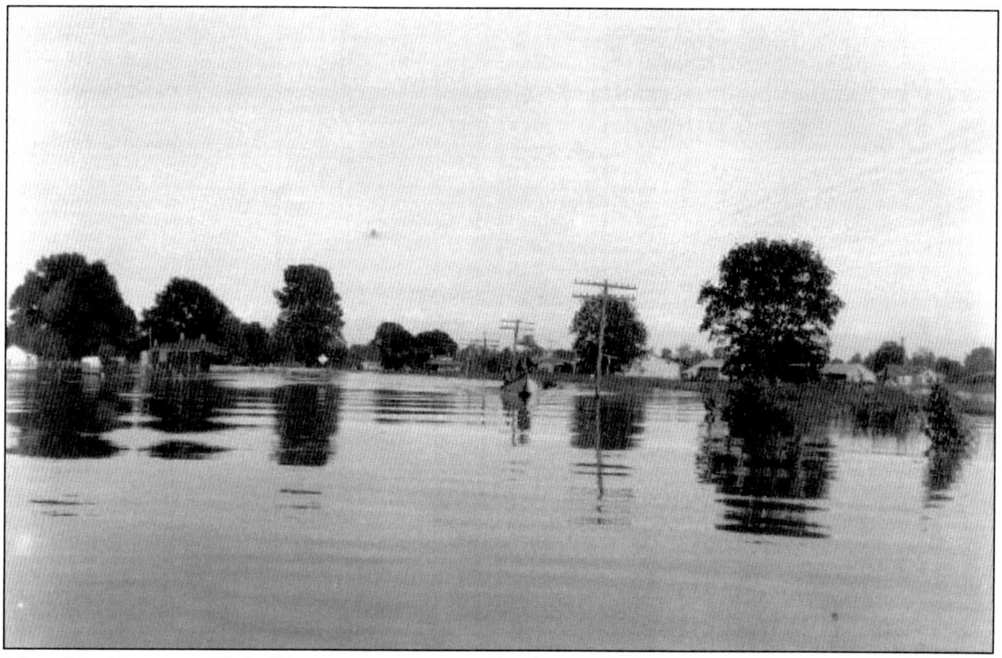

MAY 10, MOUND—U.S. HIGHWAY 80. Mound is located about 11 miles east of Tallulah and 8 miles west of Vicksburg, Mississippi. The site of the previously discussed Mound Colony and some later photos of Mound Plantation, it was named for several Indian mounds in the vicinity. (Courtesy of the USDA.)

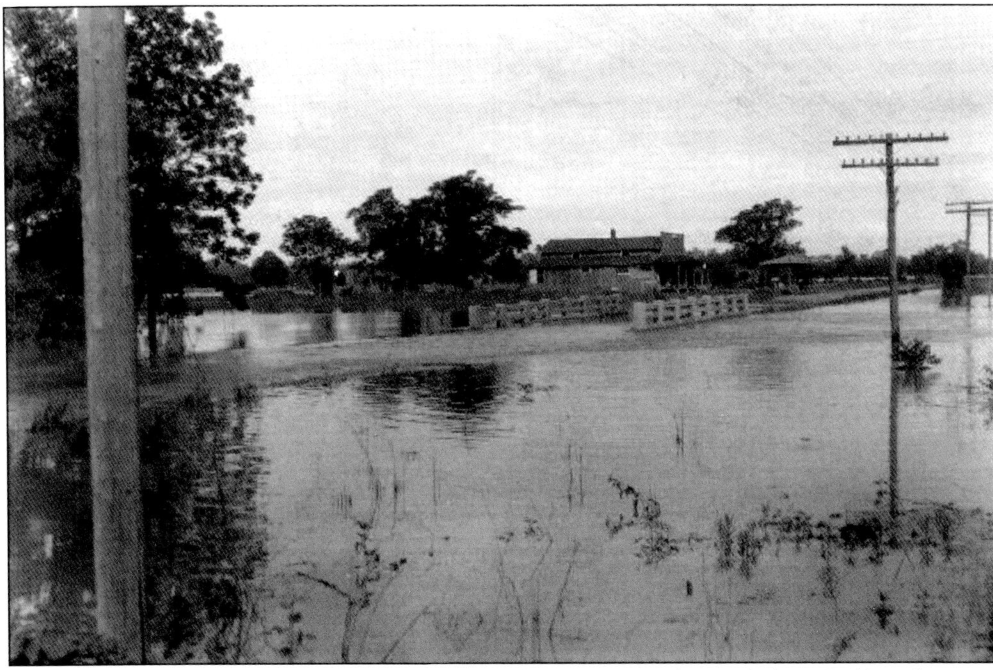

MAY 10, THOMASTOWN—U.S. HIGHWAY 80. Thomastown is located about halfway between Tallulah and Vicksburg. The old Thomastown store can be seen in the background. (Courtesy of the USDA.)

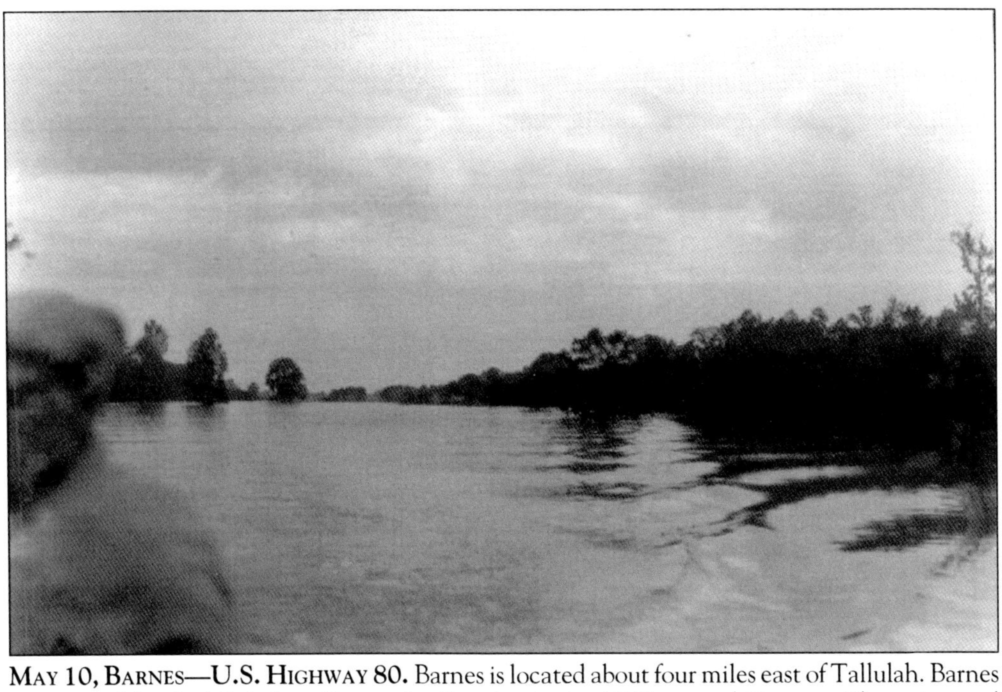

MAY 10, BARNES—U.S. HIGHWAY 80. Barnes is located about four miles east of Tallulah. Barnes was named for the Nicholson Barnes family, who in the 1830s owned Crescent Plantation and built the house at Crescent pictured earlier. (Courtesy of the USDA.)

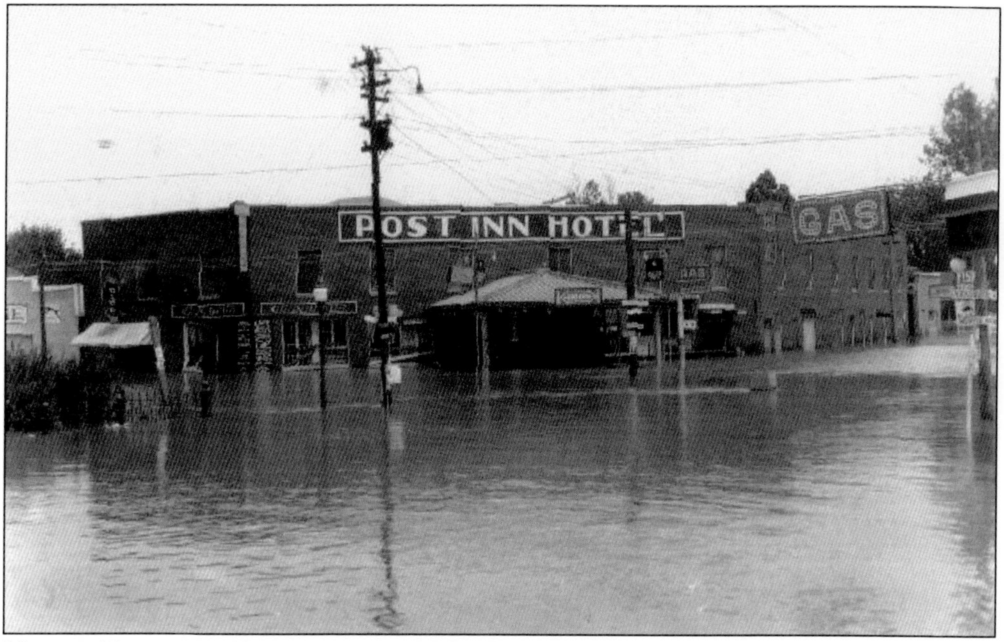

MAY 10, TALLULAH—INTERSECTION OF U.S. HIGHWAYS 65 AND 80. The Post Inn Hotel in the foreground was for many years Tallulah's only hotel. It was a "full stop shop" with a cafe and a gas station. (Courtesy of the USDA.)

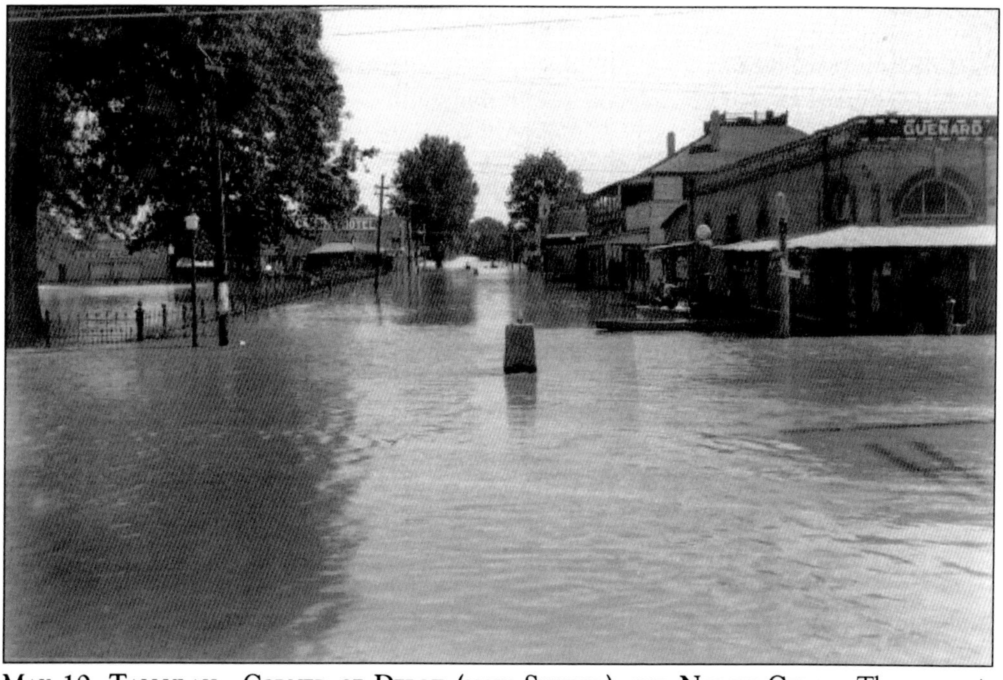

MAY 10, TALLULAH—CORNER OF DEPOT (NOW SNYDER) AND NORTH CEDAR. The water is much higher now than earlier. The view is north along U.S. Highway 65. The building on the right is the Guenard-Lucas Drugstore, and the tall building on the right center was the home of the Tallulah Social and Literary Club—where the main activity was poker playing. (Courtesy of the USDA.)

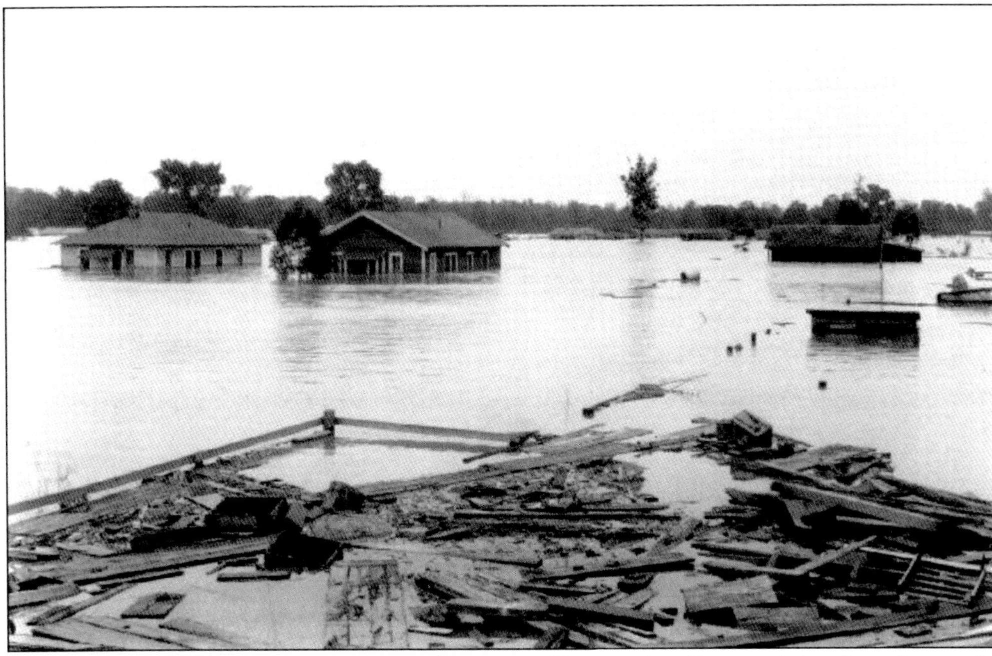

MAY 10, TALLULAH—NORTHWESTERN PART OF TOWN. As illustrated by this photo, the northern part of Tallulah was generally the lowest. Note the huge collection of debris in the foreground. (Courtesy of the USDA.)

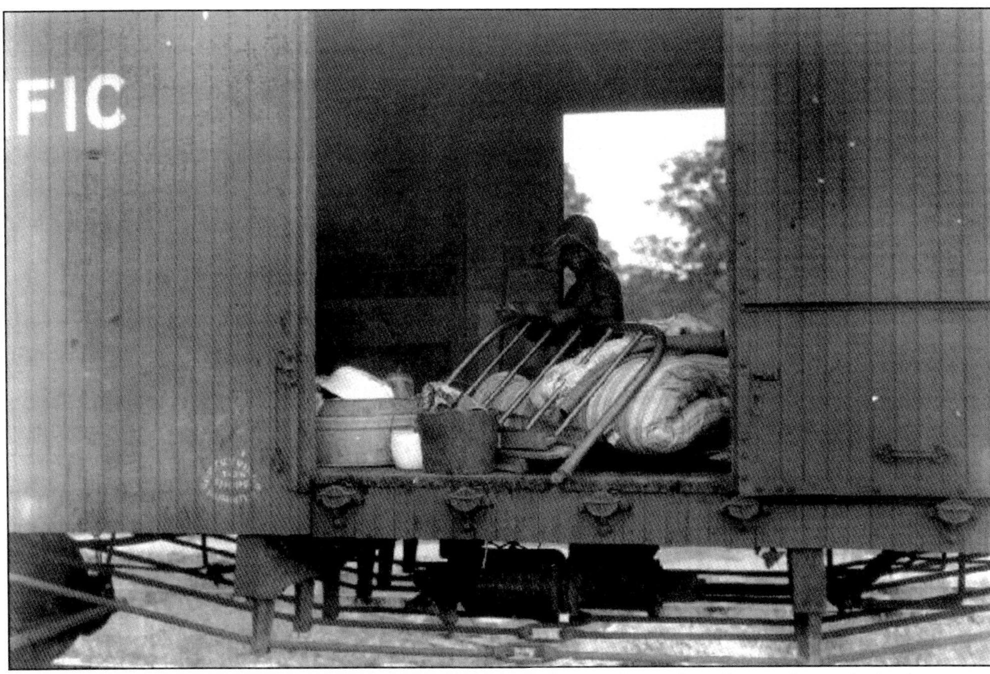

MAY 10, TALLULAH—REFUGEE LIVING IN BOXCAR. Since the railroad was the only high ground many residents spent weeks living in railroad cars. (Courtesy of the USDA.)

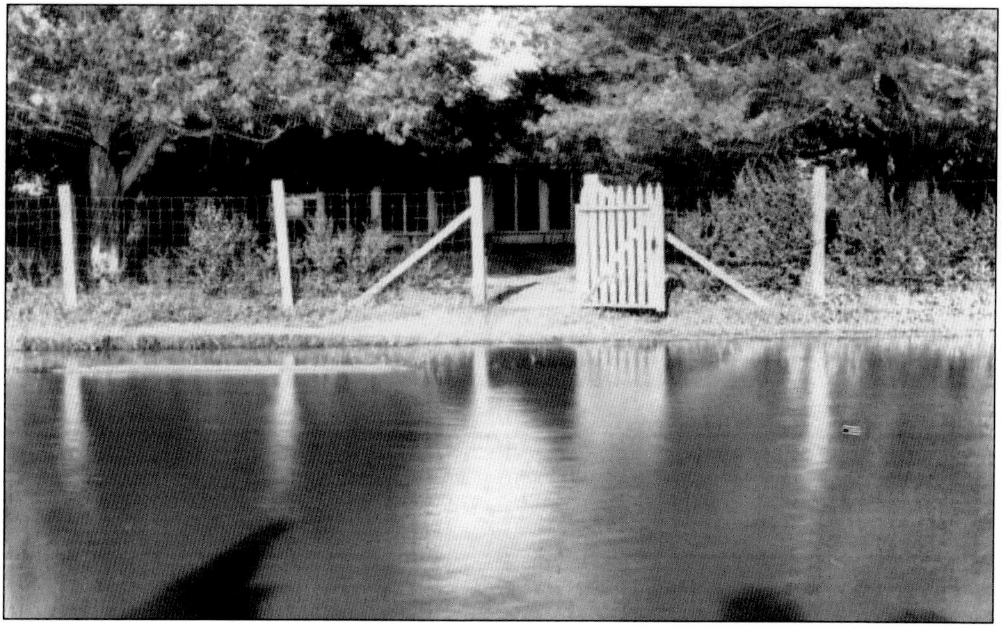

May 10, Mound—George S. Yerger Home. George S. Yerger Sr. was depicted in an earlier photo as one of the largest landowners in Madison Parish. His home was one of the few in the parish that was not flooded. (Courtesy of the USDA.)

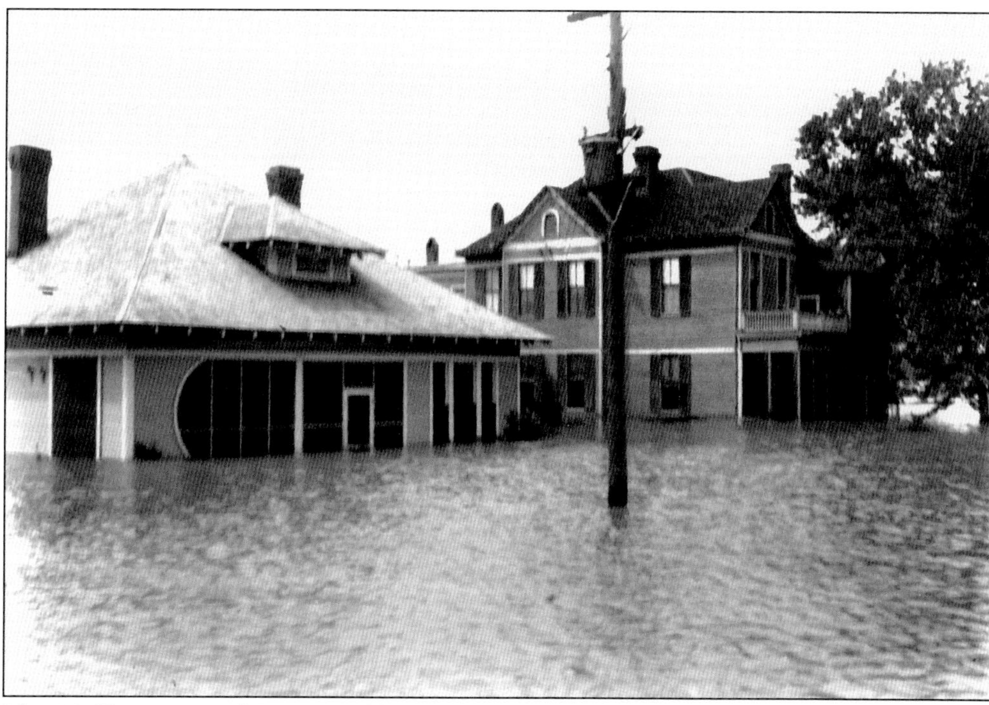

May 10, Tallulah—Claughton Home on Left, Sheriff A.J. Sevier Home on Right. Many people will remember Mrs. Claughton as a seventh-grade teacher at the Tallulah Grammar School. Andrew Jackson Sevier was sheriff of the parish for many years and was succeeded by his wife after his death. (Courtesy of the USDA.)

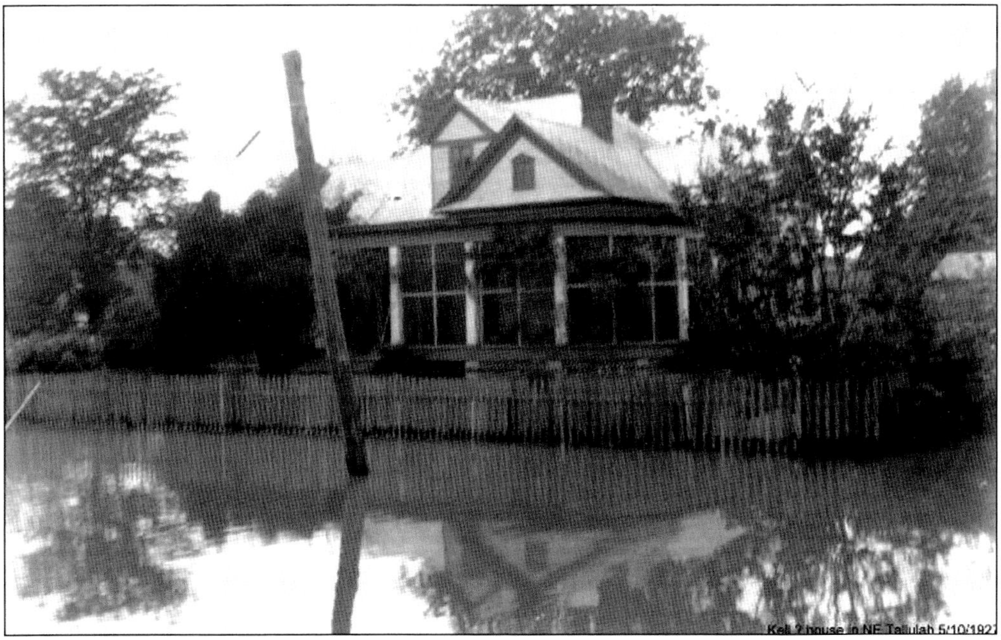

May 10, Tallulah—Kell Home. The Kell home was located in northeastern Tallulah. This was the home of Thomas Phares Kell after he moved to Tallulah. An earlier Kell home at New Carthage is pictured in the 1897 flood. (Courtesy of the USDA.)

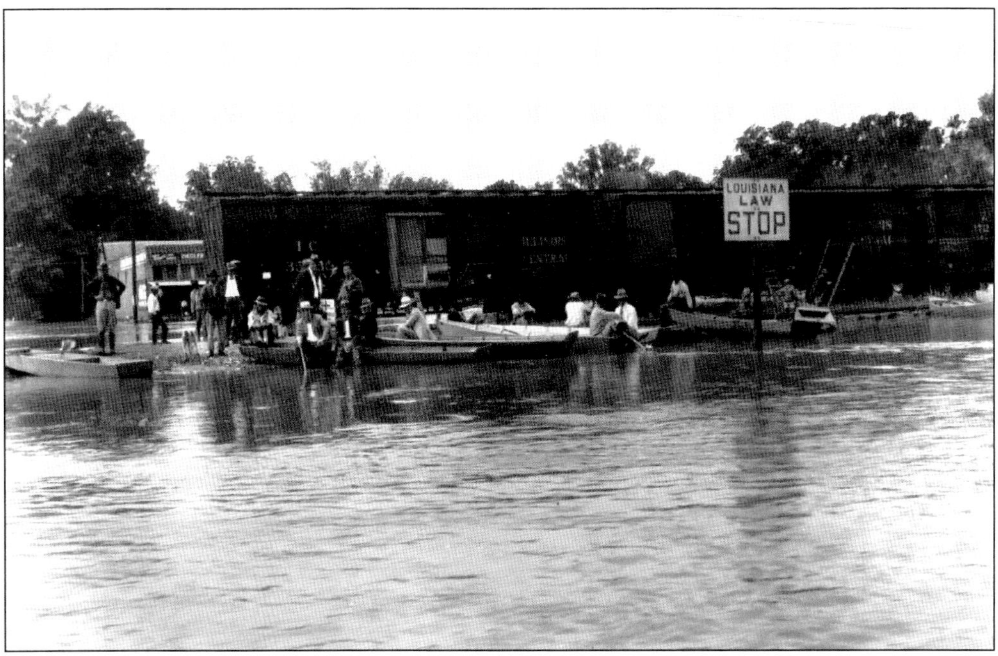

May 12, Tallulah—Boats Docked at Railroad Crossing. This is nine days since the break in the levee. Even though the railroad track was only a few feet higher than the surrounding area, it was about the only dry land available. Ziegler-Darrow Hardware can be seen behind the boxcar. (Courtesy of the USDA.)

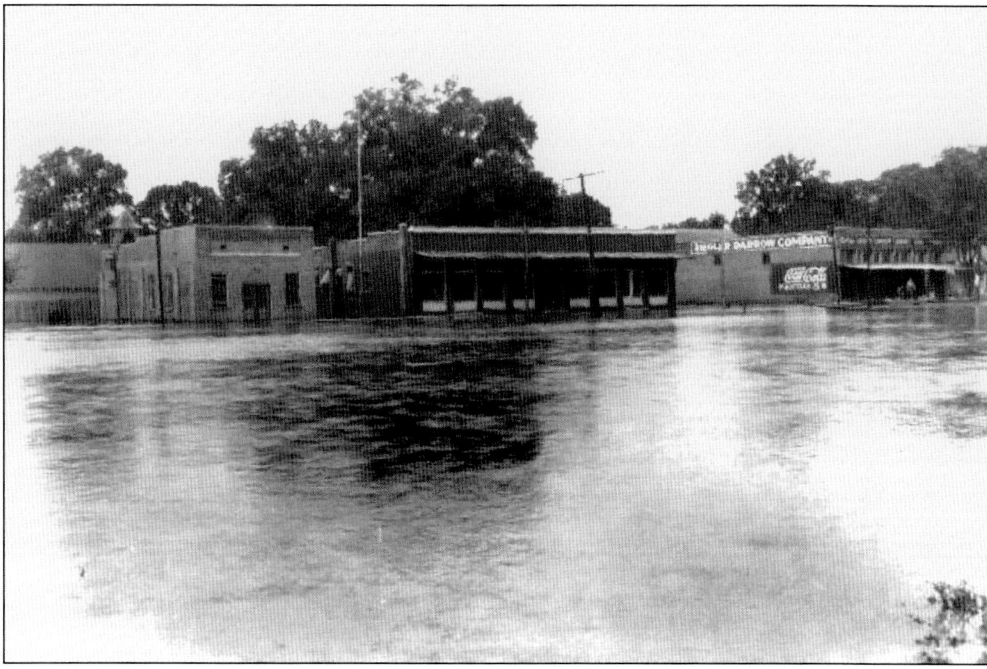

MAY 12, TALLULAH—USDA OFFICES. The USDA Agricultural Experiment Station occupied many offices, including Tallulah's first high school building, before they moved to their permanent home just south of Tallulah. The building pictured is still located on Dabney Street. (Courtesy of the USDA.)

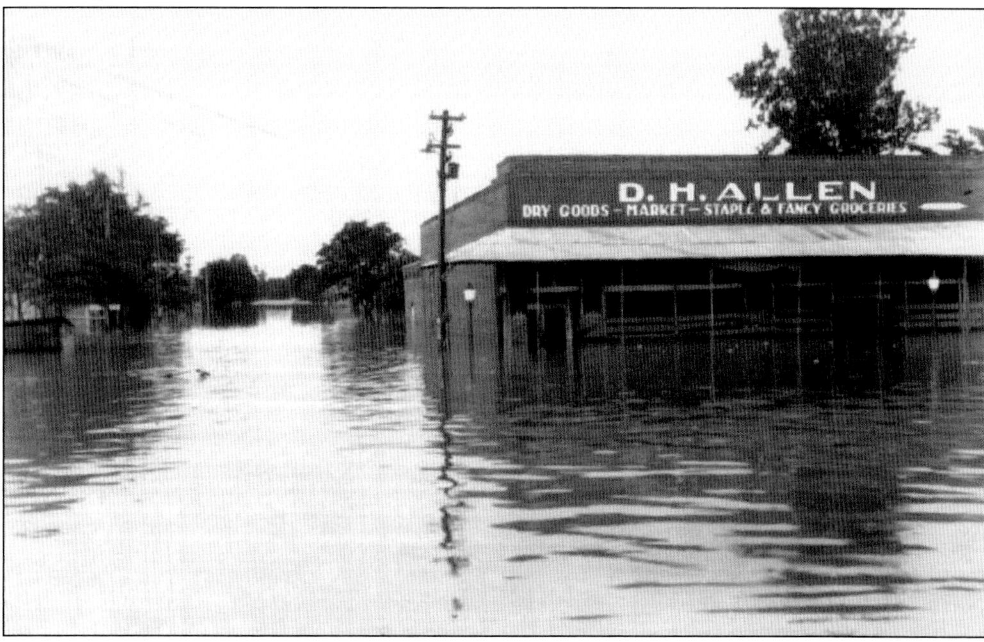

MAY 12, TALLULAH—D.H. ALLEN STORE. Dean Hall Allen owned a combination Dry Goods-Grocery store on Depot Street in Tallulah at the time of the flood. The store later changed owners, and Allen became mayor of Tallulah—a position he held for several years. (Courtesy of the USDA.)

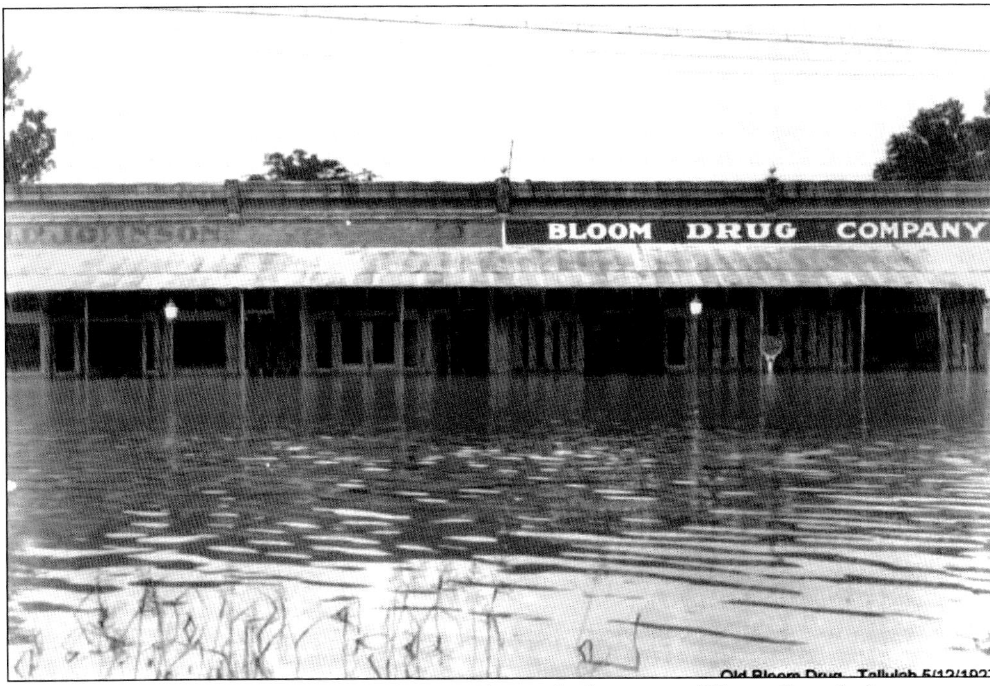

May 12, Tallulah—Bloom Drug Store. This is the location of Bloom Drug before it moved to the west end of Depot Street. Photos of the interior of the store appeared earlier. (Courtesy of the USDA.)

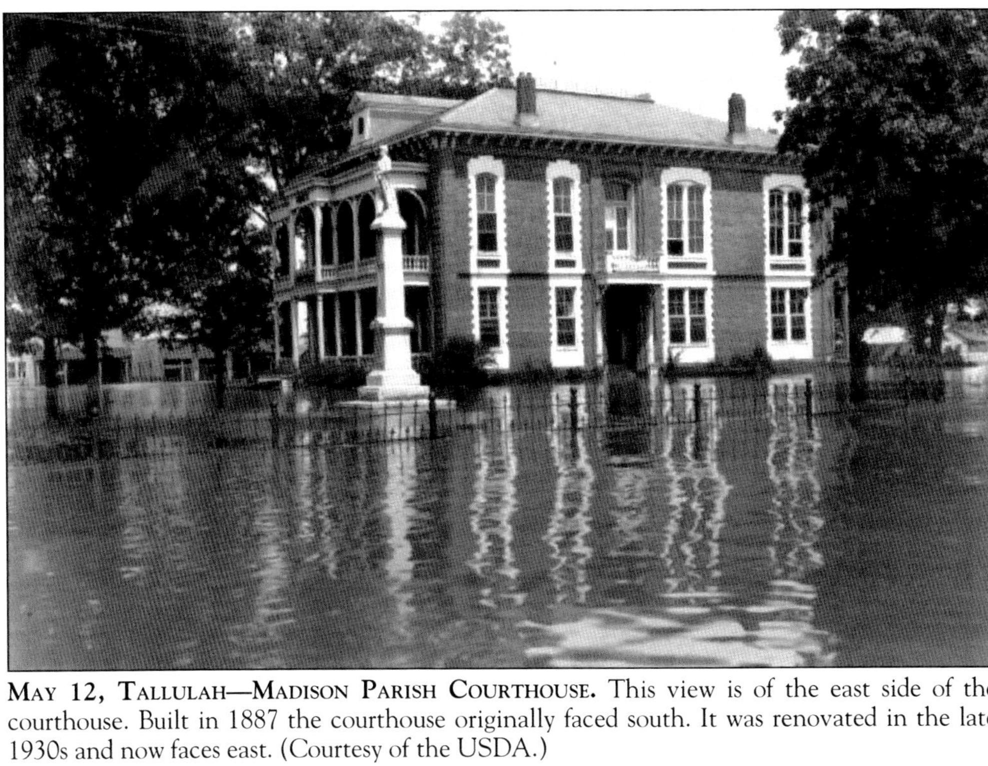

May 12, Tallulah—Madison Parish Courthouse. This view is of the east side of the courthouse. Built in 1887 the courthouse originally faced south. It was renovated in the late 1930s and now faces east. (Courtesy of the USDA.)

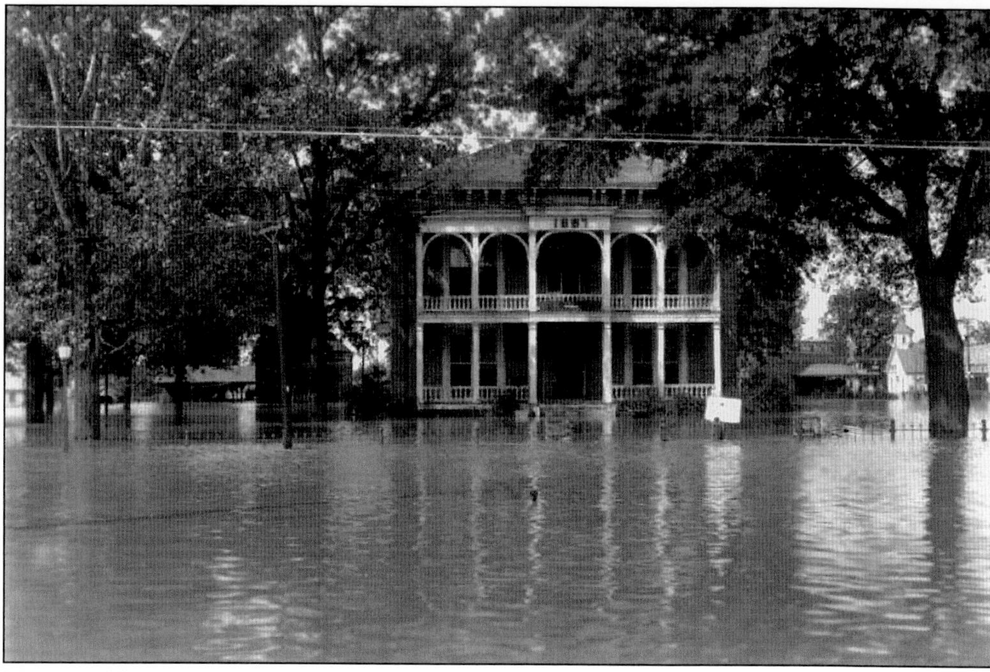

MAY 12, TALLULAH—MADISON PARISH COURTHOUSE. This view is of the south side of the courthouse. The iron fence surrounding the courthouse (the top of which is barely above water) was later moved to the George S. Yerger home at Mound. (Courtesy of the USDA.)

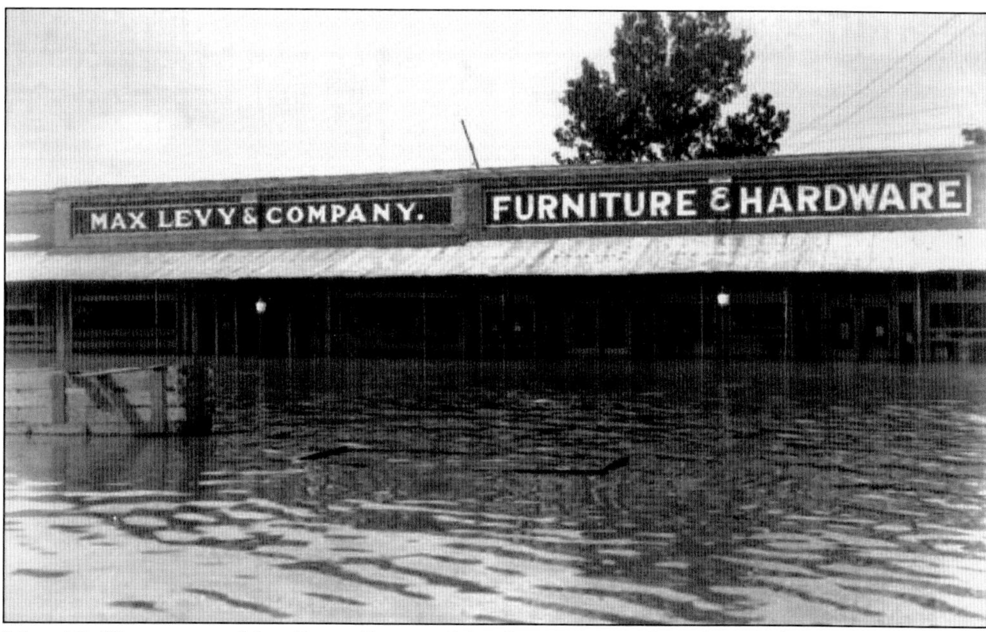

MAY 12, TALLULAH—MAX LEVY STORES. Max Levy, primarily a dry goods store, later moved to the Bloom Arcade, pictured earlier. Both of these businesses belonged to the Bloom family. (Courtesy of the USDA.)

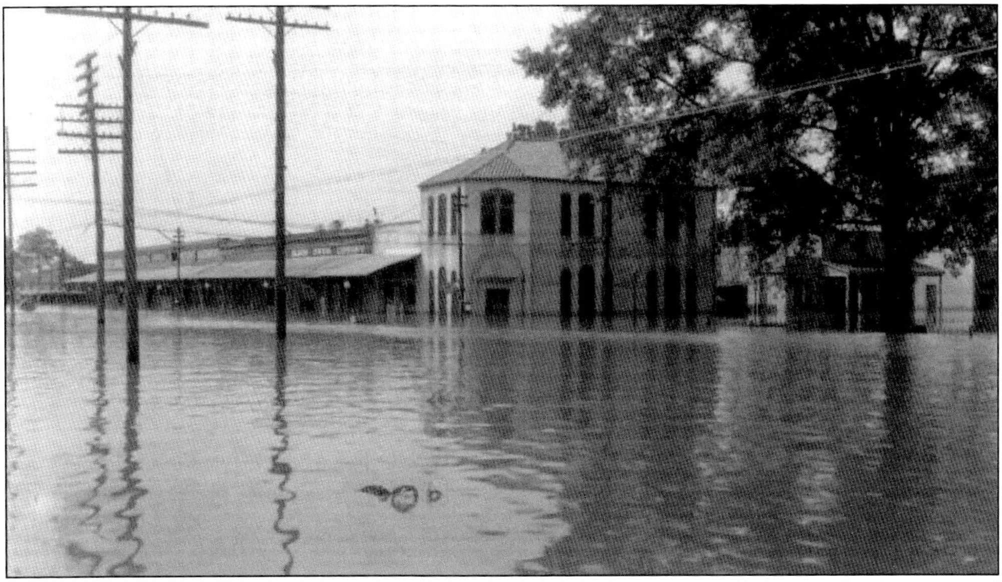

MAY 12, TALLULAH—OLD TALLULAH STATE BANK BUILDING. This was the location of the Tallulah State Bank for many years until it moved into new quarters in the 1960s. The buildings to the left were Bloom Drug and Max Levy, both pictured earlier. (Courtesy of the USDA.)

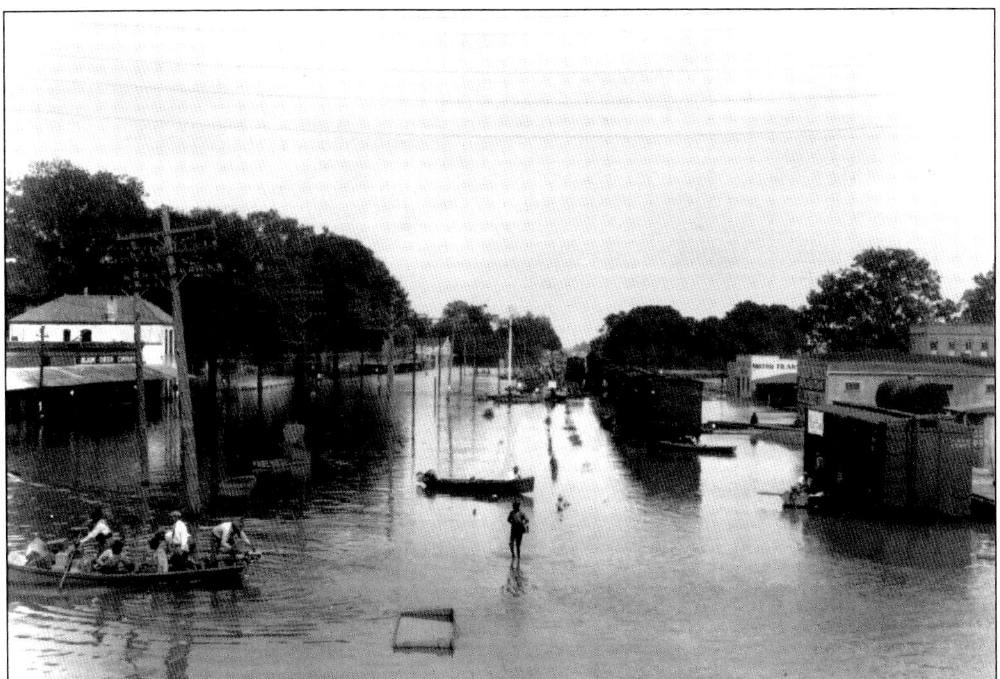

MAY 14, TALLULAH—LOOKING EAST DOWN IC RAILROAD. It has been 11 days since the break in the levee. Water has now covered the railroad tracks. Bloom Drug, Tallulah State Bank, and the courthouse are on the left. (Courtesy of the USDA.)

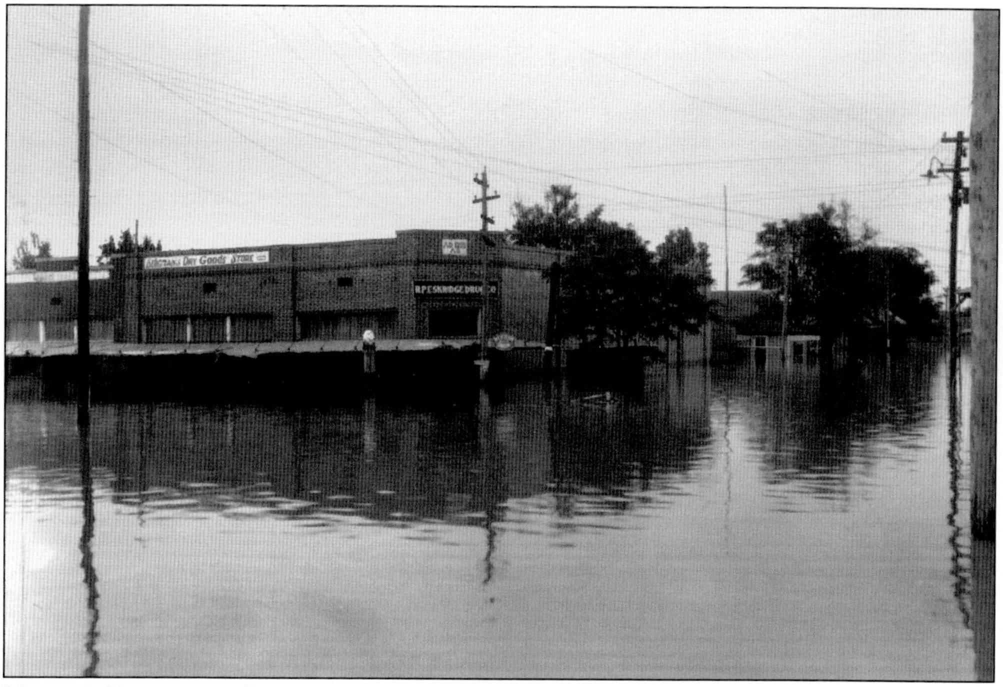

MAY 14, TALLULAH—CORNER OF DEPOT (NOW SNYDER) AND JULIA STREETS. This is the R.P. Eskridge Drug Store, which appears to have also sold gasoline (or kerosene). To the left is Seligman's Dry Goods. A small cafe appears to the right. The building was constructed in 1923. By the 1930s both of these businesses had left town. (Courtesy of the USDA.)

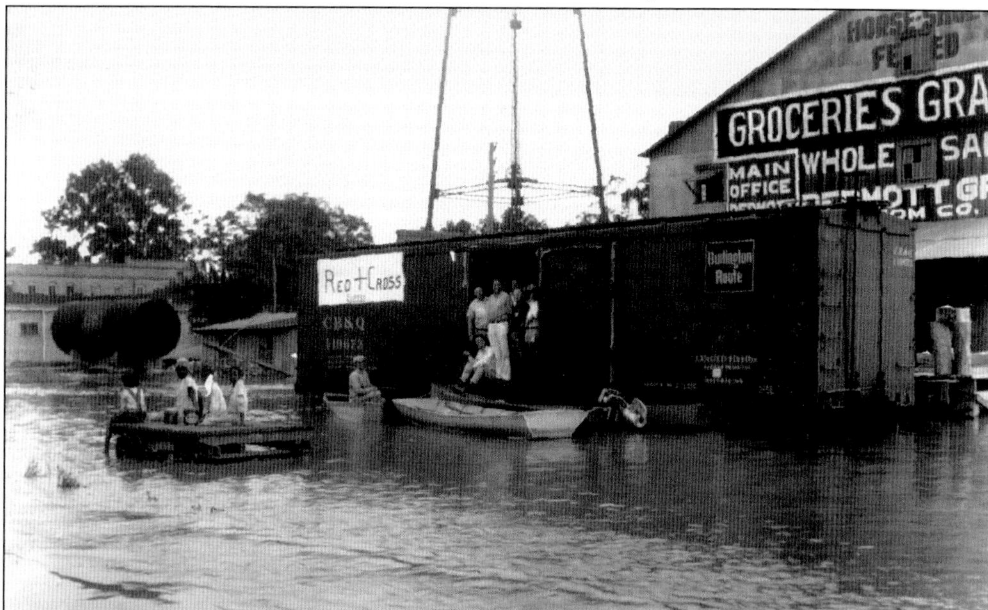

MAY 14, TALLULAH—RED CROSS SUPPLY STATION IN BOXCAR. The Red Cross supplies were stored in boxcars and delivered by boat. Later, when the water when down, the Red Cross moved into tents. The business to the right was the Dermott Wholesale Grocery. (Courtesy of the USDA.)

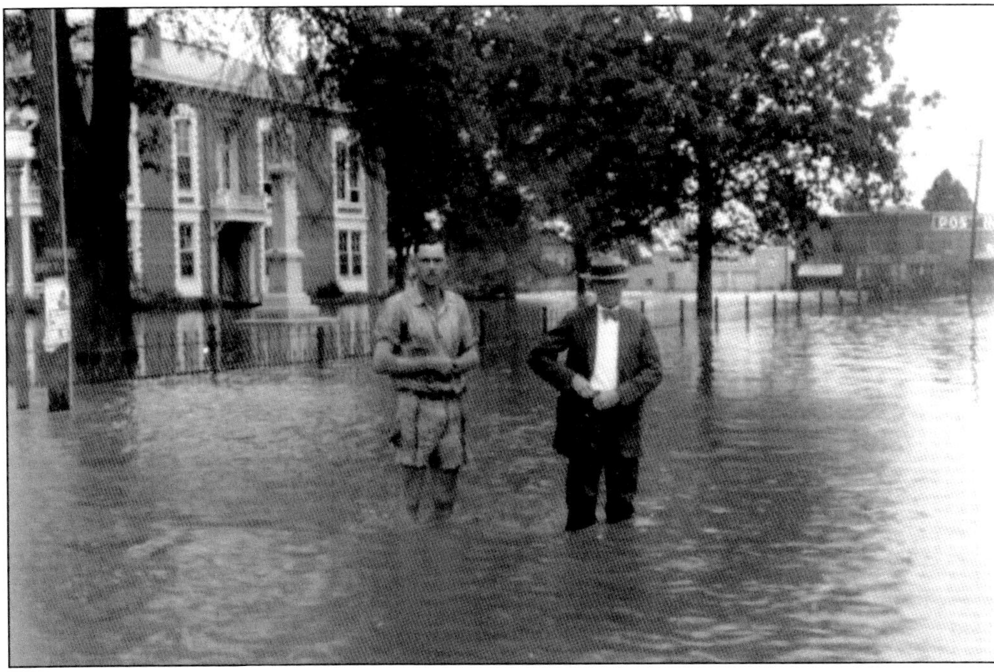

MAY 15, TALLULAH—TWO UNIDENTIFIED GENTLEMEN ON EAST SIDE OF COURTHOUSE. Twelve days have passed since the break in the levee. From the appearance of the iron fence relative to the water level it appears that the flood has receded a little. (Courtesy of the USDA.)

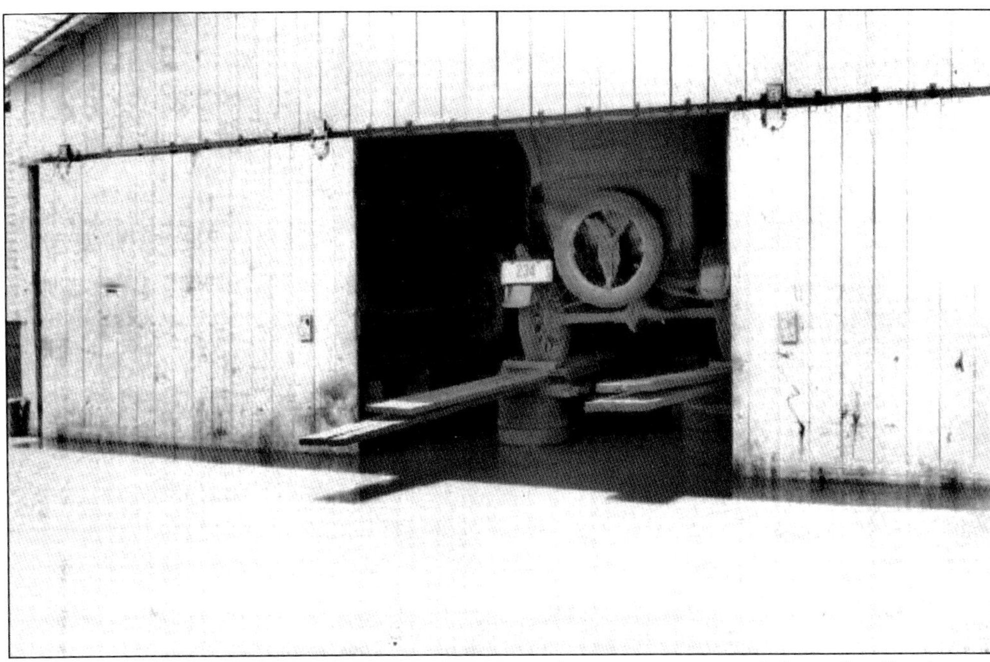

MAY 15, TALLULAH—CARS RAISED ON BARRELS. Cars were protected from the floodwaters in many ways. Here two have been hoisted onto boards suspended by barrels. (Courtesy of the USDA.)

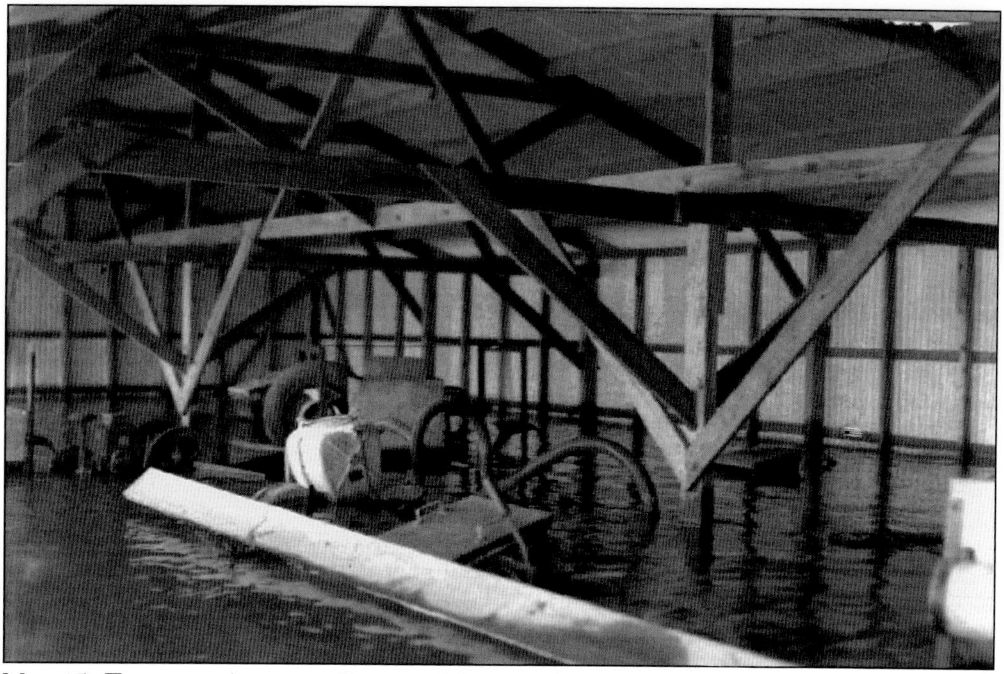

MAY 15, TALLULAH AIRPORT—DUSTING MACHINE SHED. Note that various pieces of dusting equipment have been caught in the high water. Also, much of the dusting chemical has been soaked. (Courtesy of the USDA.)

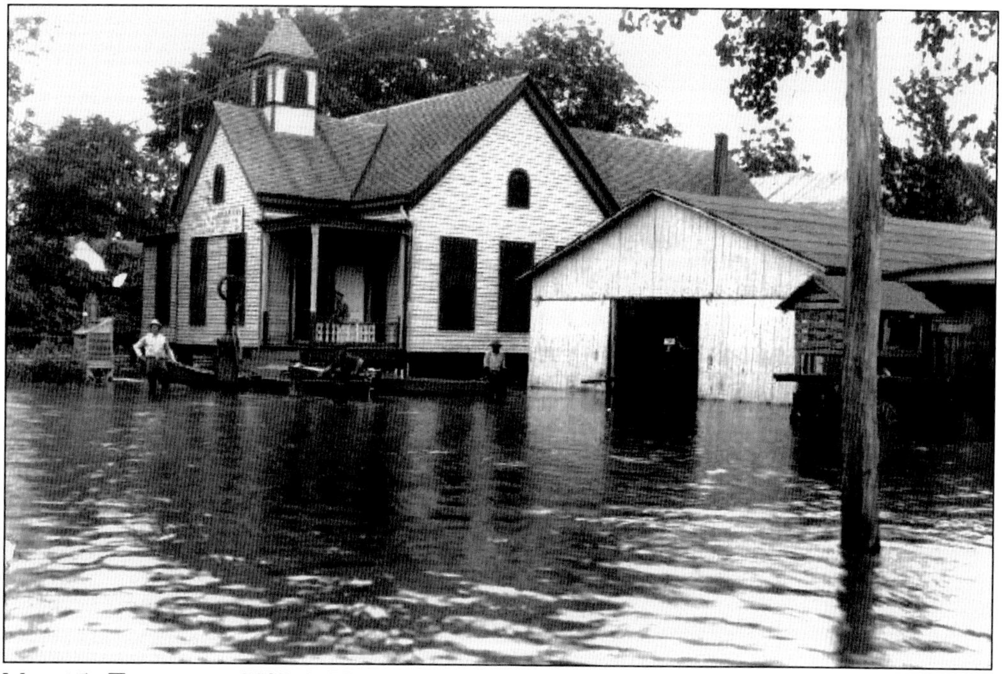

MAY 15, TALLULAH—USDA HEADQUARTERS. Note that this is the same building that was Tallulah's first school. (Courtesy of the USDA.)

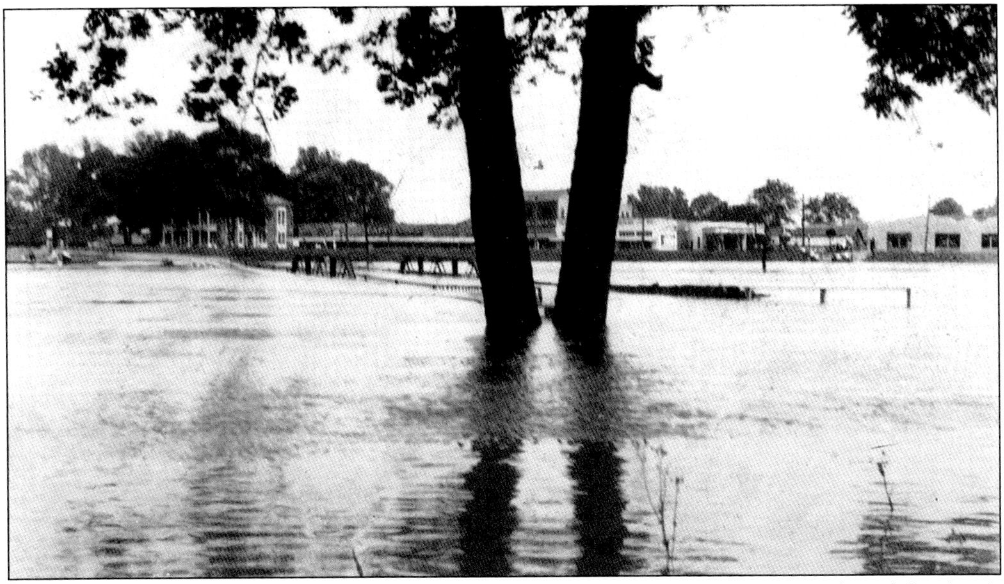

BRUSHY BAYOU BRIDGE. The courthouse is in the left background. To get an idea of the depth of the water, compare this with the same bridge shown earlier in a baptizing photograph. (Courtesy of Judy Kell Morris.)

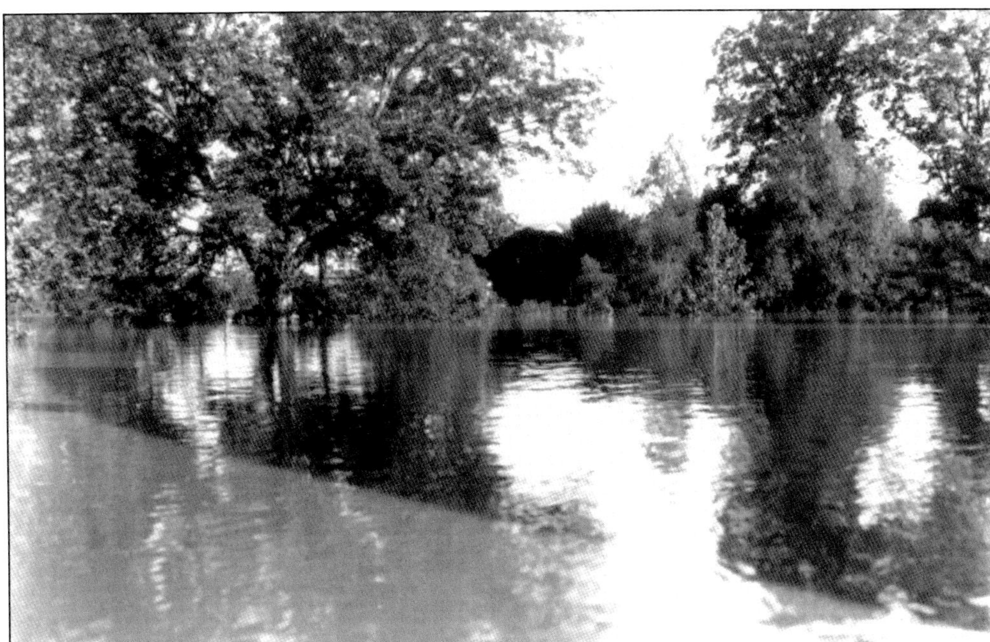

MAY 15, TALLULAH—BRUSHY BAYOU ON SOUTH LINCOLN STREET. This scene is looking southwest from the southeast side of the bayou. The edge of the bayou is indicated by darker colored water. (Courtesy of the USDA.)

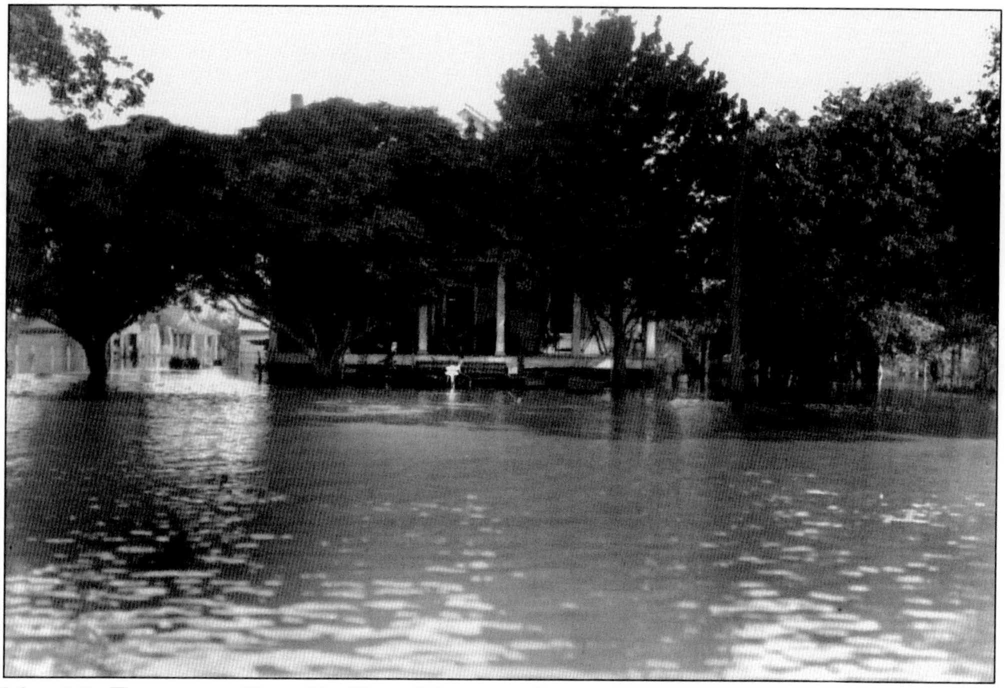

MAY 15, TALLULAH—BERT R. COAD HOME ON SOUTH LINCOLN STREET. Dr. Coad was in charge of the USDA lab in Tallulah. He was also very active in the Red Cross's attempt to rehabilitate victims of the flood. Dr. Coad's house faced Brushy Bayou. (Courtesy of the USDA.)

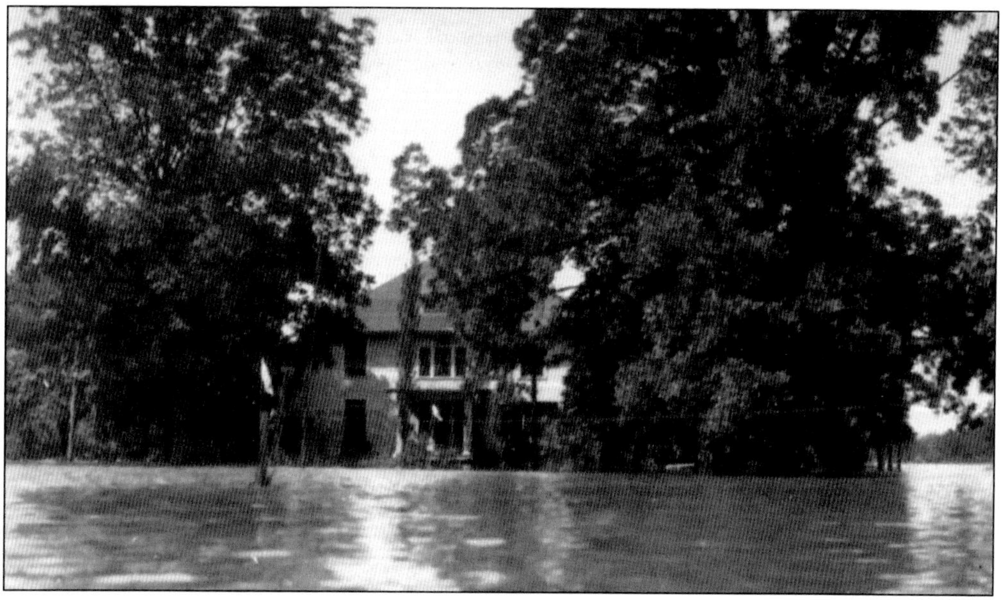

MAY 15, TALLULAH—RICHARD K. BONEY HOME ON SOUTH LINCOLN STREET. Mr. Boney was a Tallulah attorney and former Duckport planter. His father was G.L. Boney, who was discussed earlier. The top of this house can be seen in the German Airforce photo shown earlier. (Courtesy Sherrill Sevier Pirone.)

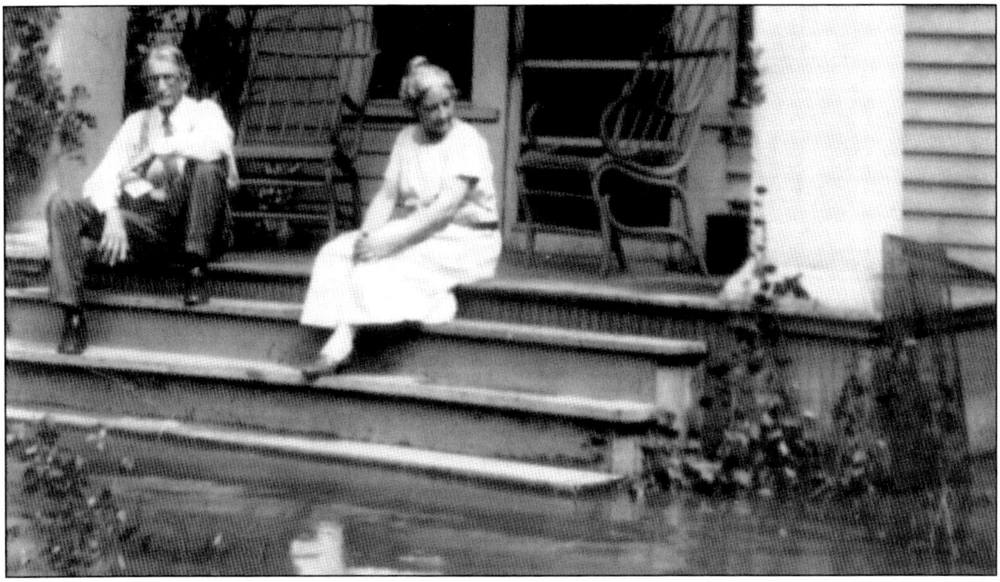

May 15, Tallulah—Mr. and Mrs. R.K. Boney Watch the Water Rise. It did not get into the house, however. Mrs. Boney was a very active clubwoman, and later became president of Louisiana Federation of Woemn's Clubs. (Courtesy Sherrill Sevier Pirone.)

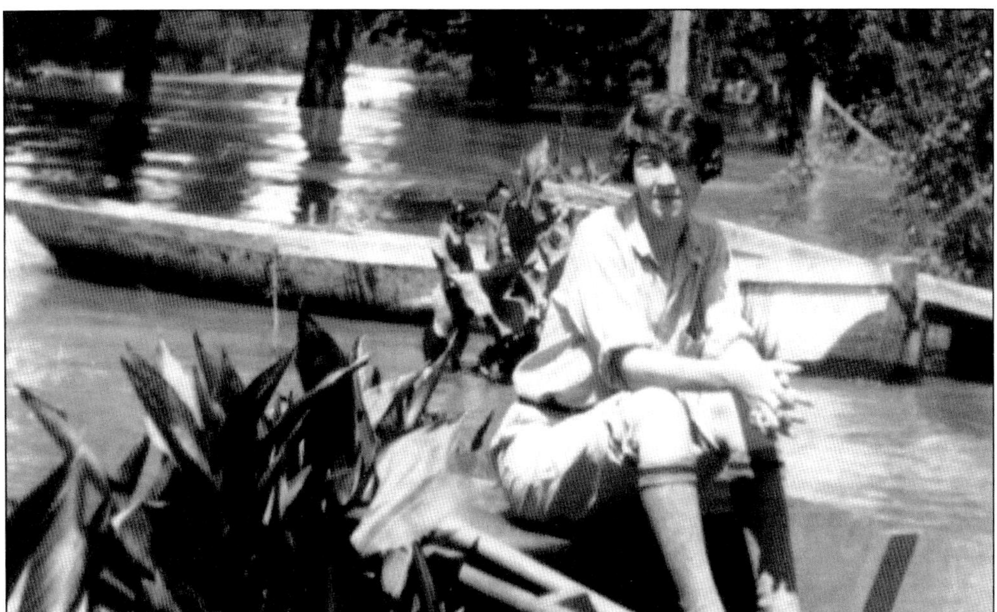

May 15, Tallulah—Martha Boney in her Front Yard. Later in 1927 Martha married W.P. "Buck" Sevier who would eventually serve many years as Tallulah's mayor. (Courtesy Sherrill Sevier Pirone.)

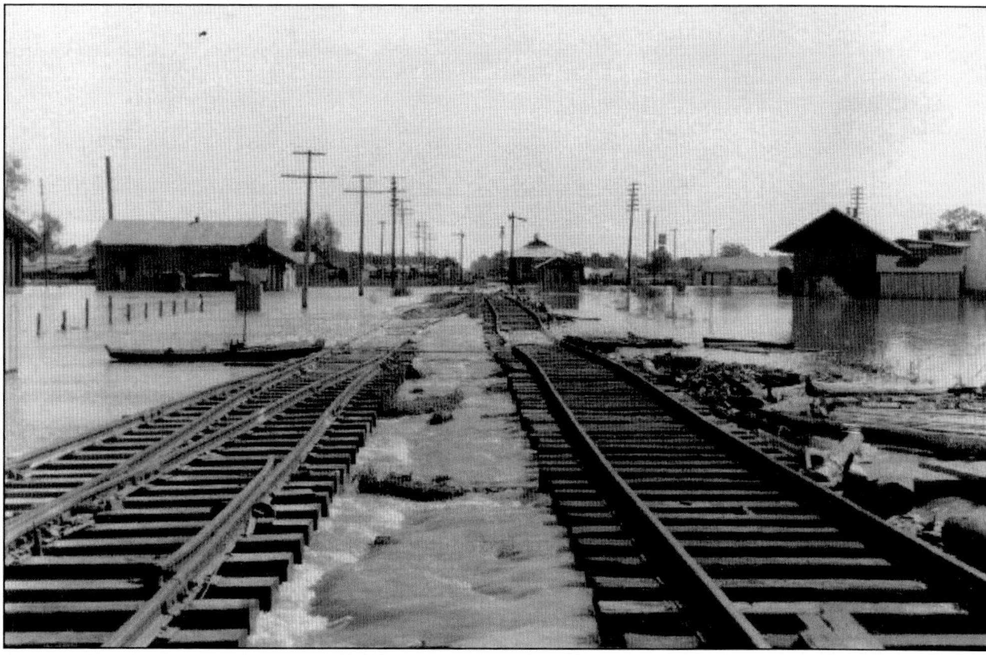

May 16, Tallulah—Looking North Up The Missouri Pacific Railroad. It has been 13 days since the levee break. This track would later become the route of one of the early "streamlined" trains—the Delta Eagle that traveled from Tallulah to Memphis each day. (Courtesy of the USDA.)

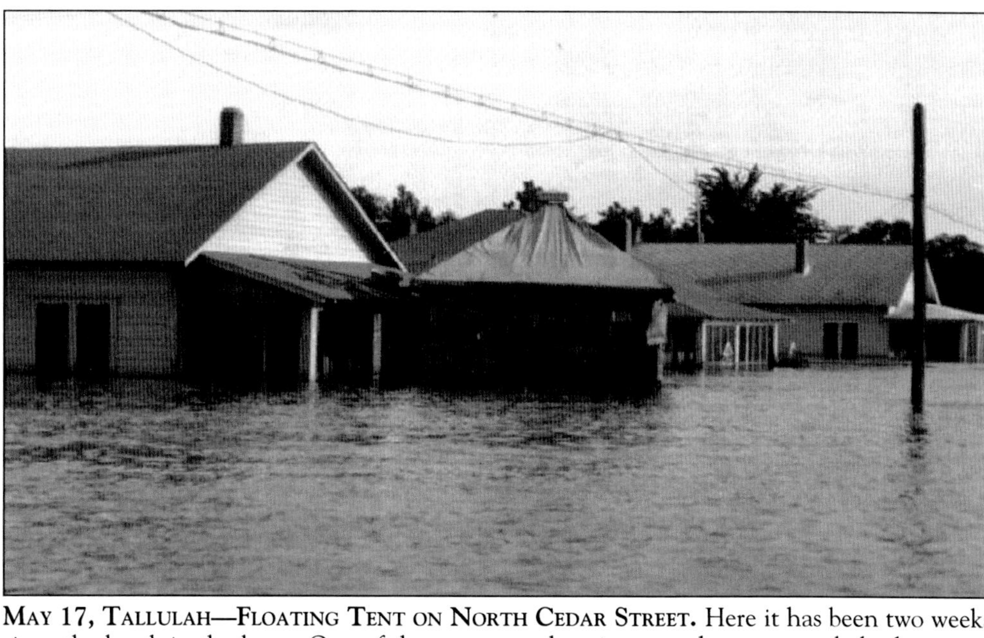

May 17, Tallulah—Floating Tent on North Cedar Street. Here it has been two weeks since the break in the levee. One of the temporary housing tents has apparently broken away from its moorings and has floated into a house. (Courtesy of the USDA.)

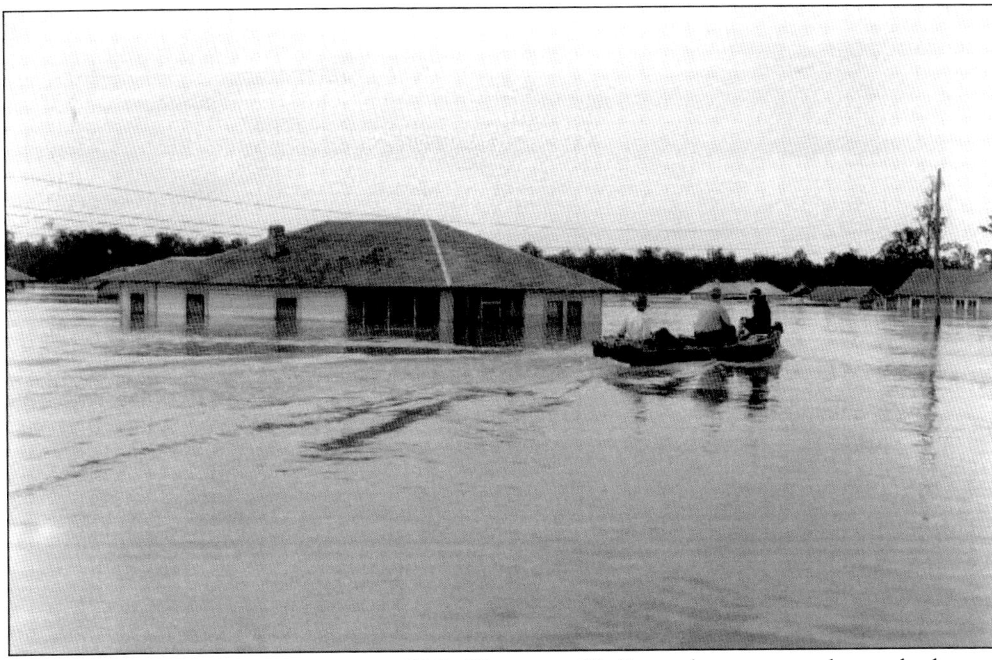

May 17, Tallulah—North along U.S. Highway 65. From the water marks on the houses it appears that the water has dropped a foot or so. Additional damage to the house was caused by the wake of motorboats. (Courtesy of the USDA.)

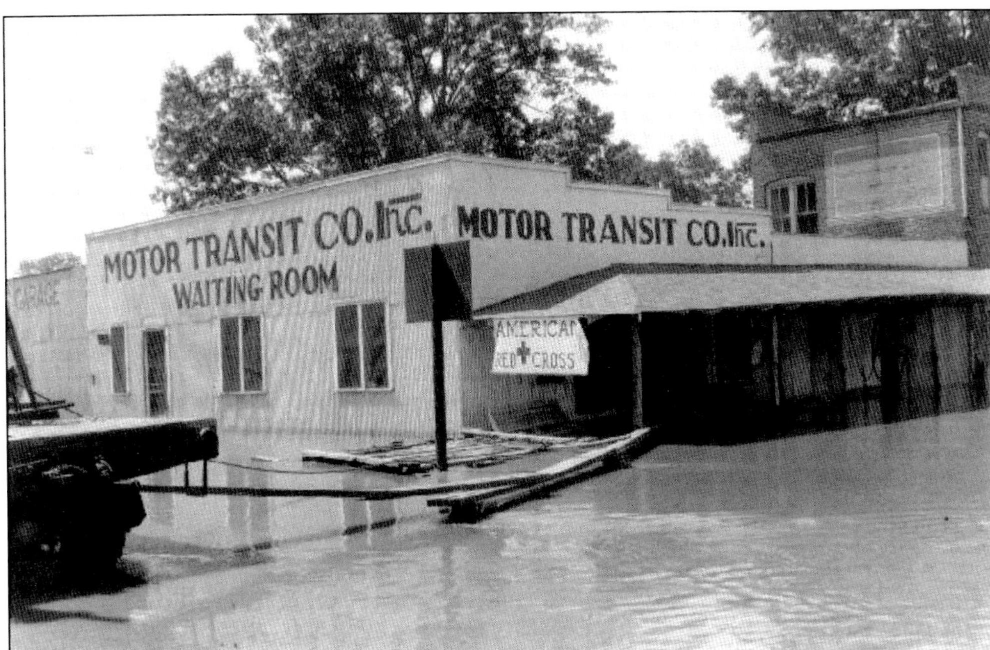

May 17, Tallulah—Red Cross Site at the Bus Station. This was one of several Red Cross locations. Note the planks used to get from the vehicle in the foreground to the building. (Courtesy of the USDA.)

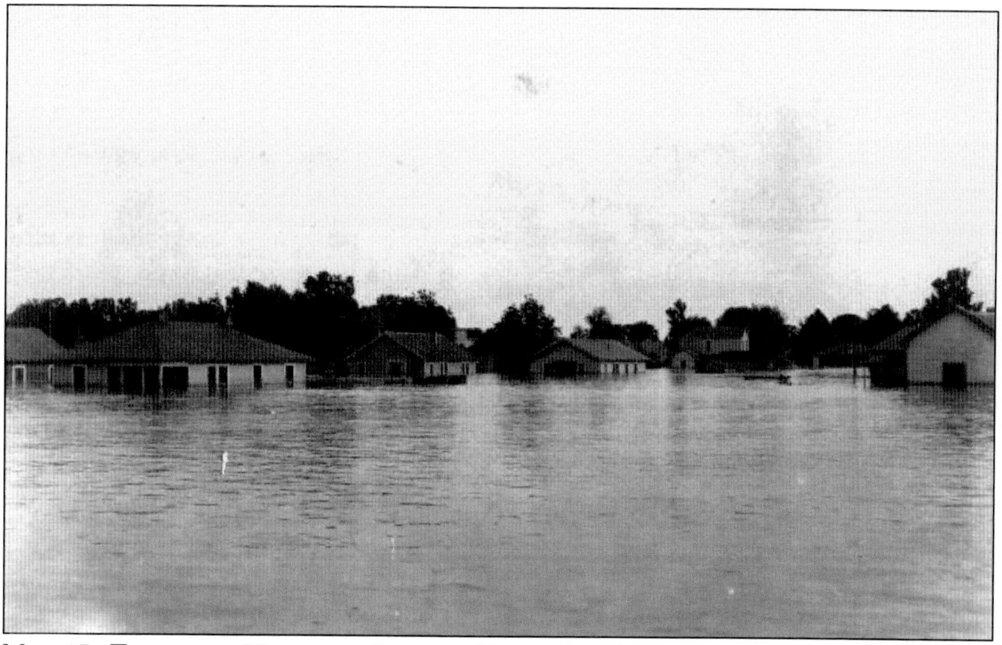

MAY 17, TALLULAH—NORTHERN PART OF TOWN. Another scene shows houses with flood water halfway up to the roofs in the lower, northern part of town. (Courtesy of the USDA.)

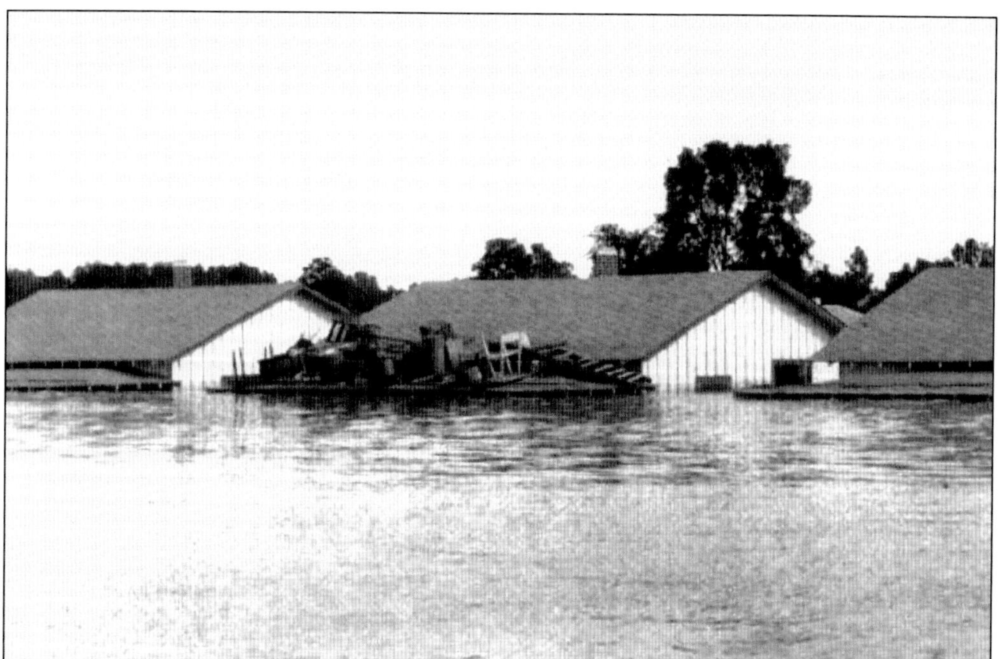

MAY 17, TALLULAH—NORTHERN PART OF TOWN. Note the furniture on the roof. Many people lost their furniture when it floated away. (Courtesy of the USDA.)

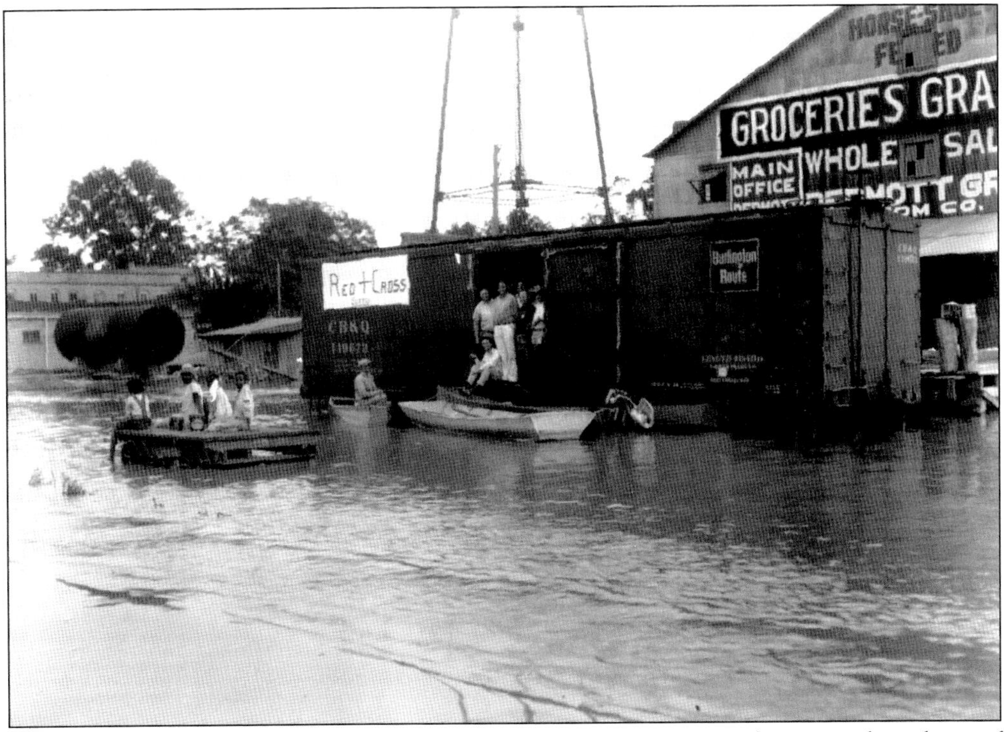

MAY 17, TALLULAH—RED CROSS STATION IN A RAILROAD CARD. This is another photo of the Red Cross supply station in a railroad car. The water is still over tracks as evidenced by the sidecar loaded with refugees. (Courtesy of the USDA.)

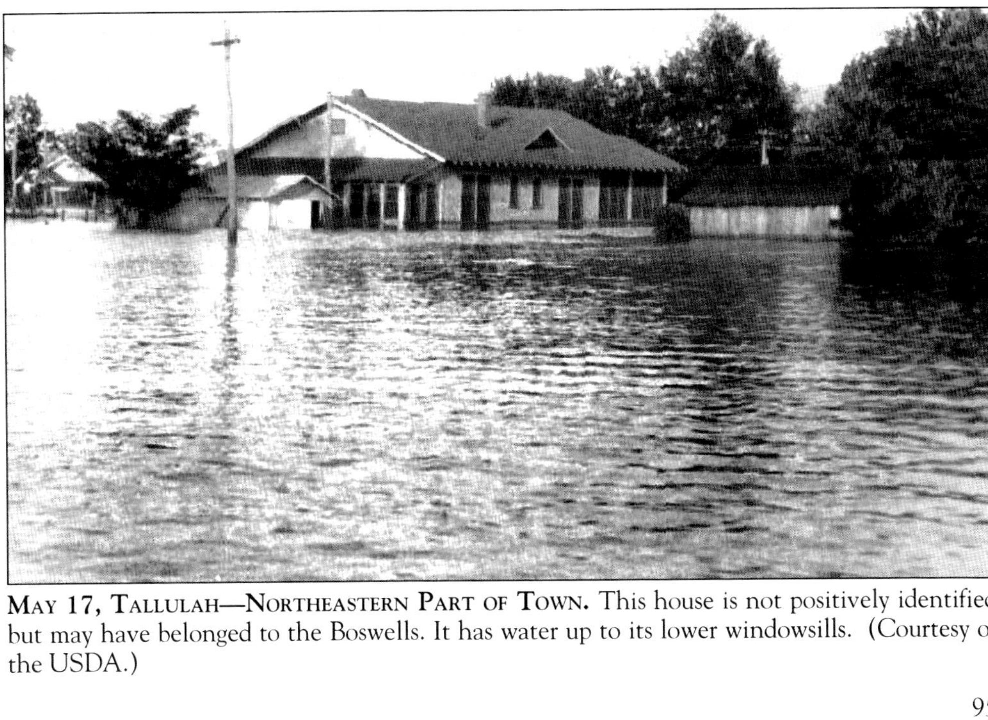

MAY 17, TALLULAH—NORTHEASTERN PART OF TOWN. This house is not positively identified but may have belonged to the Boswells. It has water up to its lower windowsills. (Courtesy of the USDA.)

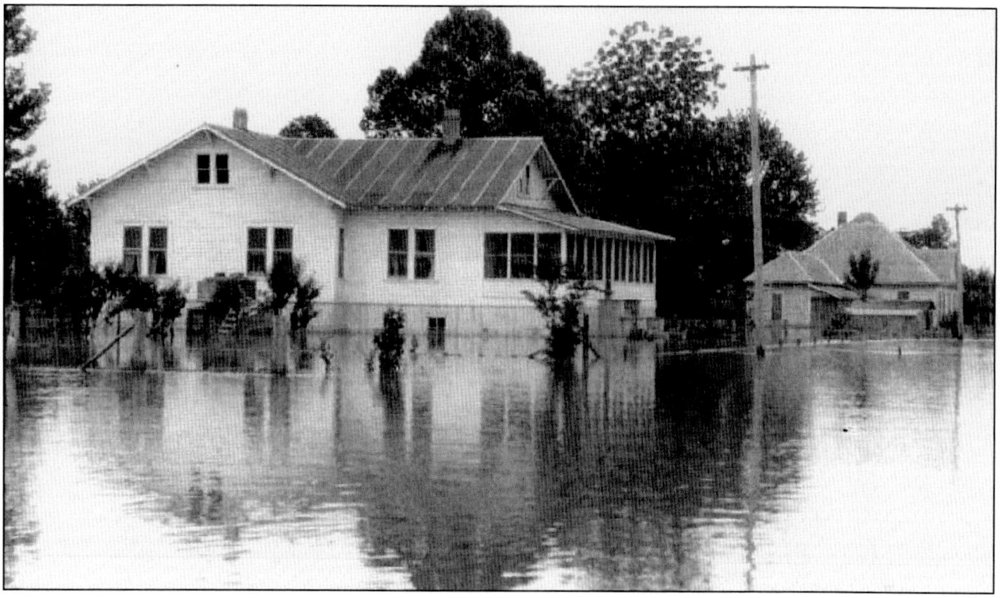

MAY 17, TALLULAH—NORTHEASTERN PART OF TOWN. This appears to be the Percy O. Benjamin House. The main portion was built high enough off the ground to avoid damage. However the lower portion seems to be inundated. (Courtesy of the USDA.)

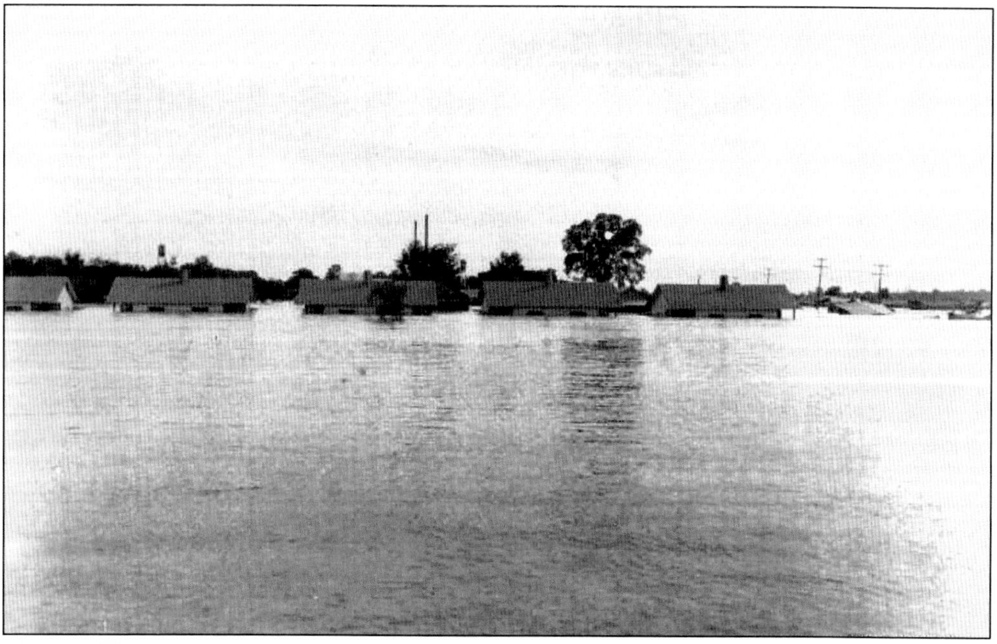

MAY 17, TALLULAH—NORTHWESTERN PART OF TOWN. As mentioned before the northwestern part of Tallulah, being the lowest experienced the most flood damage. These houses all had floodwater almost up to their roofs. (Courtesy of the USDA.)

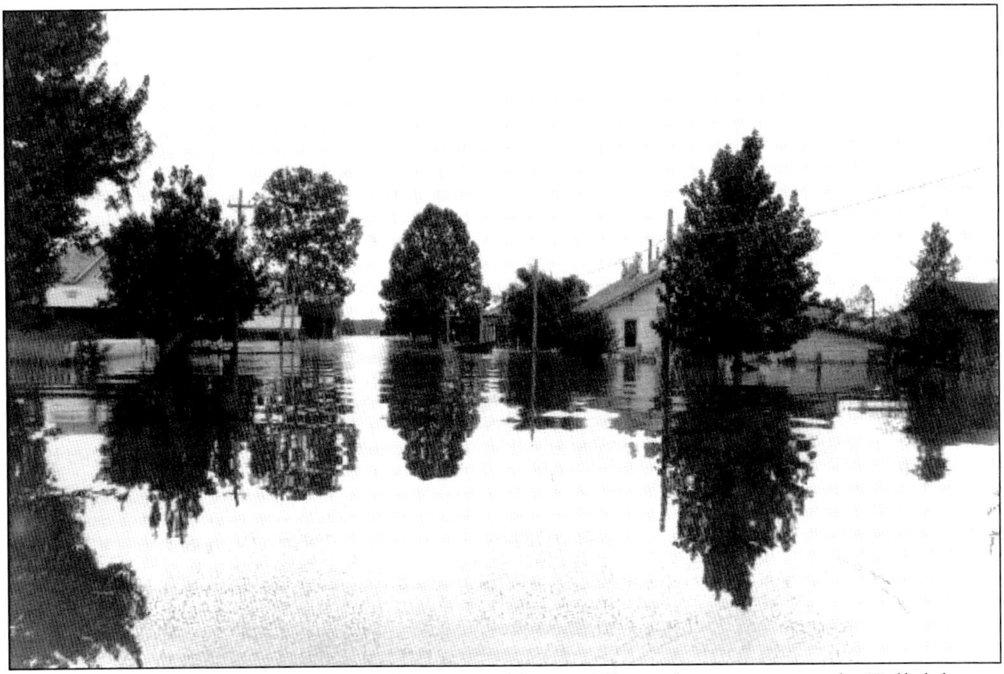

MAY 17, TALLULAH—SOUTHERN PART OF TOWN. These houses in south Tallulah are unidentified. (Courtesy of the USDA.)

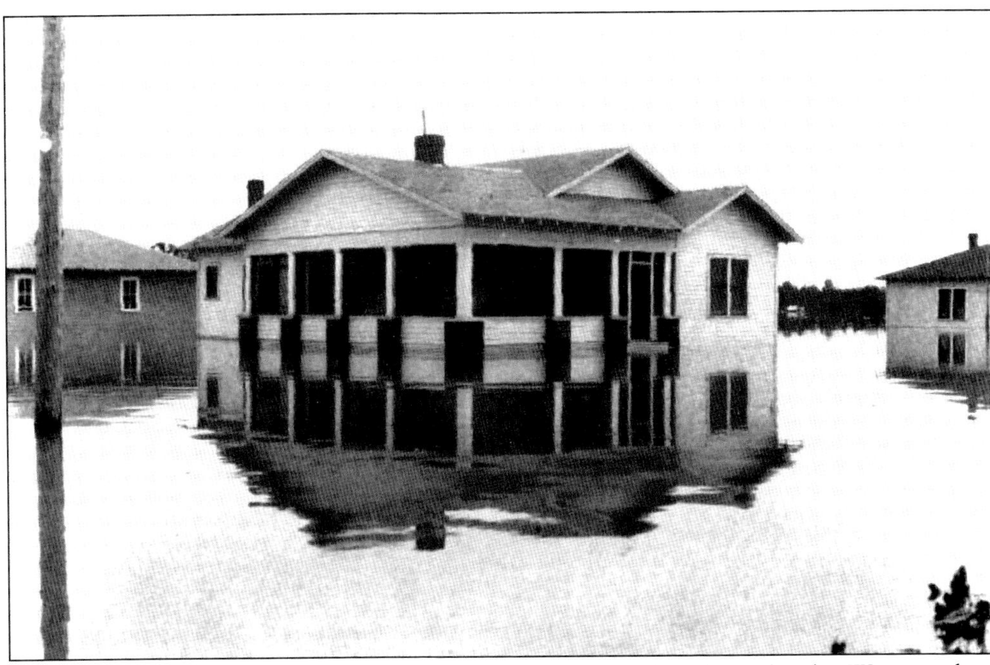

MAY 17, TALLULAH—SOUTHERN PART OF TOWN. This is thought to be the Westmoreland House on LaSalle Street. The house appears to have been built high enough off the ground that it sustained less damage than most. (Courtesy of the USDA.)

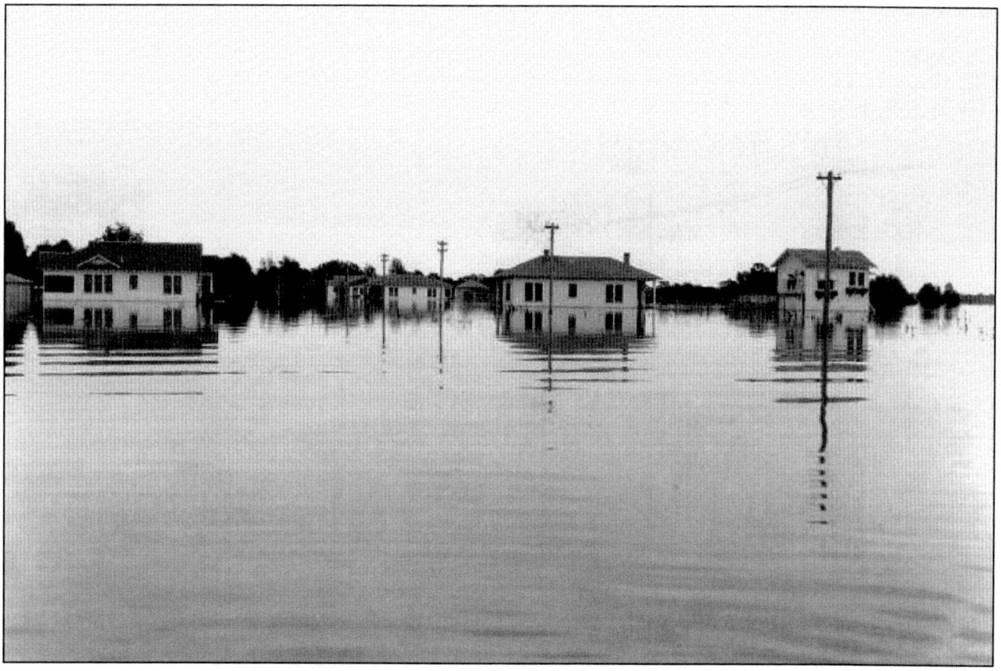

May 17, Tallulah—Southern Part of Town. This view is north on South Walnut Street. The house on the left was that of W.P. Sevier Sr. In the middle of the image is the Purdy home, and the house on the right belonged to Mr. T.H. Harris. (Courtesy of the USDA.)

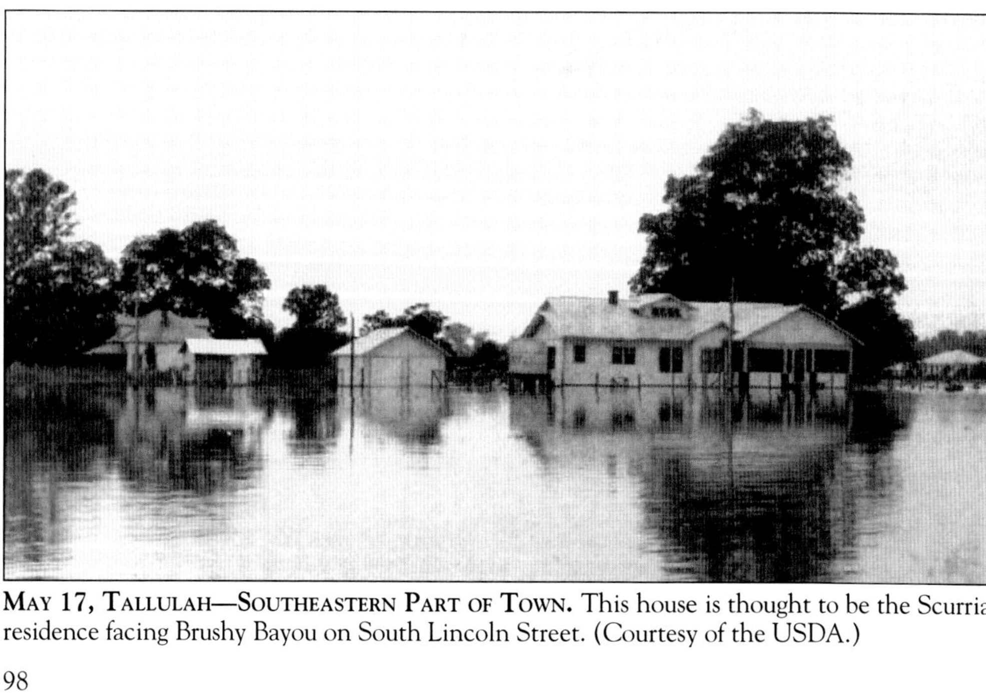

May 17, Tallulah—Southeastern Part of Town. This house is thought to be the Scurria residence facing Brushy Bayou on South Lincoln Street. (Courtesy of the USDA.)

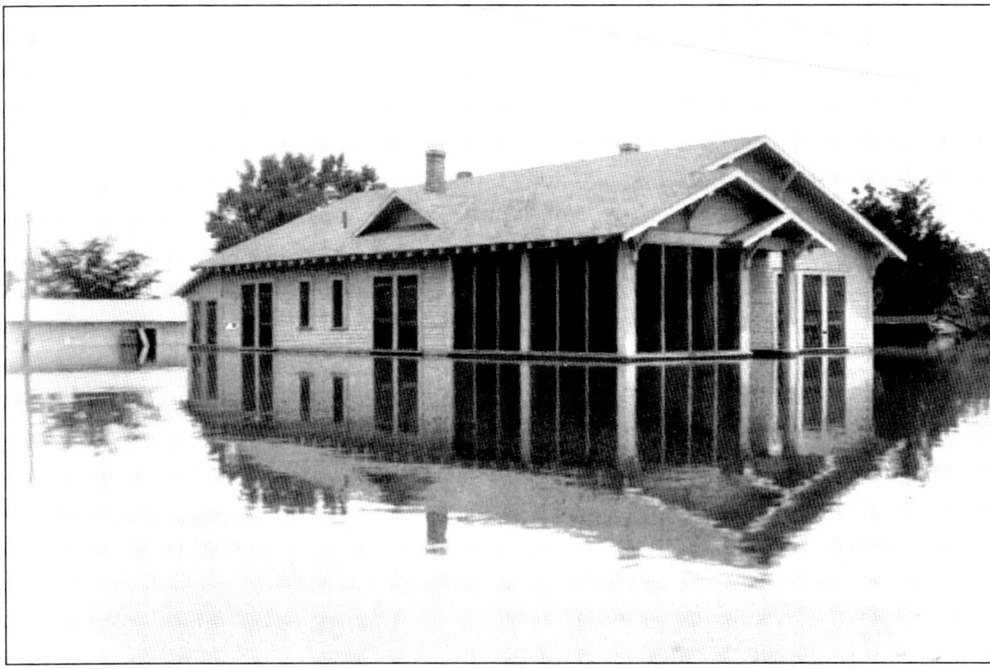

MAY 17, TALLULAH—SOUTHEASTERN PART OF TOWN. This home is unidentified. (Courtesy of the USDA.)

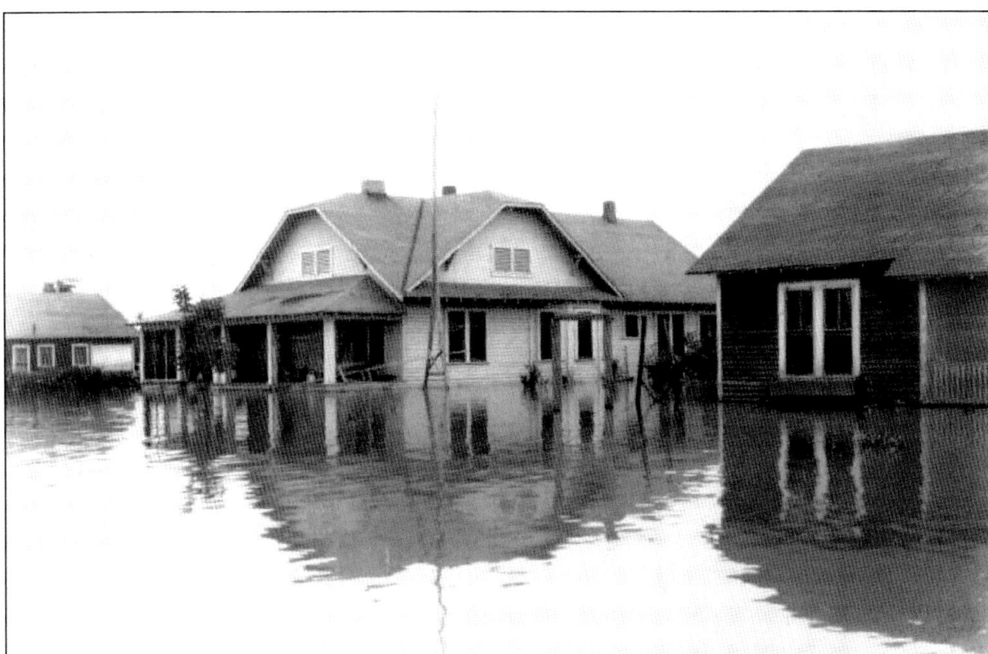

MAY 17, TALLULAH—SOUTHEASTERN PART OF TOWN. This home is unidentified. (Courtesy of the USDA.)

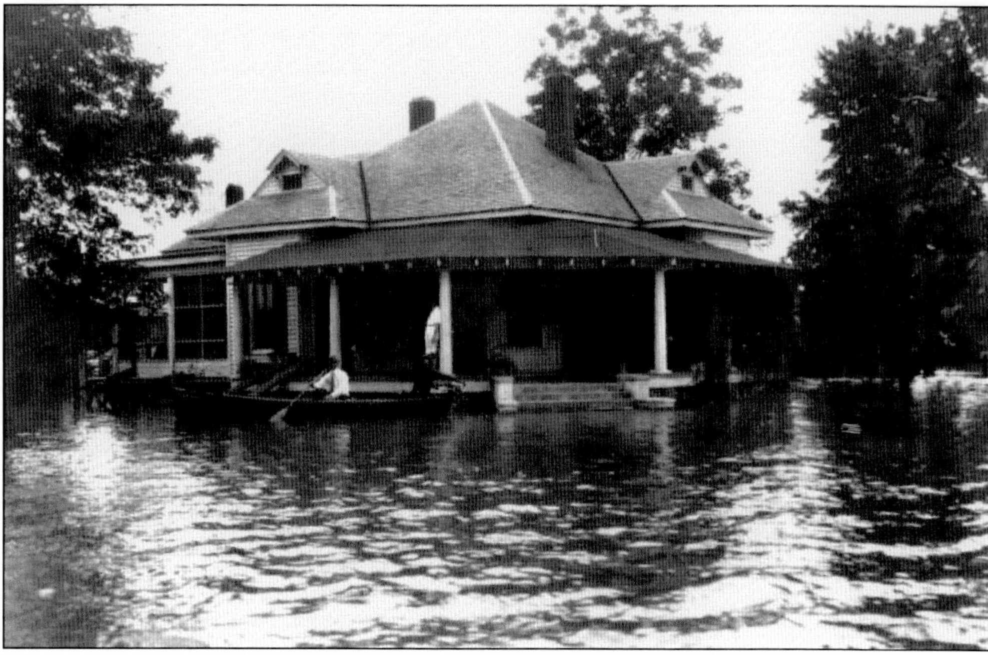

MAY 17, TALLULAH—CASON HOUSE ON SOUTH LINCOLN STREET. The Cason house was located on the corner of South Lincoln and Johnson Streets, just east of the bridge (pictured earlier) across Brushy Bayou. (Courtesy of the USDA.)

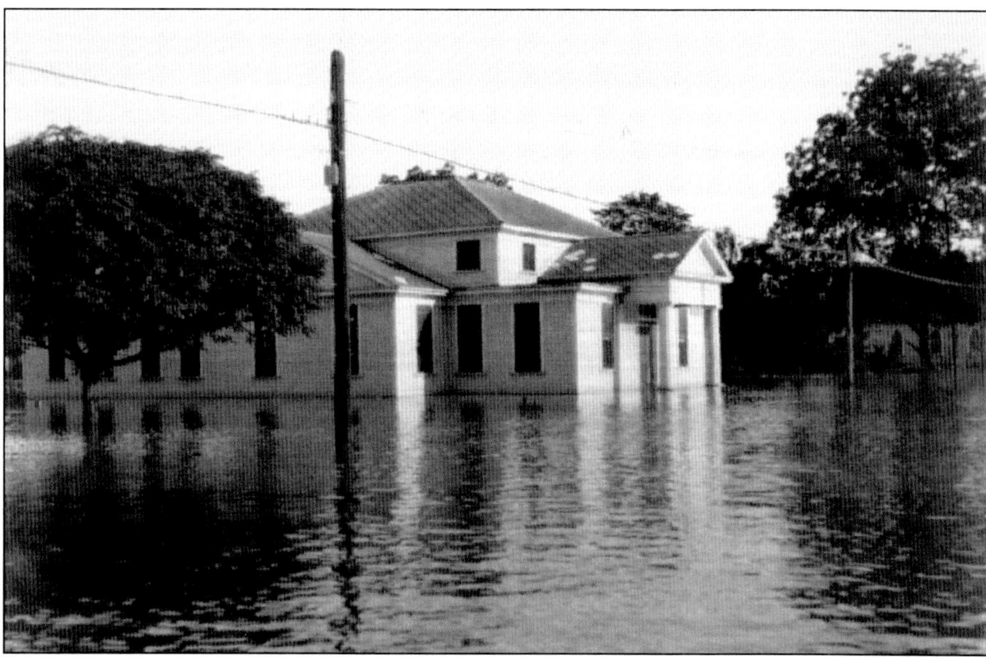

MAY 17, TALLULAH—FIRST BAPTIST CHURCH ON NORTH CEDAR STREET. This was the original location of the First Baptist Church. In 1951 the church moved to its present location on Bayou Drive. The site is currently occupied by the Hibernia Bank. (Courtesy of the USDA.)

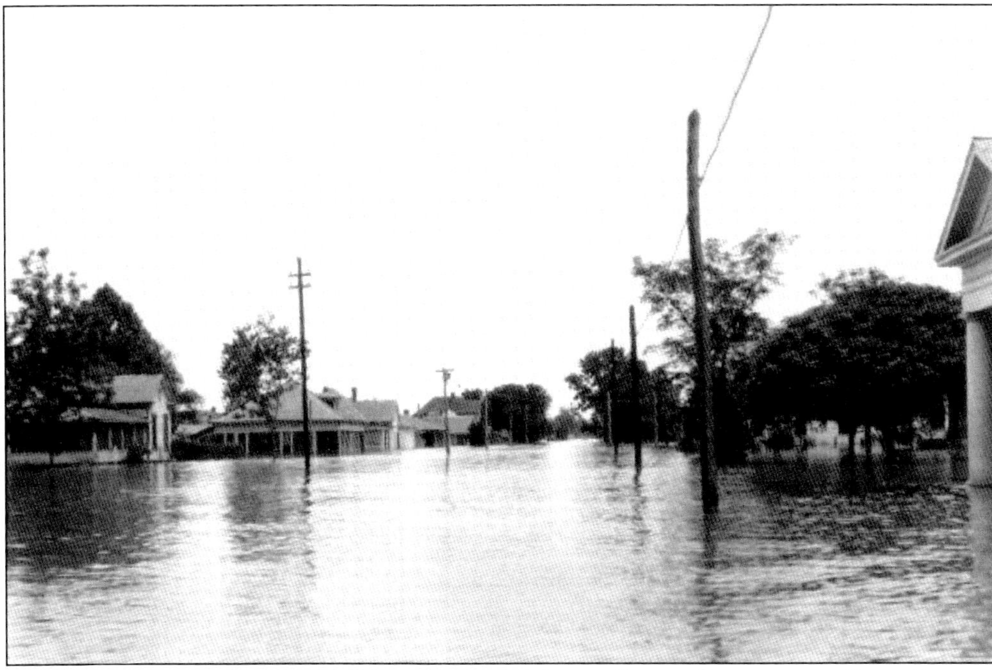

May 17, Tallulah—Looking North along North Cedar Street from First Baptist Church. This is now the northbound lane of U.S. Highway 65. Commercial buildings have now replaced most of the houses seen here. (Courtesy of the USDA.)

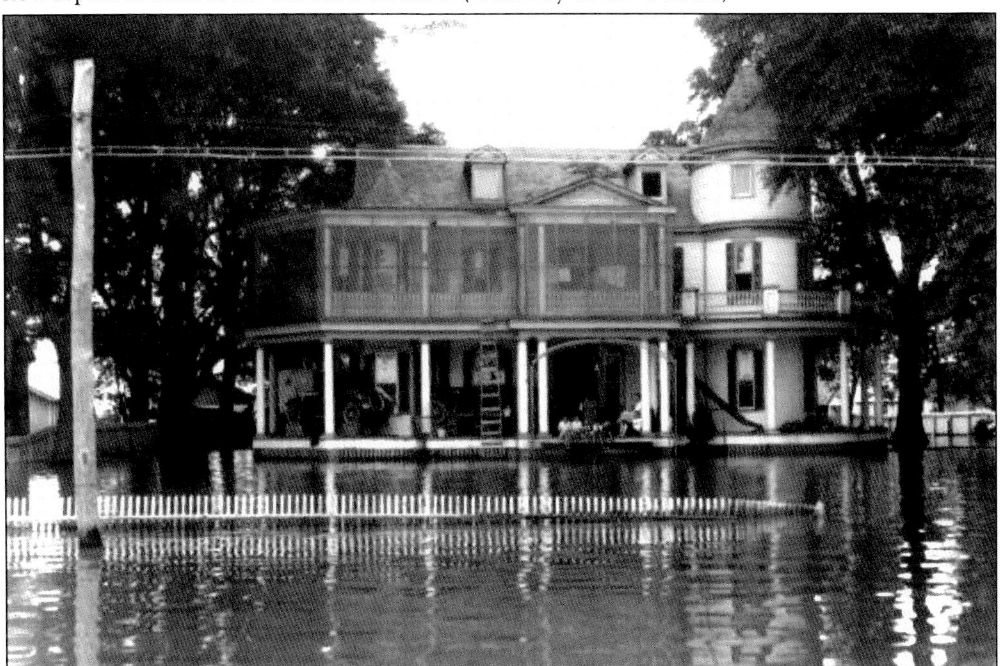

May 17, Tallulah—Dr. Gaines's House. Dr. Gaines lived on North Mulberry Street, and during the flood was probably the most active doctor in town. All through the flood period he made house calls in a boat. (Courtesy of the USDA.)

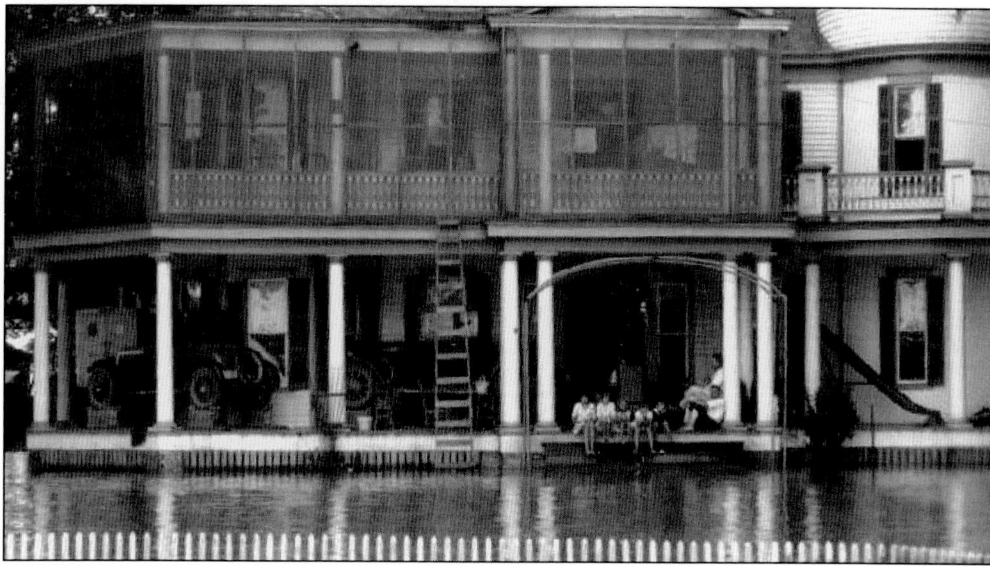

May 17, Tallulah—Close-up of Dr. Gaines's House. In the enlargement of the previous photo two automobiles and an ambulance can be noted on the front porch. (Courtesy of the USDA.)

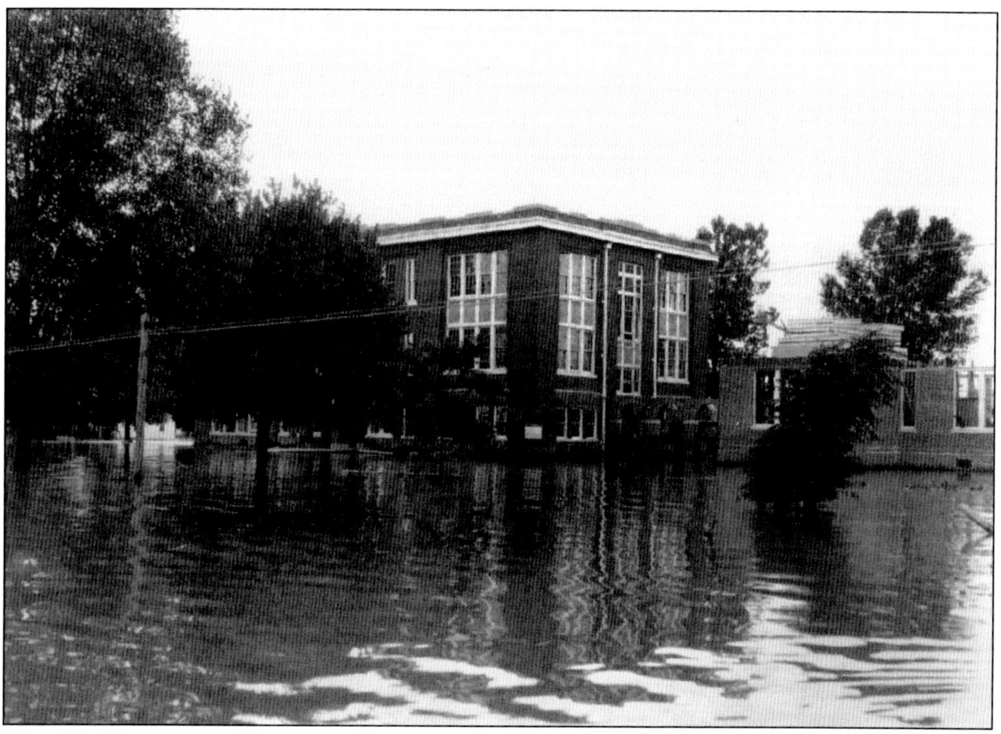

May 17, Tallulah—Tallulah Grammar School. The school building was in use until the 1950s when a new grammar school was built on Johnson Street. The building on the right is a portion of the high school being constructed at that time. (Courtesy of the USDA.)

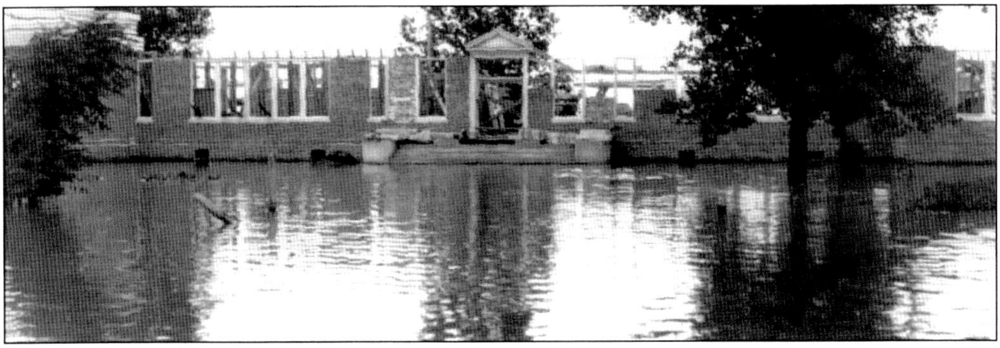

May 17, Tallulah—Tallulah High School Under Construction. Construction on the first floor of Tallulah High School had just begun when the 1927 flood hit. The high school is still in use today. (Courtesy of the USDA.)

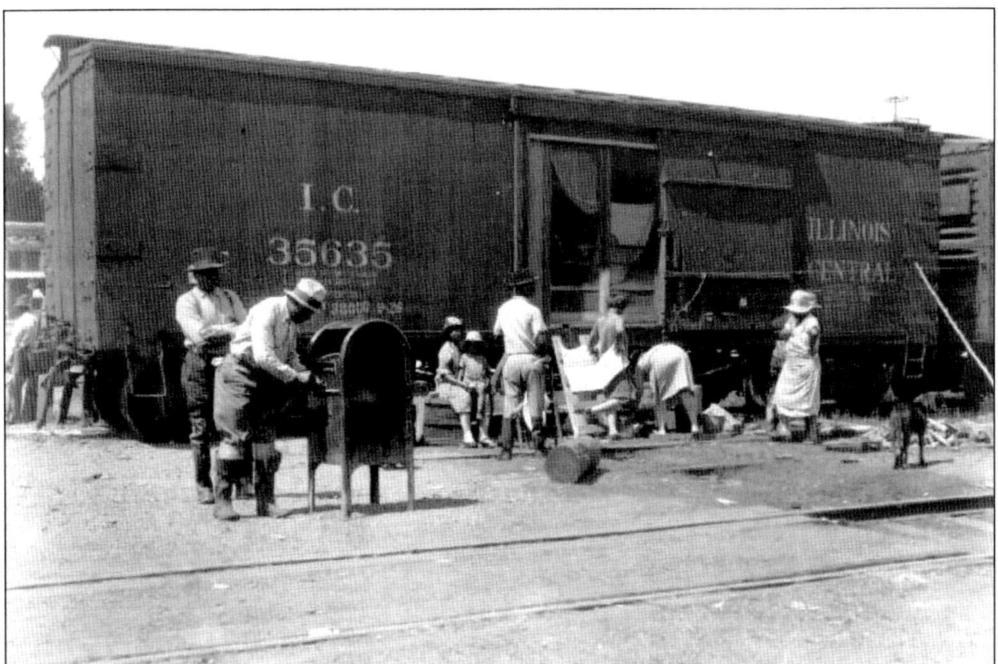

May 17, Tallulah—Mailbox on Illinois Central Railroad Track. The mailbox located on the railroad tracks near the intersection of Depot Street and U.S. Highway 65 seemed to be a meeting place as well as a postal drop. (Courtesy of the USDA.)

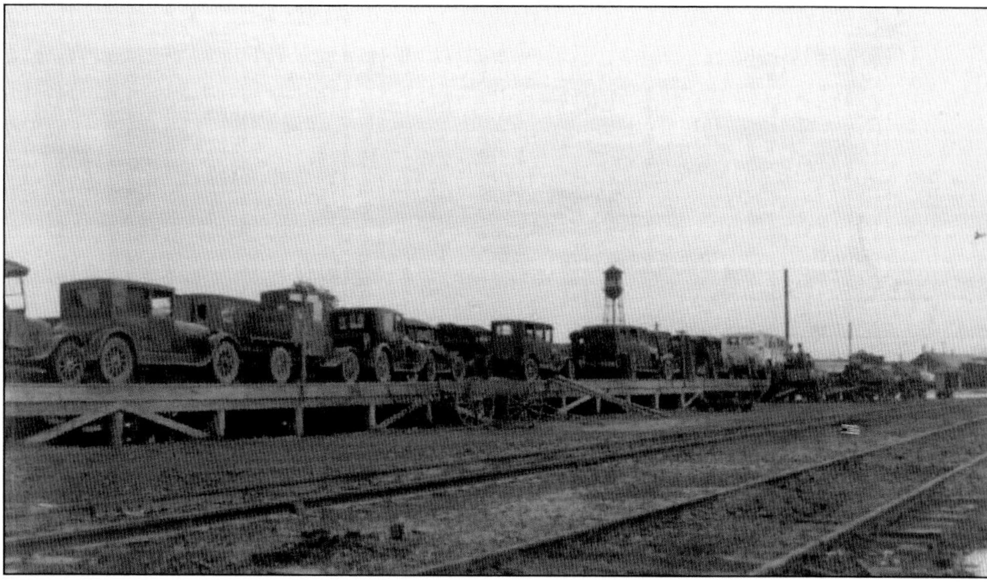

May 17, Tallulah—Automobiles Stored along the Railroad Track. To keep their vehicles high and dry, many people stored them on a ramp along the railroad. (Courtesy of the USDA.)

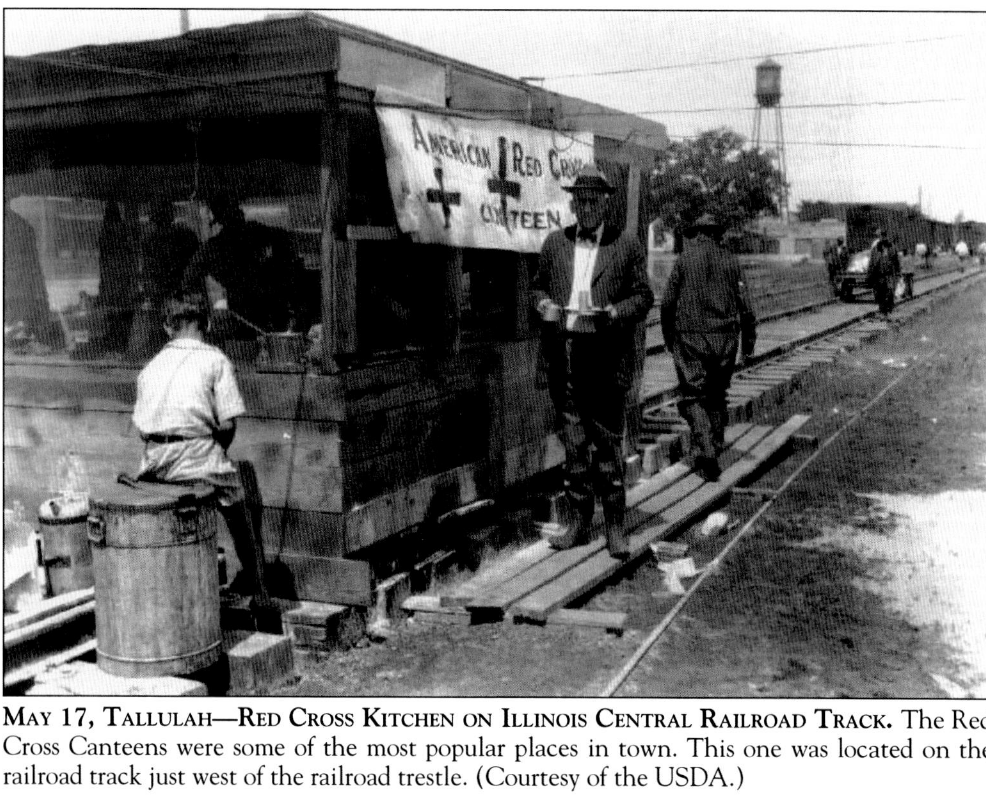

May 17, Tallulah—Red Cross Kitchen on Illinois Central Railroad Track. The Red Cross Canteens were some of the most popular places in town. This one was located on the railroad track just west of the railroad trestle. (Courtesy of the USDA.)

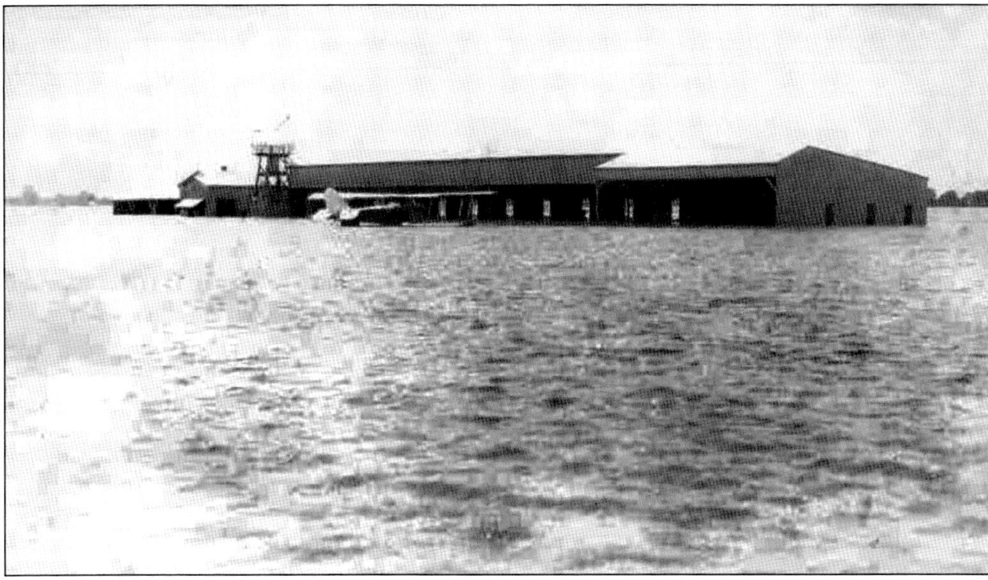

Tallulah Airport c. May 17. Note the lone Huff-Daland duster surrounded by water. (Courtesy of Reid Foster.)

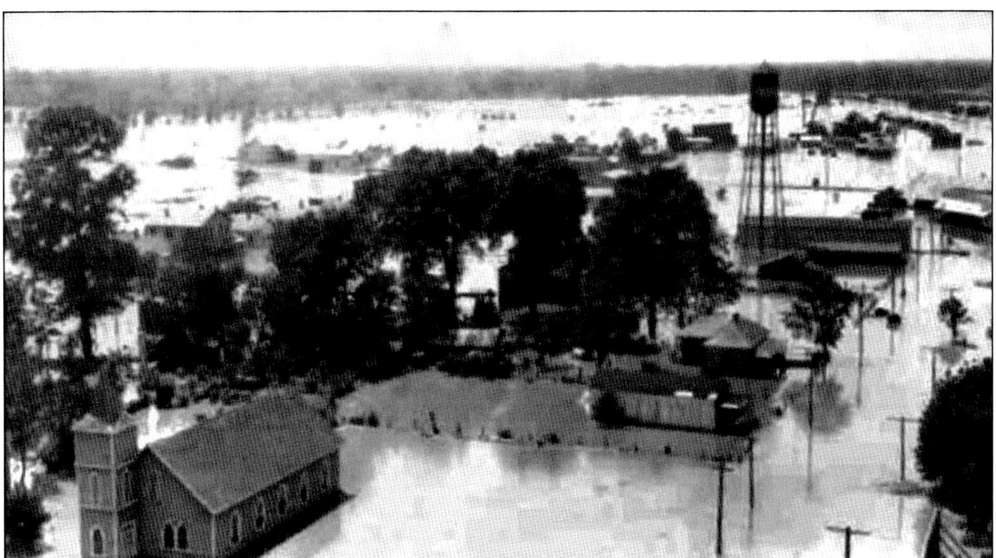

Tallulah c. May 17. This is an aerial view of an unidentified area in Tallulah. (Courtesy of Reid Foster.)

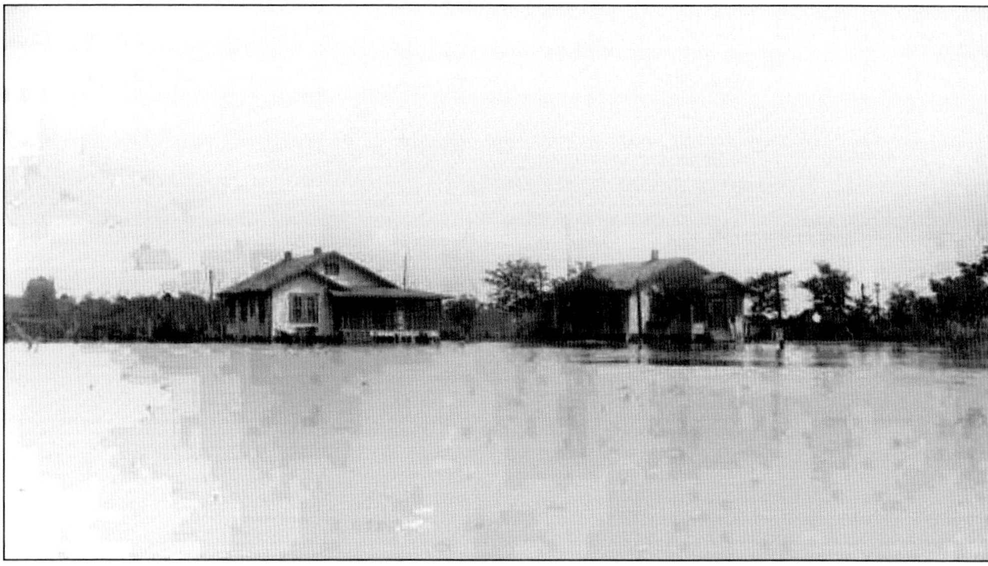

TALLULAH C. MAY 17. The home of Tom and Kitty Foster is to the right This view is on Brushy Bayou, two blocks south of the southern bridge, which had not yet been built. (Courtesy of the Reid Foster.)

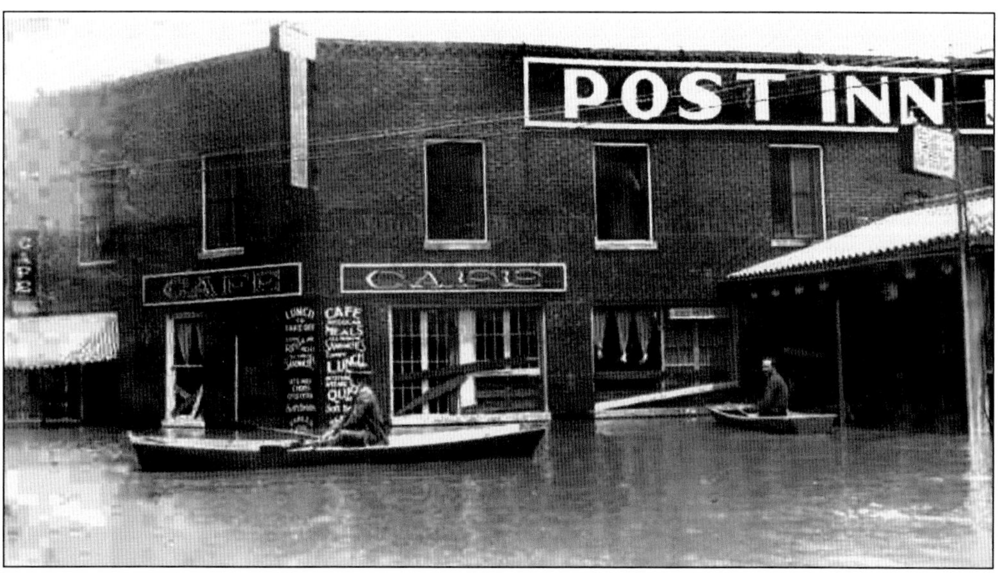

TALLULAH C. MAY 17. This view of the Post Inn Hotel Cafe also shows a well-dressed gentleman out for an afternoon paddle. Note the attempt to board the windows. (Courtesy of Reid Foster.)

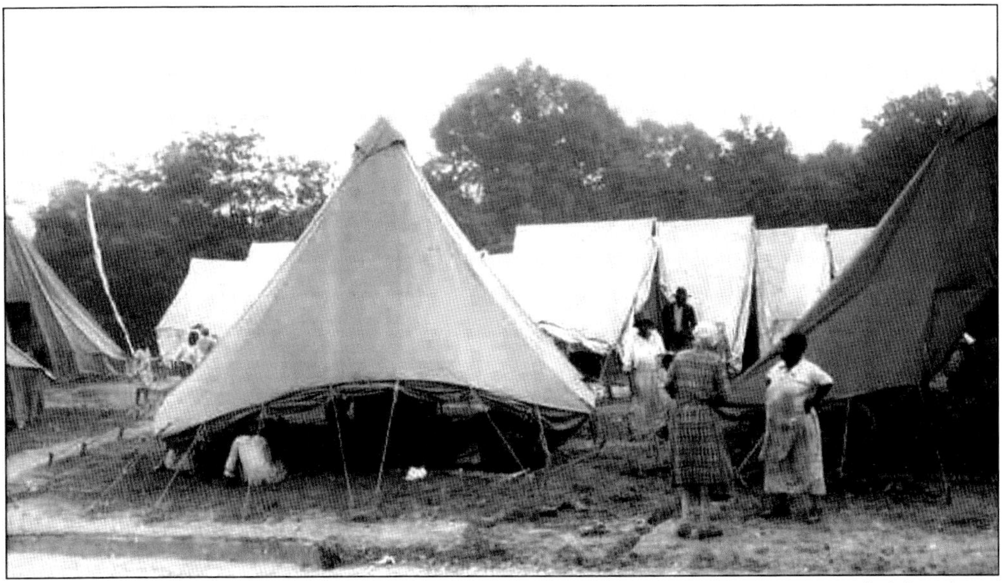

TALLULAH C. MAY 17—REFUGEE CAMP. This is a view of people visiting at the Tallulah refugee camp. (Courtesy of Reid Foster.)

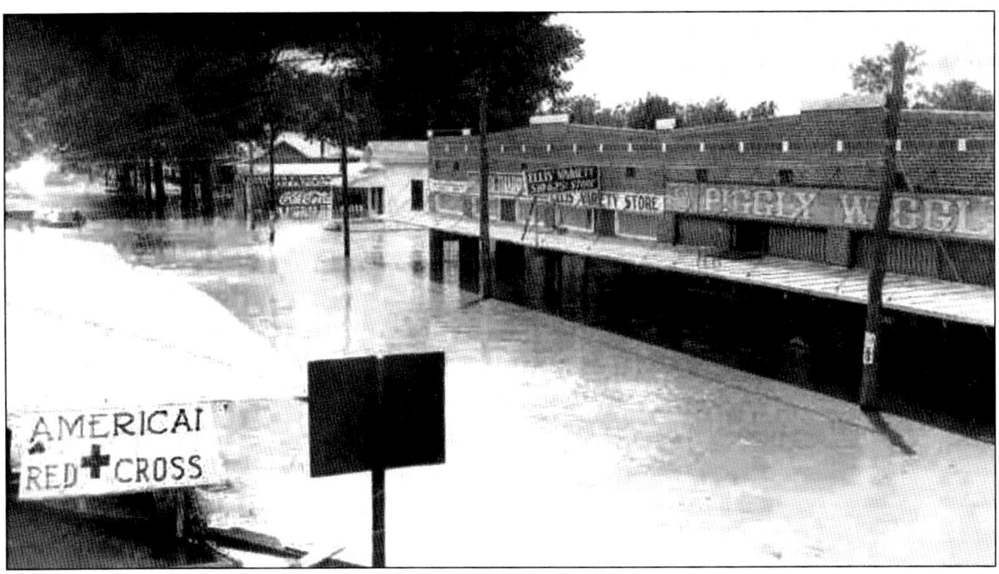

TALLULAH C. MAY 17—PIGGLY WIGGLY GROCERY. This view on Depot Street shows the Piggly Wiggly Grocery and the Ellis Variety stores. A Red Cross Station can be seen on the lower left. (Courtesy of Reid Foster.)

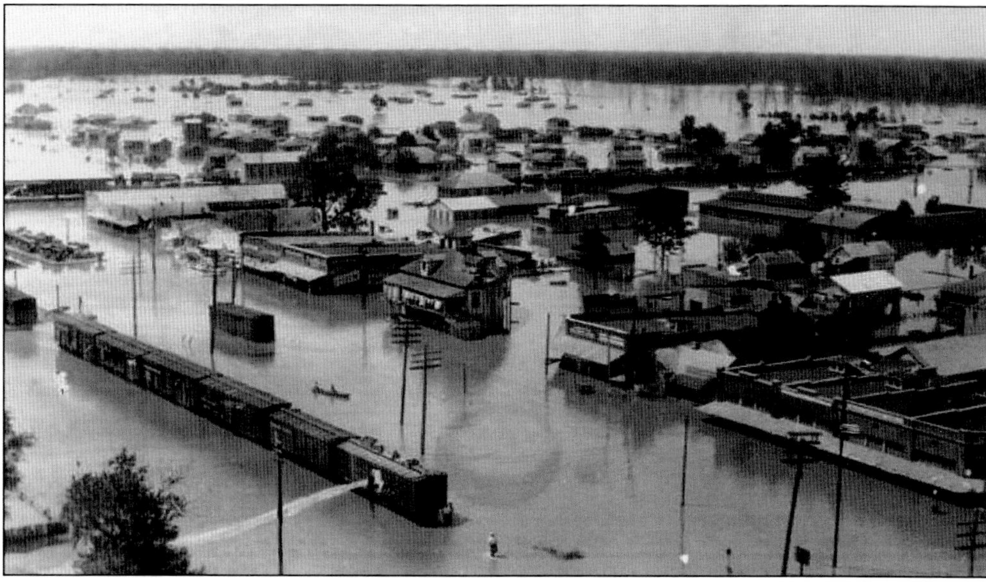

TALLULAH C. MAY 17—AERIAL VIEW OF DOWNTOWN TALLULAH. This northwesterly aerial view of downtown Tallulah shows the Illinois Central railroad, which parallels Depot Street. The Missouri Pacific Line can be seen across the top third of the photo. (Courtesy of Bea Neill.)

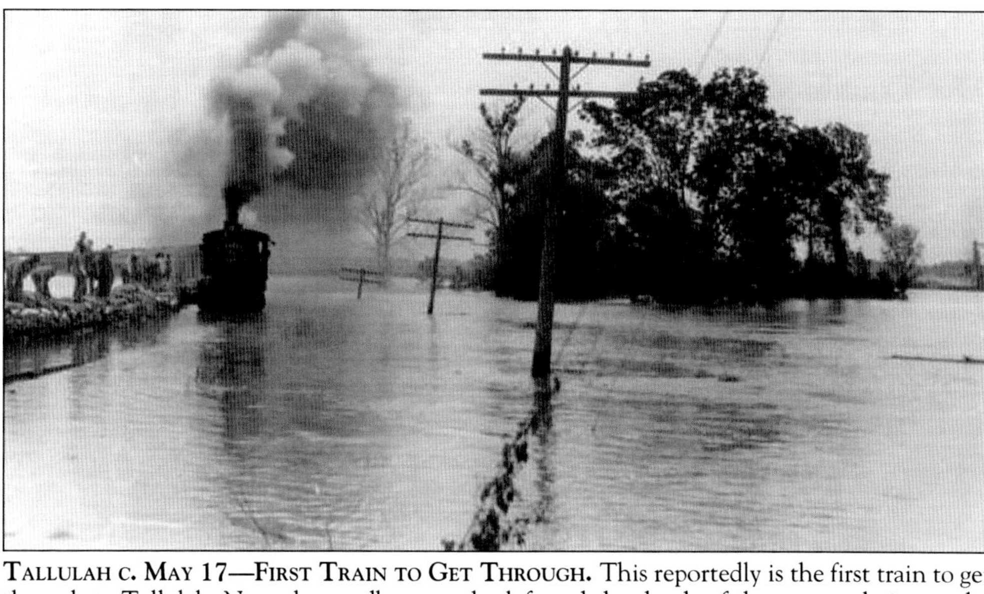

TALLULAH C. MAY 17—FIRST TRAIN TO GET THROUGH. This reportedly is the first train to get through to Tallulah. Note the sandbags on the left and the depth of the water relative to the telephone poles in the left center. (Courtesy of Bea Neill.)

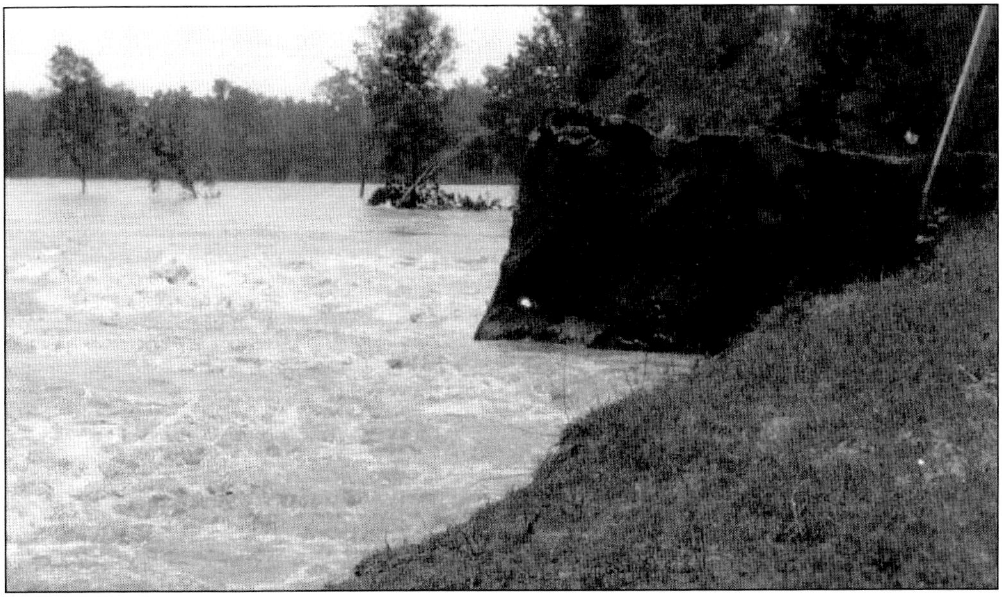

May 18, Cabin Teele. The Cabin Teele Crevasse occurred on May 3rd. This photo shows the crevasse 15 days after the break in the levee. (Courtesy of USDA.)

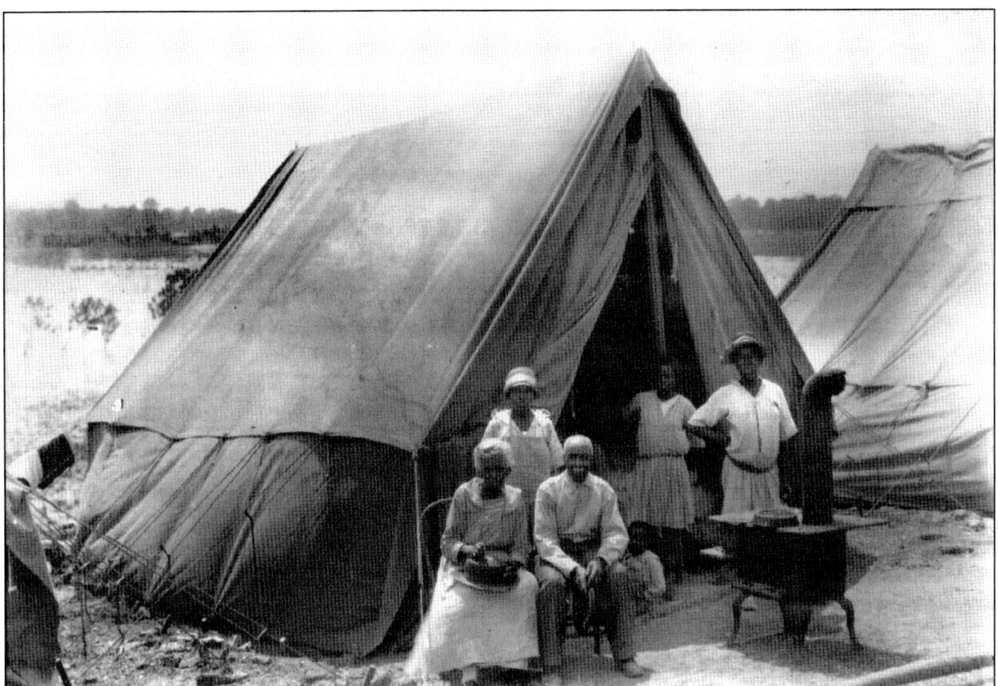

May 18, Milliken's Bend—Refugee Camp. Jim Pendleton and his wife, shown here, had been in every flood since 1874. Note the pot-bellied stove on the right. (Courtesy of USDA.)

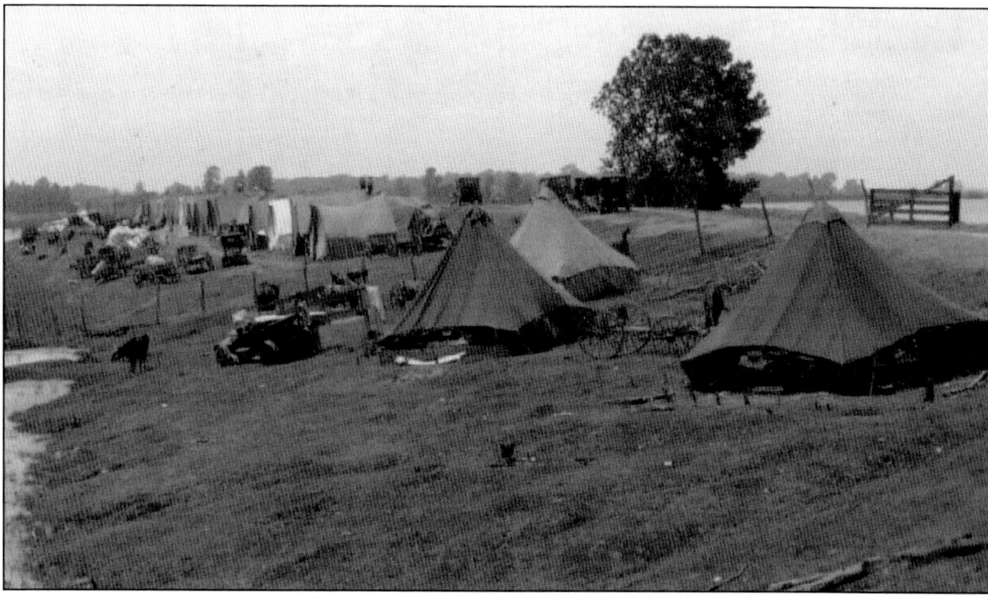

May 18, Milliken's Bend—Refugee Camp. Refugee camps were established by the Red Cross at several location including those at Tallulah and on the levee near Milliken's Bend. Today the town of Milliken's Bend is only a memory. (Courtesy of USDA.)

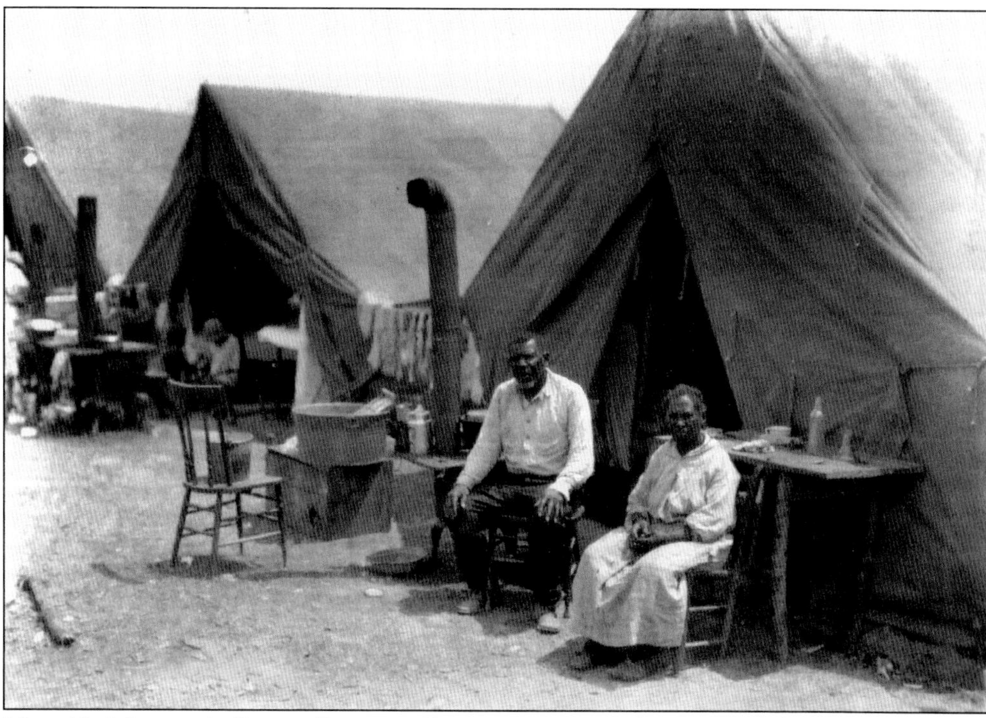

May 18, Milliken's Bend—Refugee Camp. Here is another view of the refugee camp on the levee at Milliken's Bend. Because of Mississippi River encroachment, Milliken's Bend was forced to be abandoned in the early 1900s. Most of the residents moved to Tallulah. (Courtesy of USDA.)

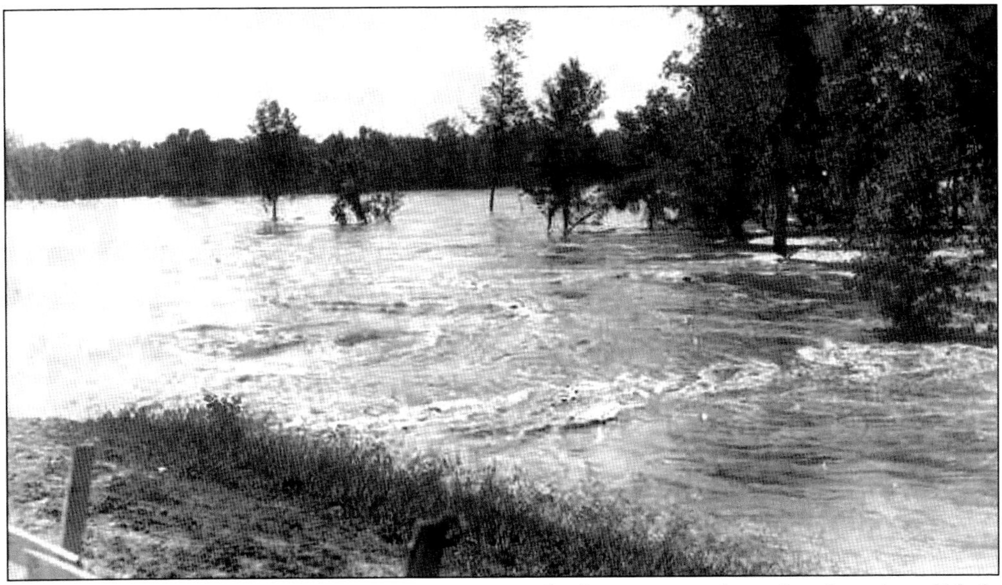

Cabin Teele c. May 19. Water continues to rush the crevasse through a location slightly different from the one shown previously. (Courtesy of Reid Foster.)

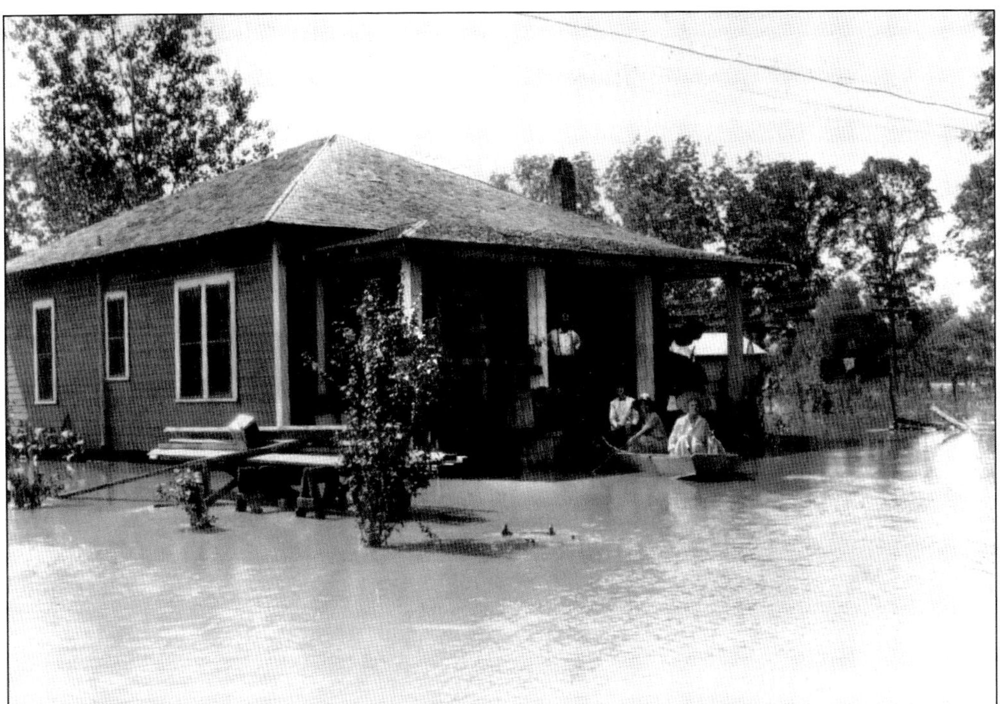

May 19, Tallulah—Devine Home. This was taken 16 days after the break in the levee. Mrs. Devine will be remembered as the owner of Tallulah's Ideal Flower Shop during the 1930s and 1940s. (Courtesy of USDA.)

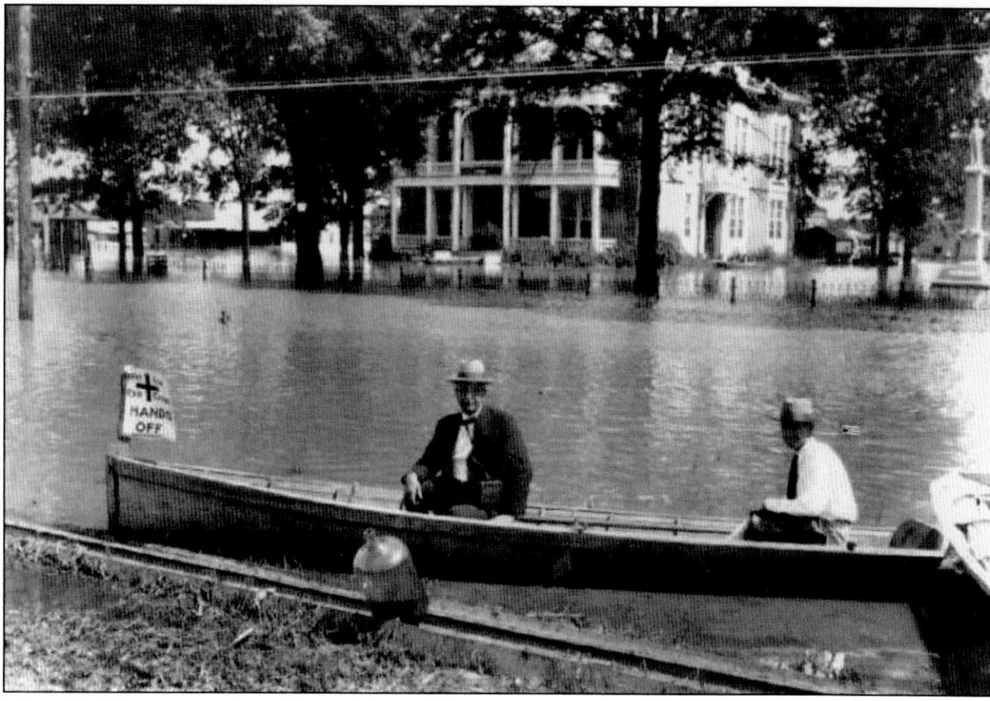

MAY 19, TALLULAH—RED CROSS BOAT. This was one of the official Red Cross Inspection boats. Note the "hands off" sign. The Madison Parish Courthouse is in the background. (Courtesy of USDA.)

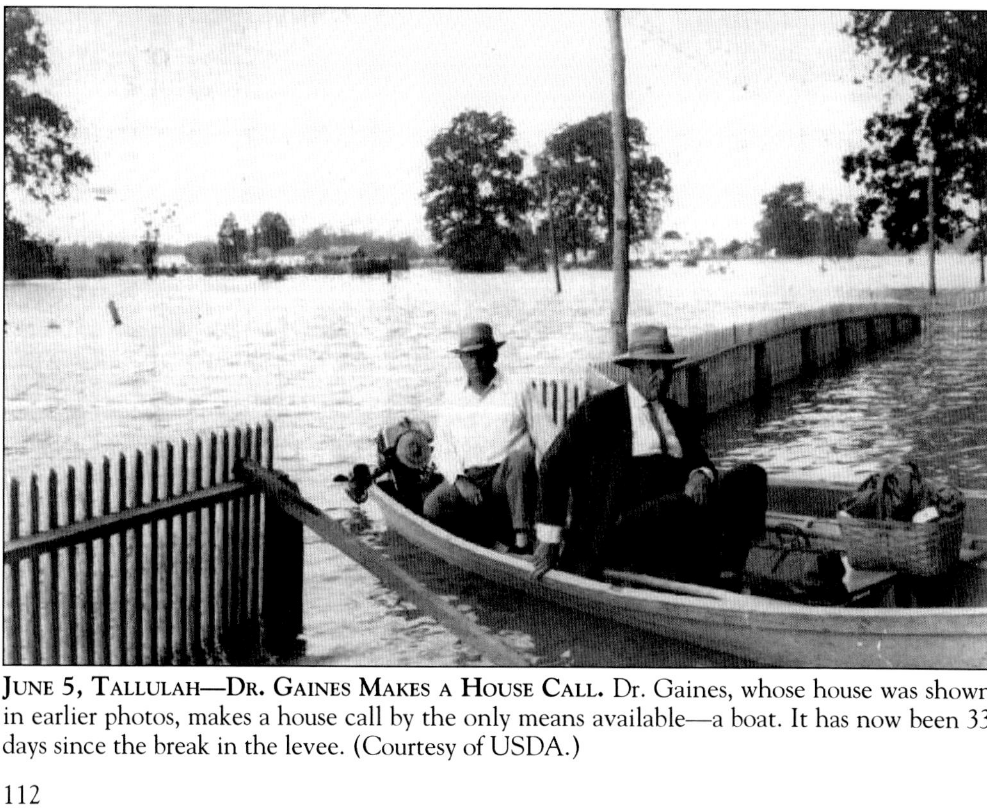

JUNE 5, TALLULAH—DR. GAINES MAKES A HOUSE CALL. Dr. Gaines, whose house was shown in earlier photos, makes a house call by the only means available—a boat. It has now been 33 days since the break in the levee. (Courtesy of USDA.)

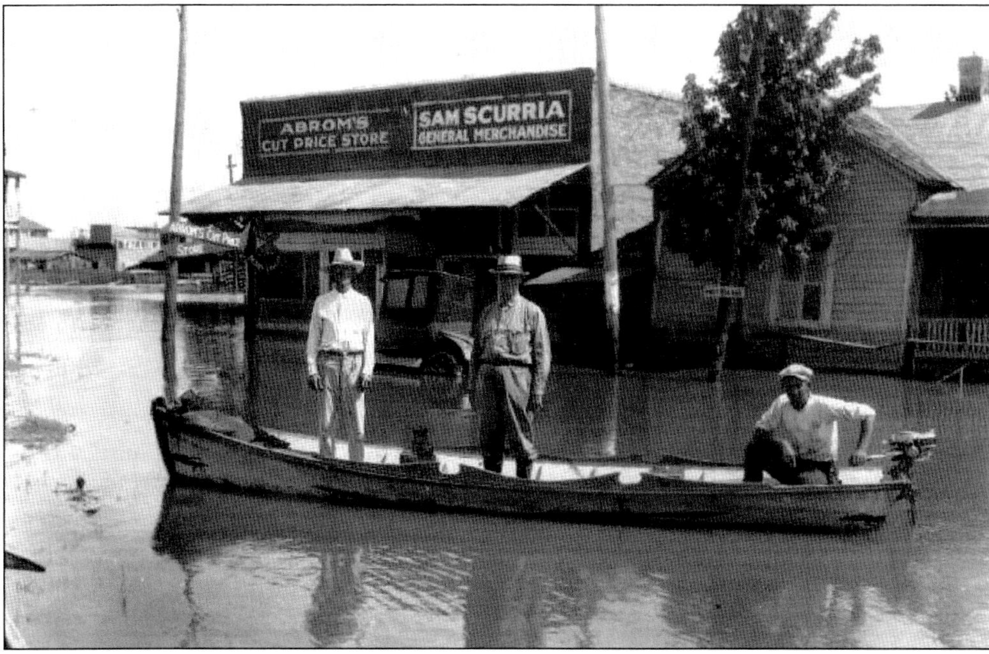

June 6, Tallulah—Abroms and Scurria Stores. Thirty-four days after the break in the levee water still stands in Abrom's Cut Price Store and Sam Scurria's General Merchandise. Neither of these stores exists today. (Courtesy of USDA.)

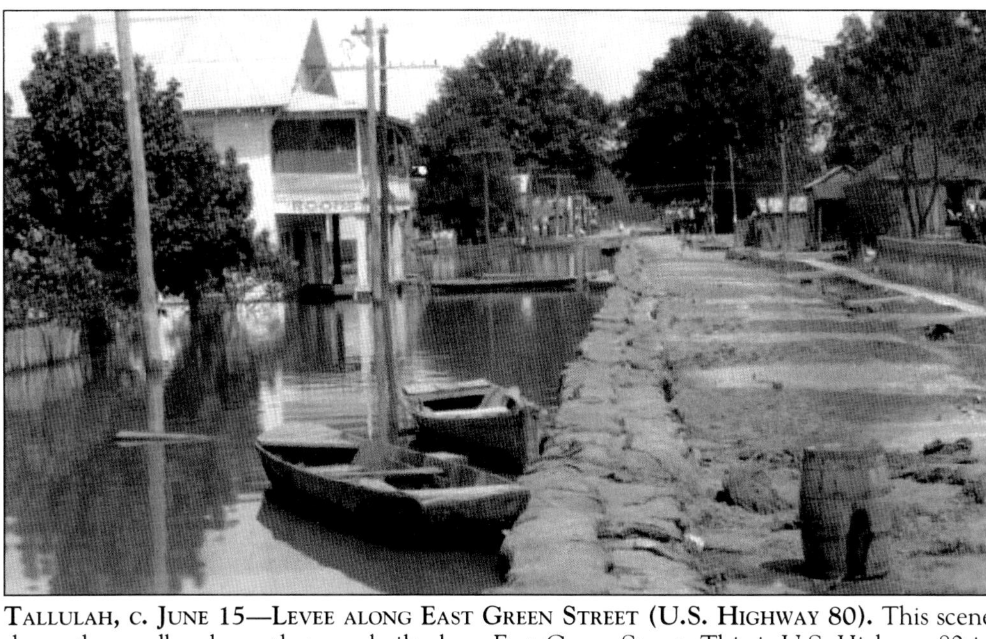

Tallulah, c. June 15—Levee along East Green Street (U.S. Highway 80). This scene shows the sandbag levee that was built along East Green Street. This is U.S. Highway 80 in western Tallulah. (Courtesy of USDA.)

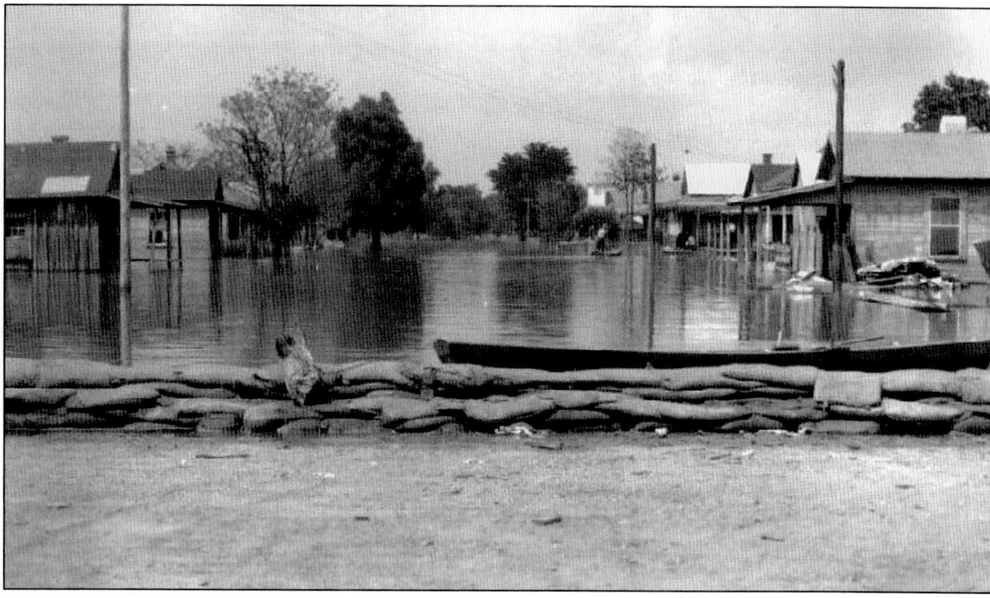

Tallulah, c. June 15. Another sandbag scene along East Green Street shows that even six weeks after the flood, water was still standing. (Courtesy of USDA.)

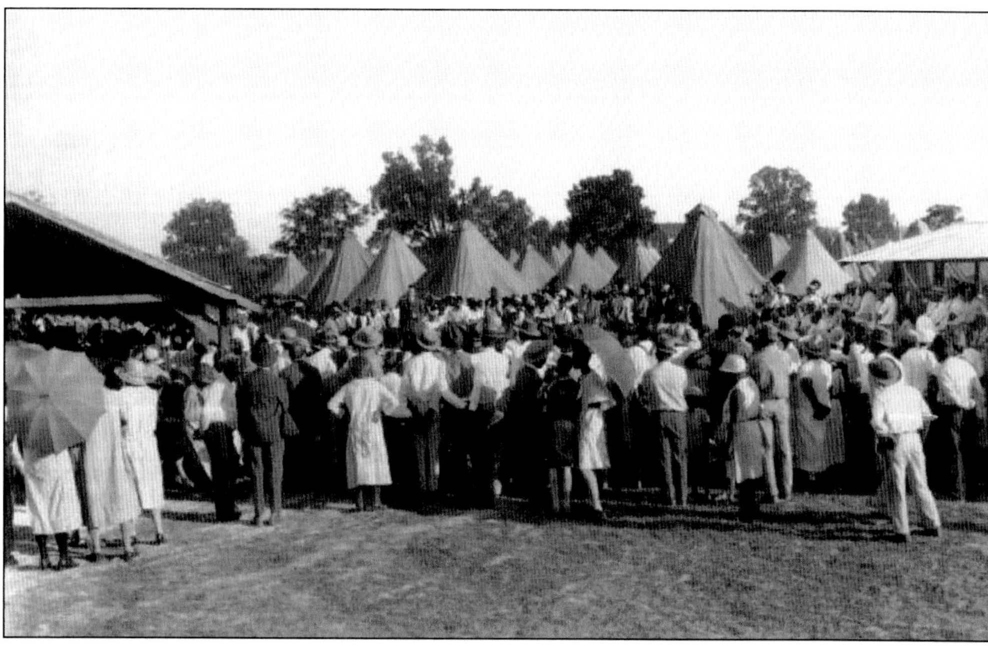

July 4, Tallulah—Flood Refugees. Even 62 days after the levee break, many refugees still lived in tents. This must have been a special July 4th celebration. Fourth of July celebrations in Madison Parish were rare until the late 1940s because that was the date of Vicksburg's Civil War surrender. (Courtesy of USDA.)

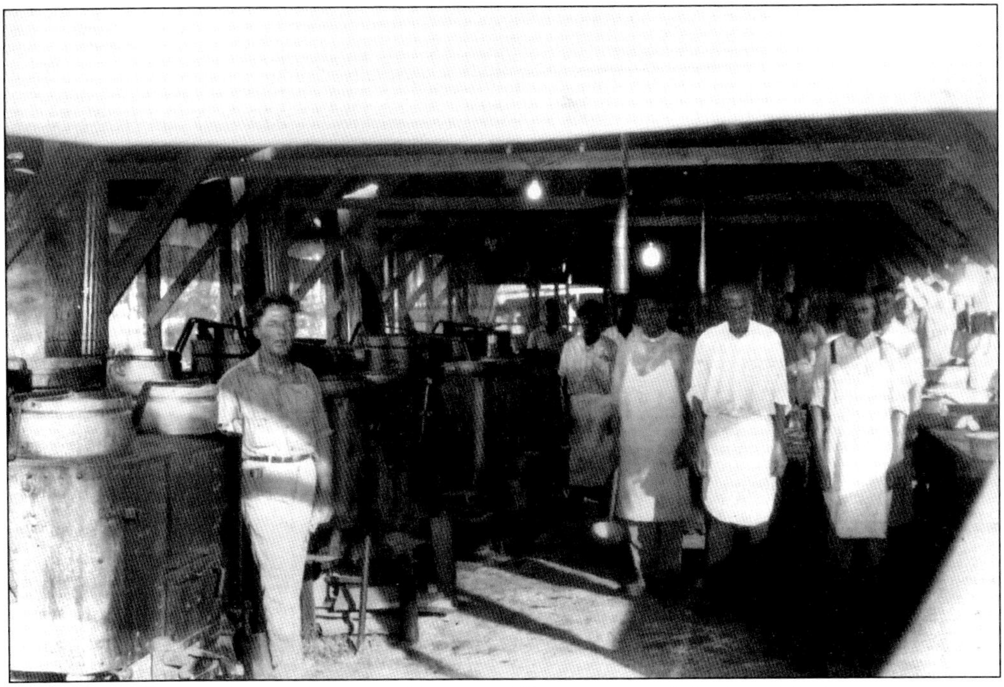

July 4, Tallulah—Flood Refugee Kitchen. This was one of the large kitchens necessary to feed so many displaced persons. Notice the sizeable amount of kitchen equipment on the left side of the photo. (Courtesy of USDA.)

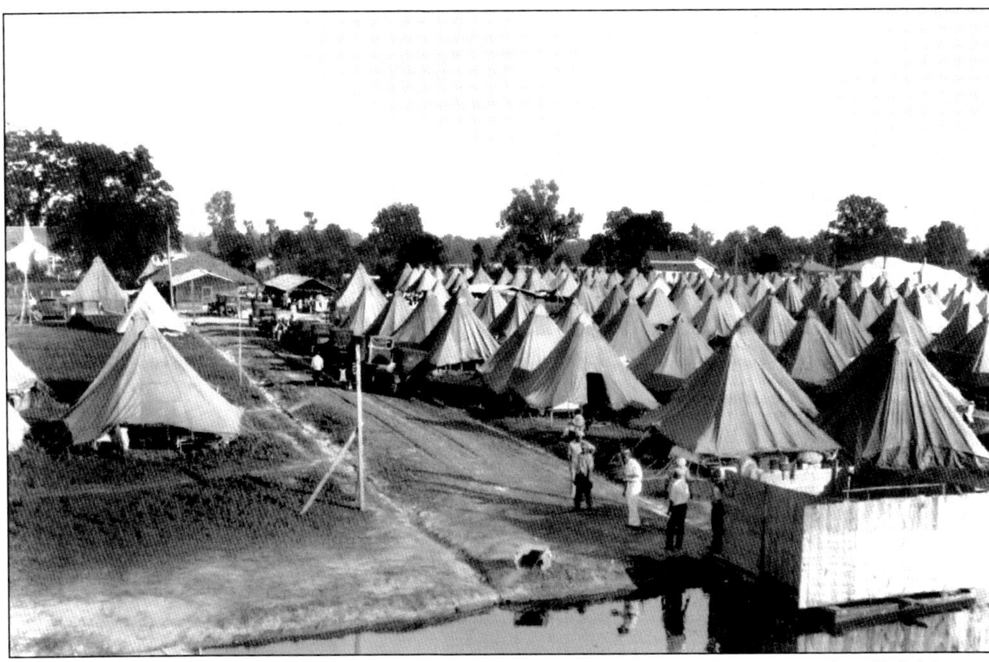

July 4, Tallulah—Flood Refugee "Tent City." This is another view of Tallulah's tent city. The enclosed area in the right foreground was probably an outdoor bathroom. (Courtesy of USDA.)

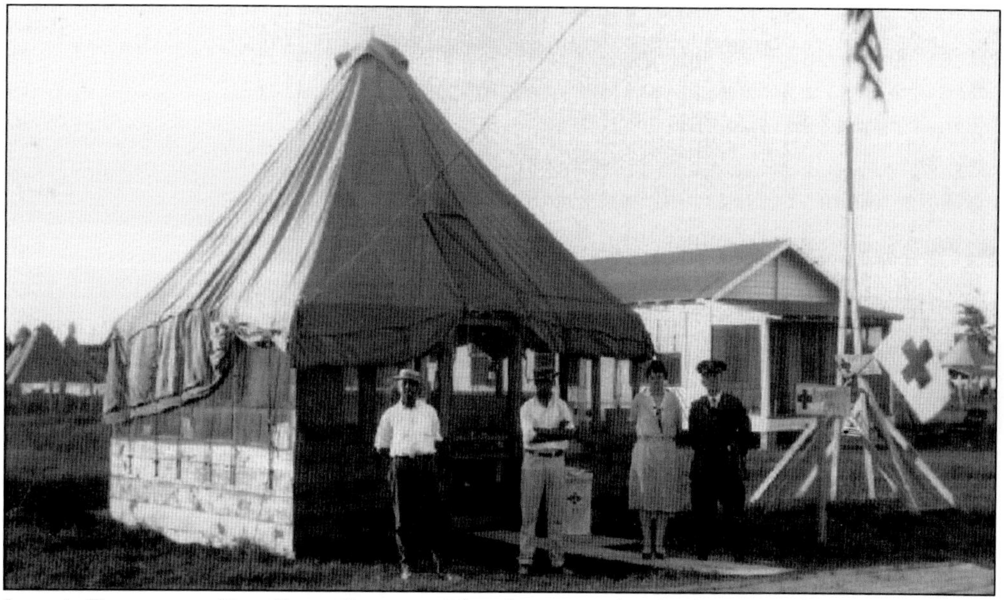

JULY 4, TALLULAH—RED CROSS STATION. This shows another Red Cross Aid Station. This one seems to be equipped with a nurse and a policeman. (Courtesy of USDA.)

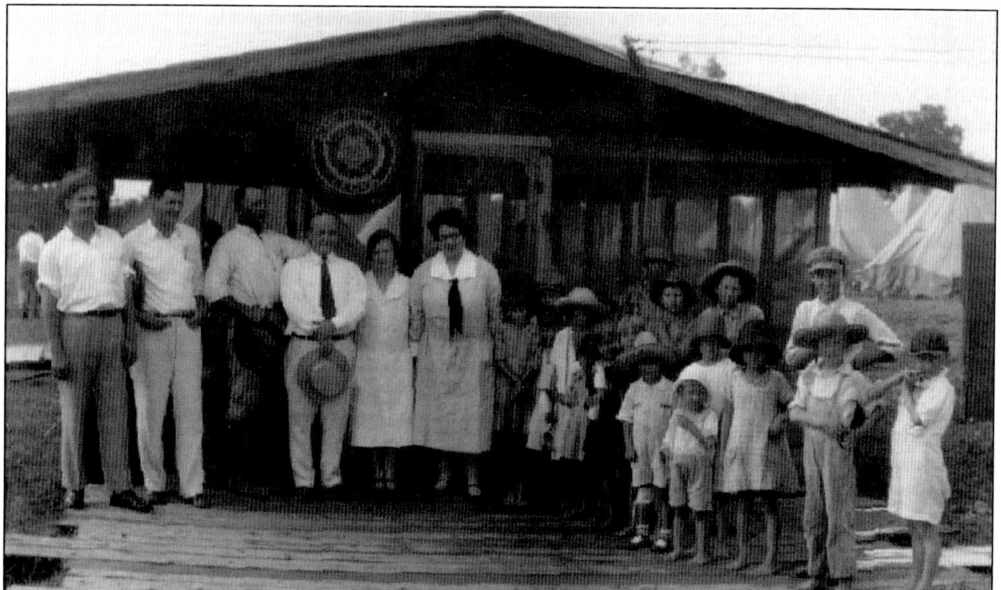

JULY 4, TALLULAH—AMERICAN LEGION STATION. The American Legion also had an aid station. The only person possibly identified in this picture is the nurse in the center who is believed to be Hazel Jean Moberly. (Courtesy of USDA.)

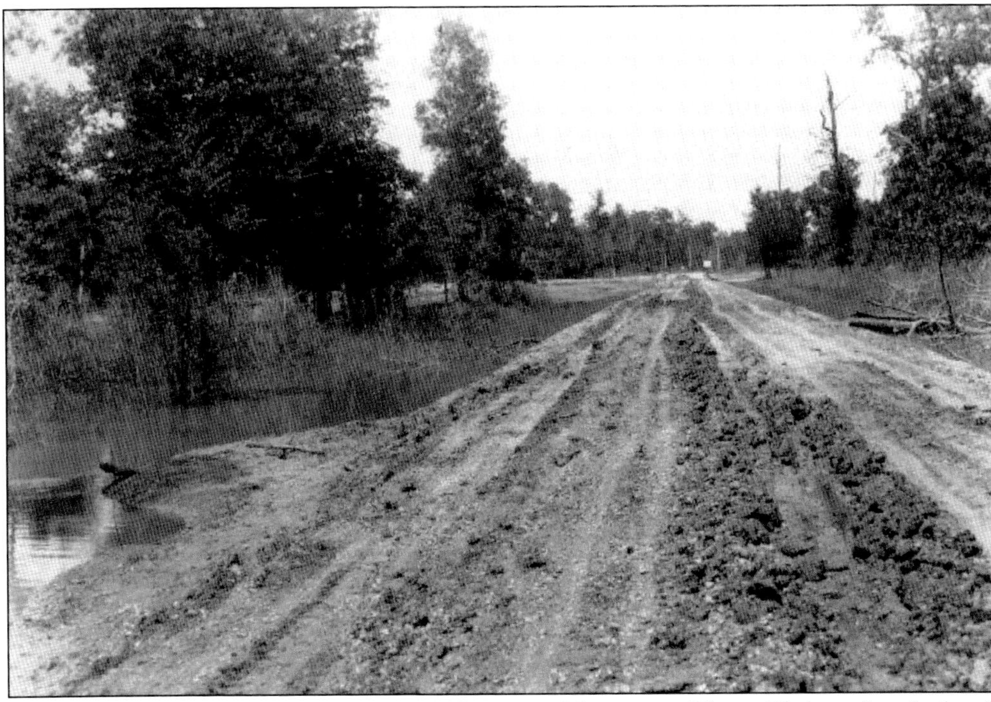

JULY 21, TALLULAH—U.S. HIGHWAY 65 NORTH OF TALLULAH. This is 79 days after the break in the levee. By now the public roads were completely destroyed. (Courtesy of USDA.)

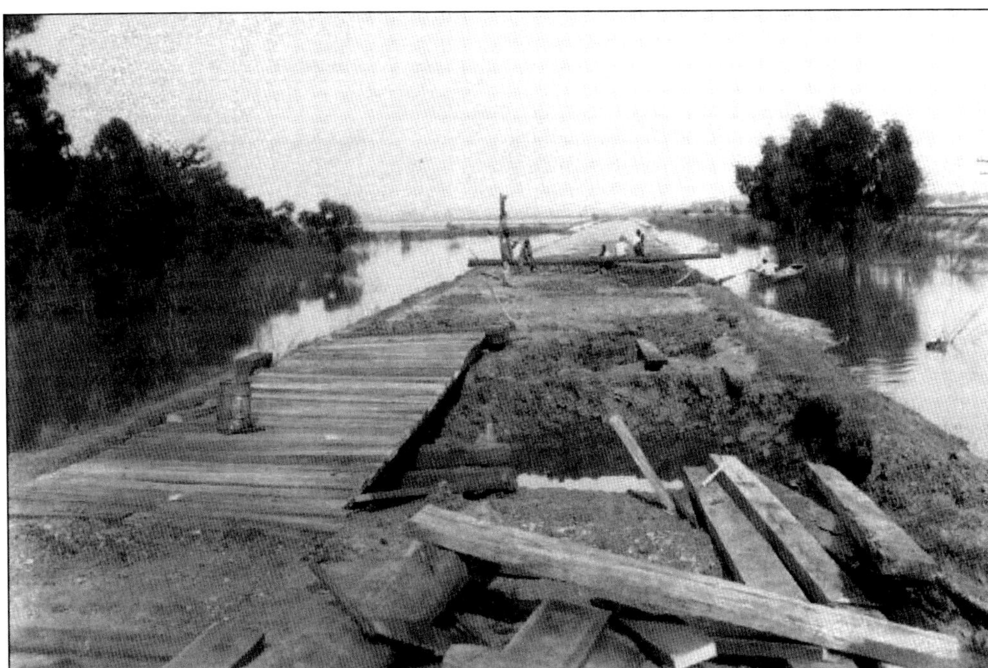

JULY 21, TALLULAH—ROAD DAMAGE. This is U.S. Highway 80 one mile east of Tallulah where water still stood on both sides of the roadbed. (Courtesy of USDA.)

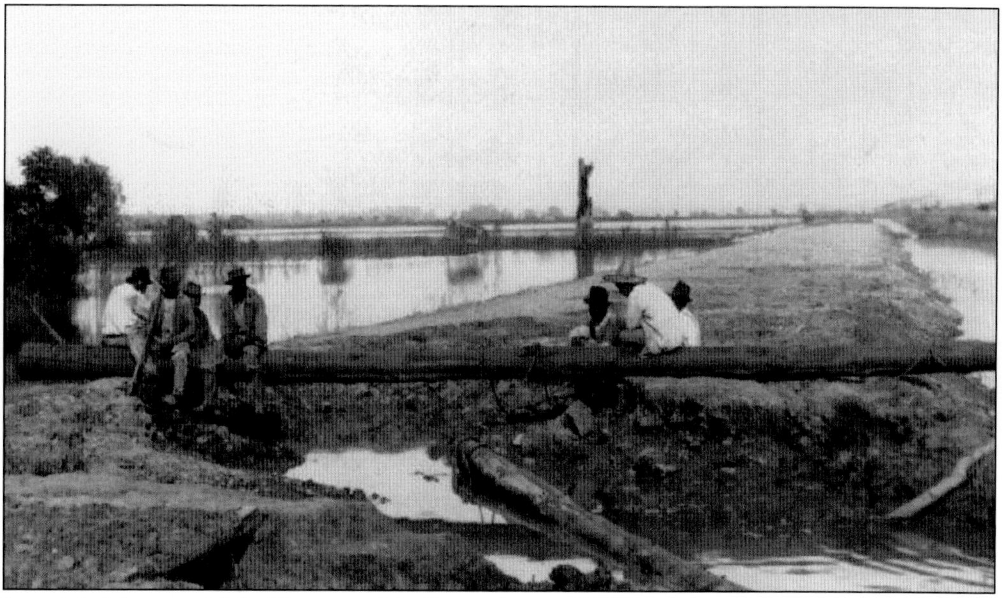

July 21, Mound—U.S. Highway 80. Shown here is U.S. Highway 80 near Mound about 11 miles east of Tallulah. The workers must be taking a break. (Courtesy of USDA.)

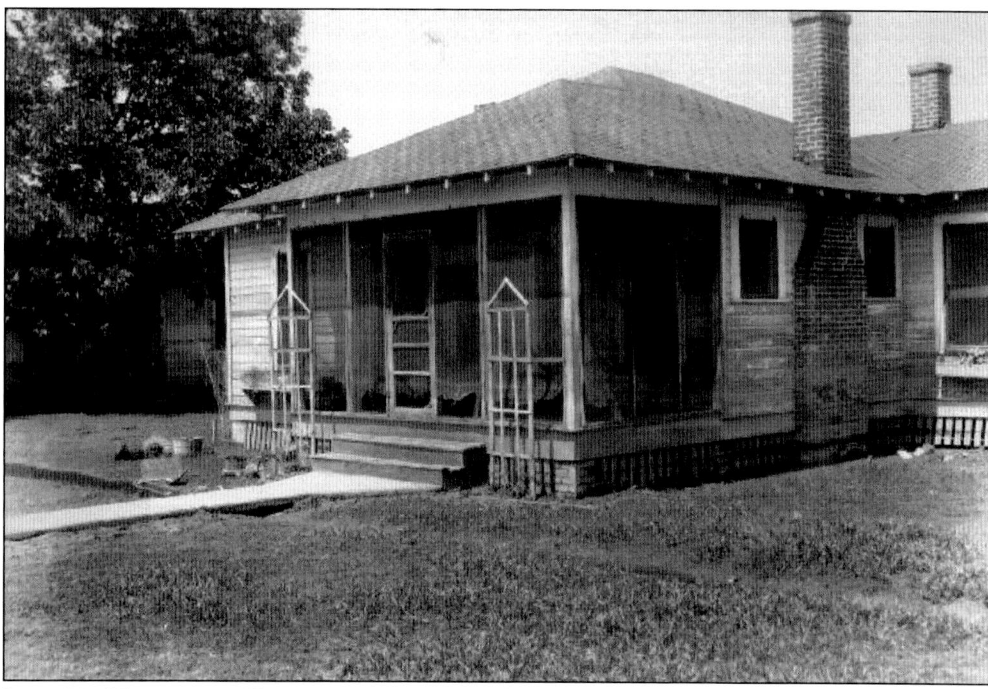

July 22, Tallulah—House Damage. Note the water line about halfway up house in this photograph taken 80 days after the levee broke. (Courtesy of USDA.)

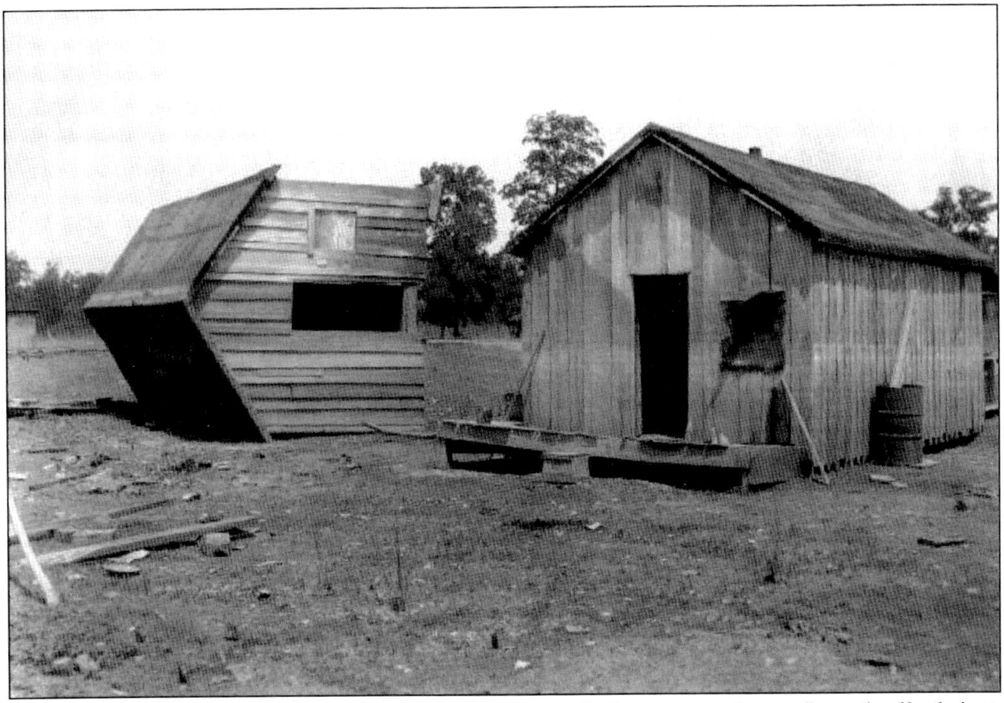

JULY 22, TALLULAH—HOUSE DAMAGE. These two sheds seem to have floated off of their original locations. One has been turned on its side. (Courtesy of USDA.)

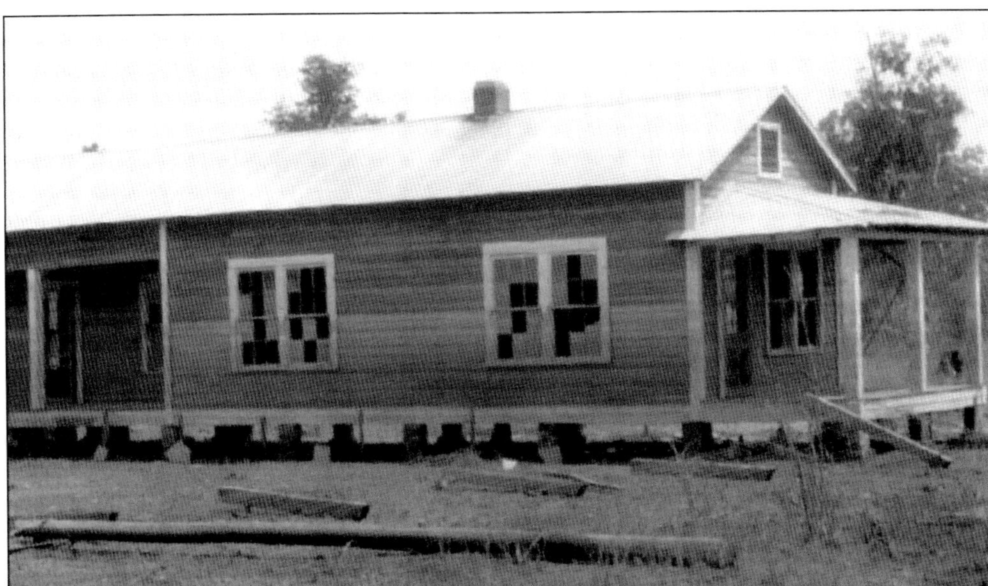

JULY 22, TALLULAH—HOUSE DAMAGE. This Tallulah house did not seem to be moved, but many windows have been broken out. The lumber in the foreground may have supported a walkway during the high water. (Courtesy of USDA.)

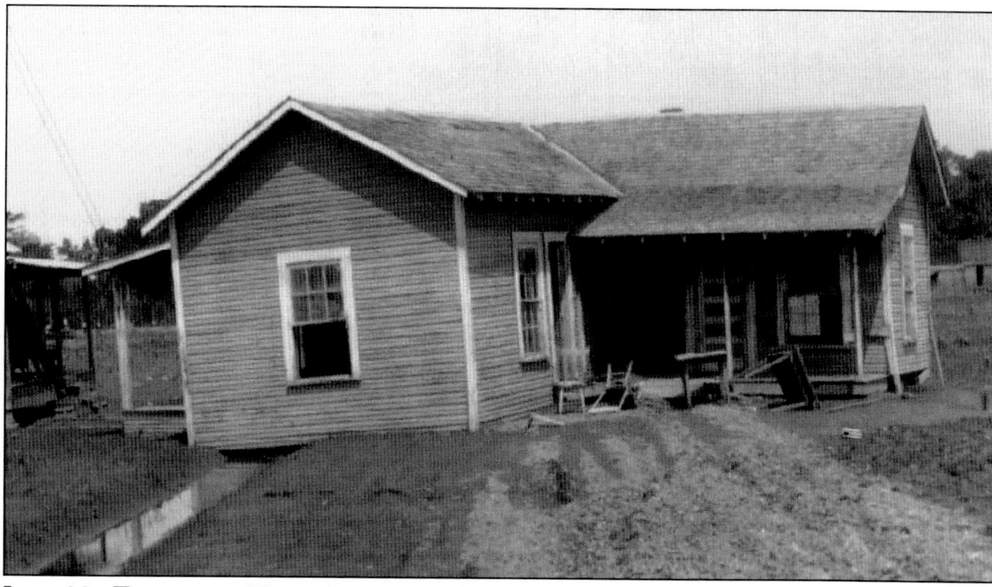

July 22, Tallulah—House Damage. This house has been picked up and moved off its location, and the furniture appears to have been damaged. A ditch now runs beneath the left side. (Courtesy of USDA.)

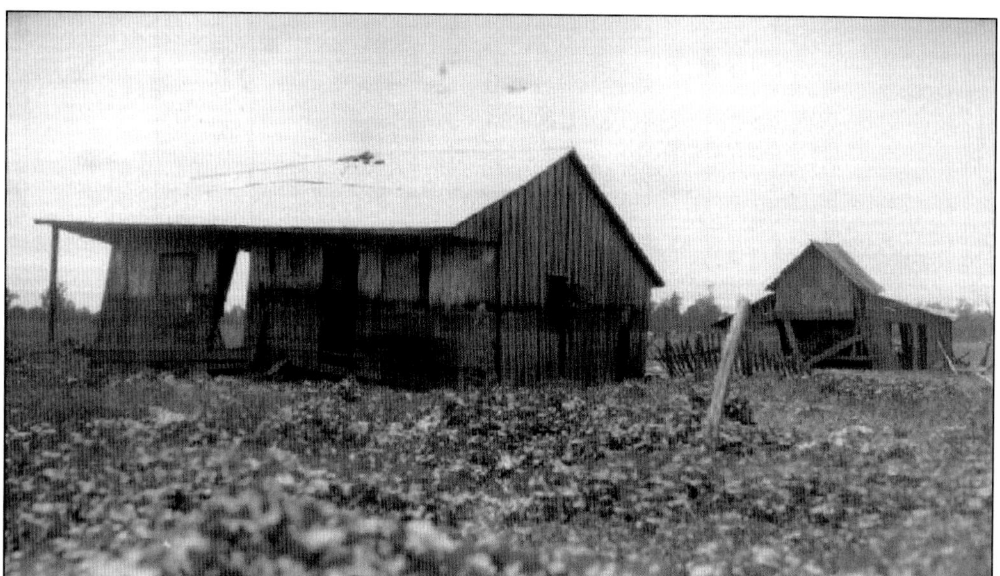

July 27, Mound—House and Barn Damage. The house and barn were both heavily damaged and appear ready to collapse. This photo was taken 85 days after the break in the levee. (Courtesy of USDA.)

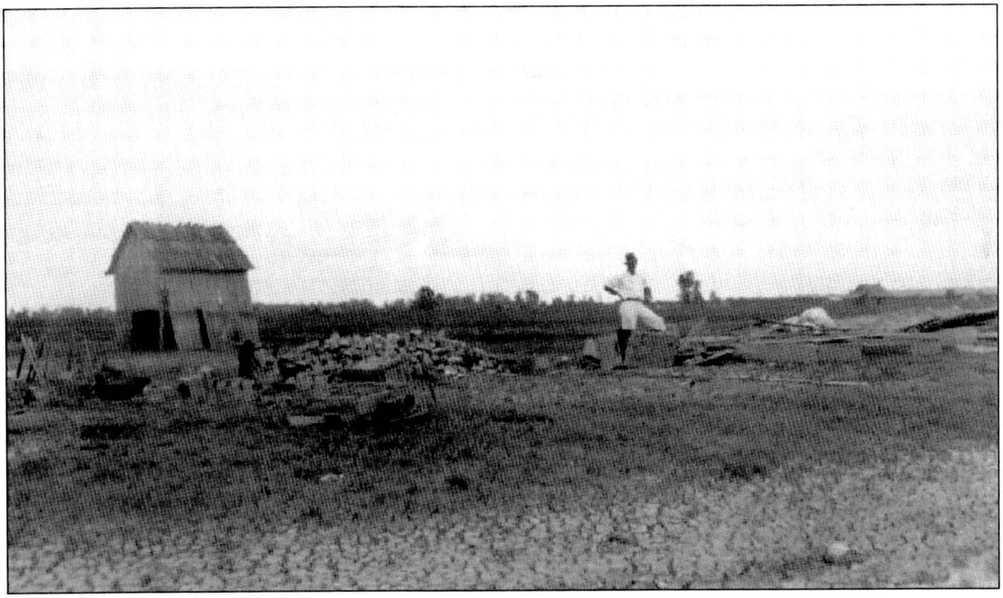

JULY 27, MOUND. The house is gone, but the pile of bricks that used to be a chimney remains. The barn in the left background is leaning precariously to the left. (Courtesy of USDA.)

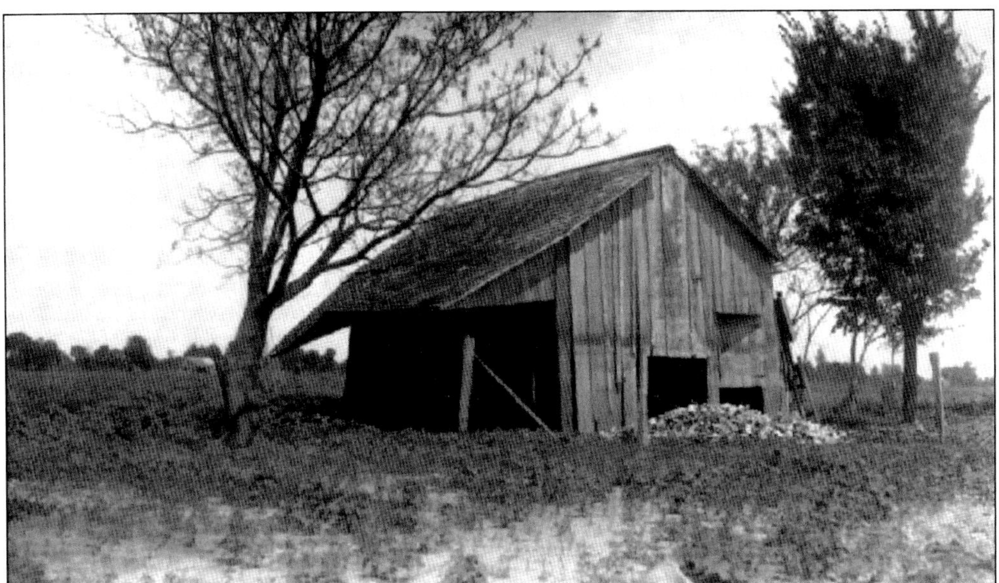

JULY 27, MOUND. This house is still standing, but the chimney is destroyed. The tree to the left appears to be leaning over the house. (Courtesy of USDA.)

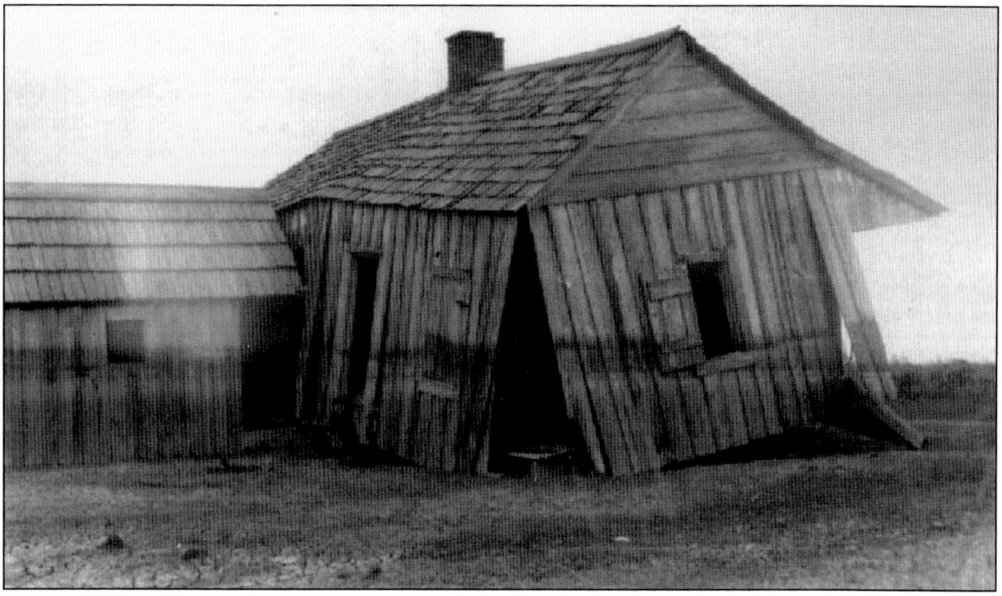

July 27, Mound—House Damage. Here a house is split open. From the appearance of the water marks, the house apparently split after the water had reached its highest point. (Courtesy of USDA.)

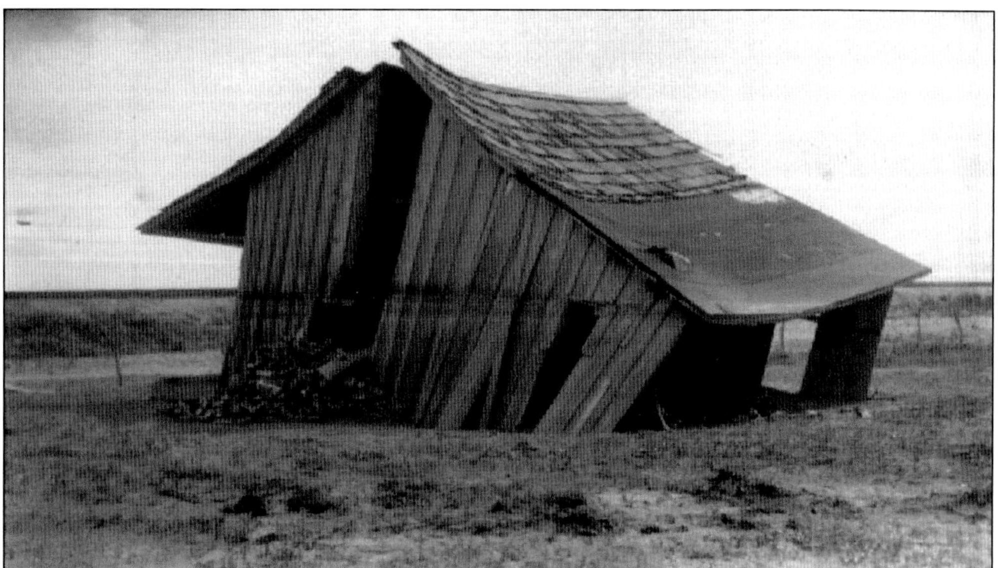

July 27, Mound. This house is barely standing, and the chimney is gone. (Courtesy of USDA.)

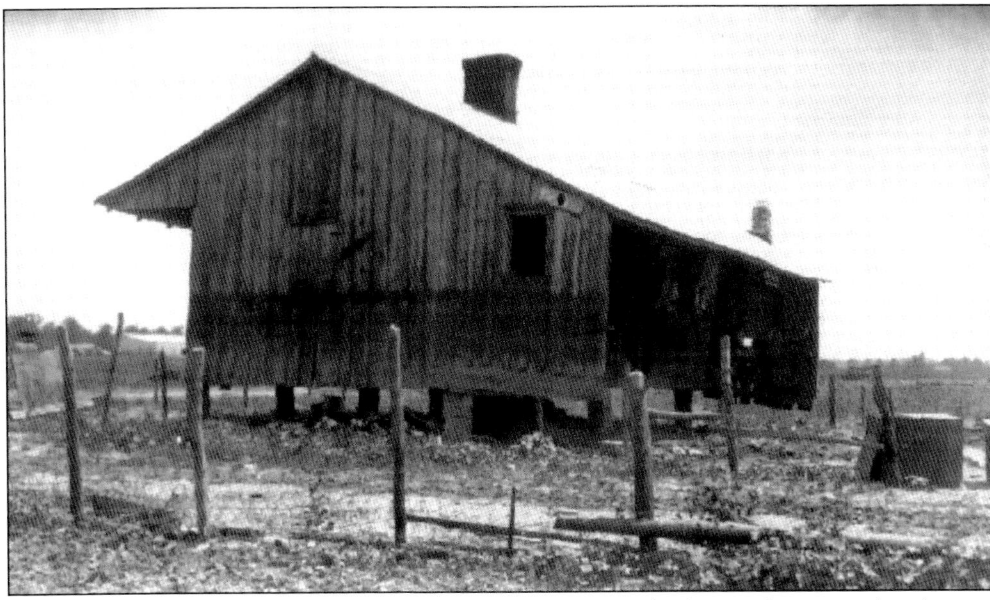

July 27, Mound. Part of the rear end of this house has washed away; however, the chimney is still standing. Also it appears that some of the support pillows on the right back are missing. (Courtesy of USDA.)

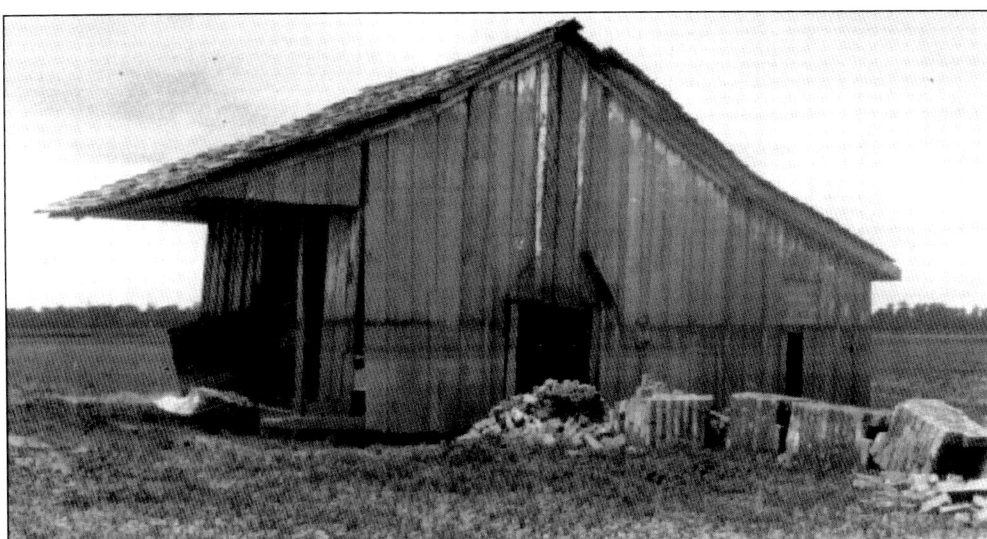

July 27, Shirley Plantation. This house is standing, but the chimney has fallen. Several of the support pillows may have washed away. Shirley Plantation was the site of the Tallulah Airport. (Courtesy of USDA.)

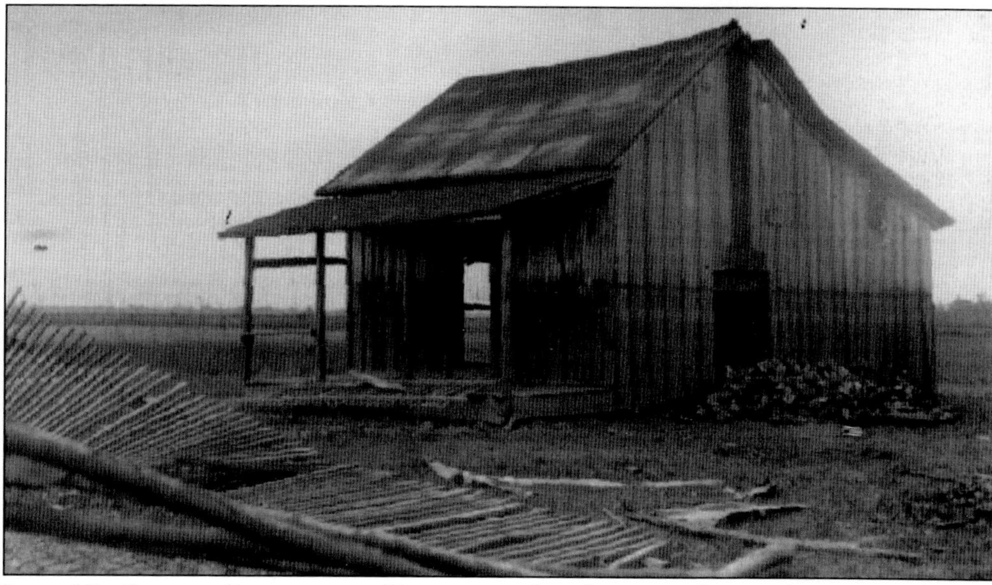

July 27, Shirley Plantation. Here is another house with no chimney. (Courtesy of USDA.)

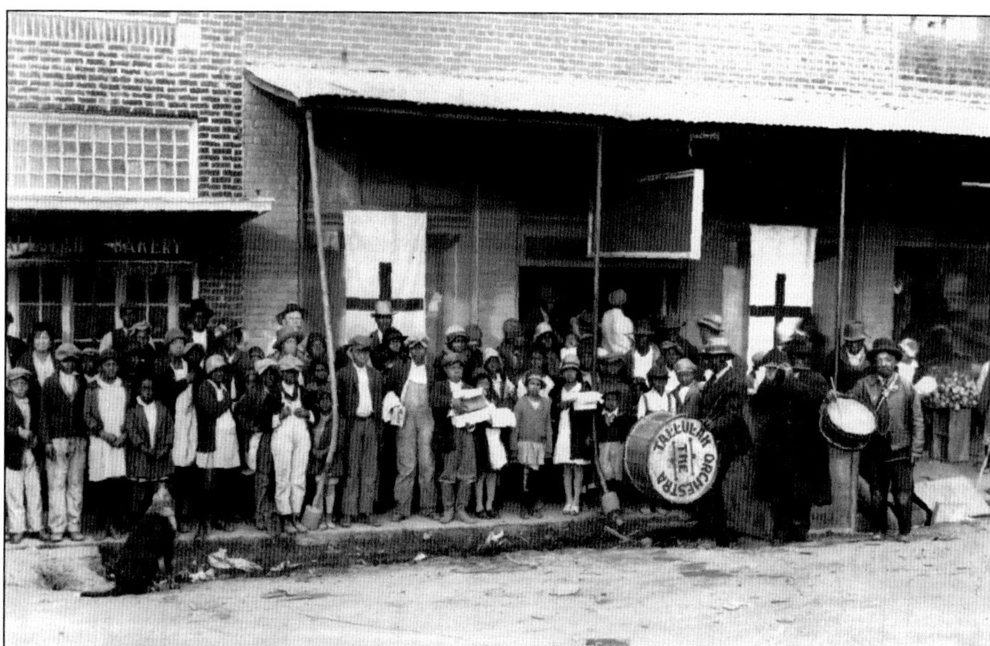

Red Cross Station c. September 30. This is where clothing and furniture were handed out to the needy. This picture is from 119 days after the levee broke. (Courtesy of USDA.)

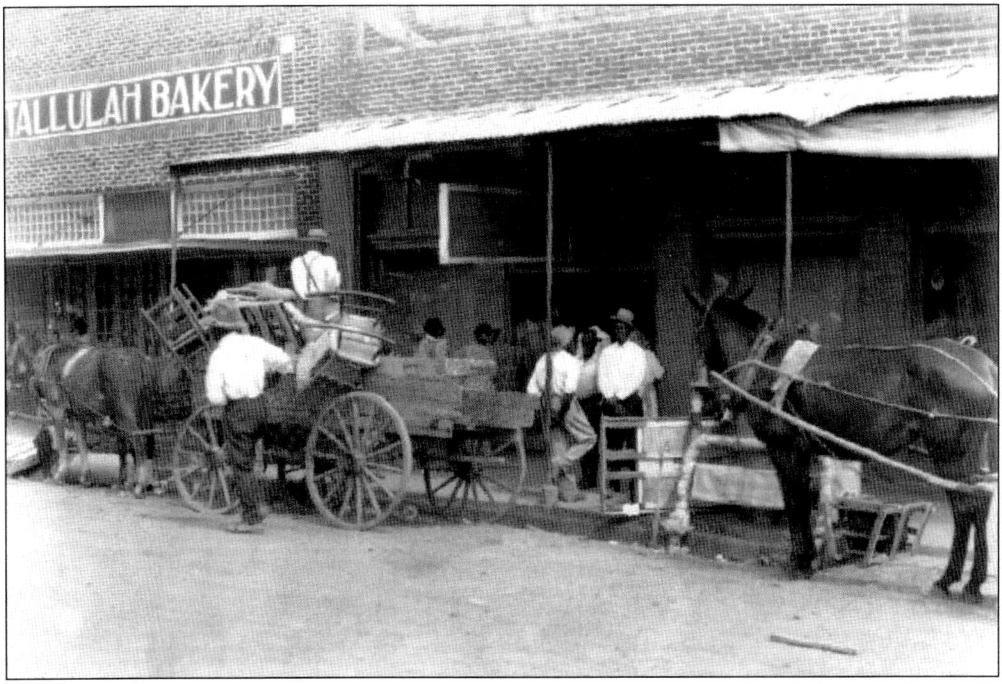

RED CROSS STATION c. SEPTEMBER 30. Furniture and clothing is being handed out to the needy and carried away in mule-drawn wagons. (Courtesy of USDA.)

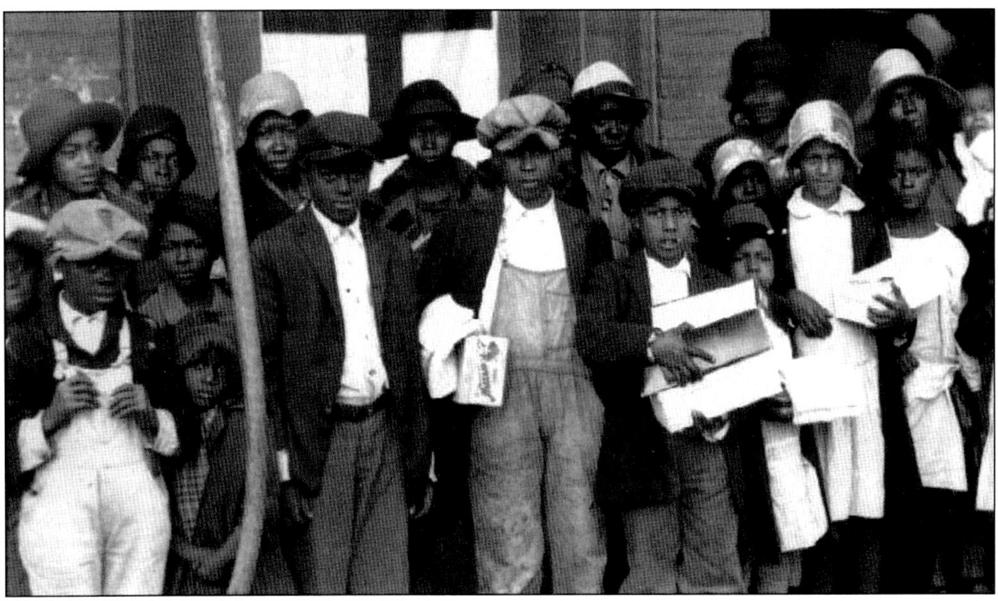

RED CROSS STATION c. SEPTEMBER 30. Here refugees have received clothing from the Red Cross. Most of these people lost practically everything they had to the flood. (Courtesy of USDA.)

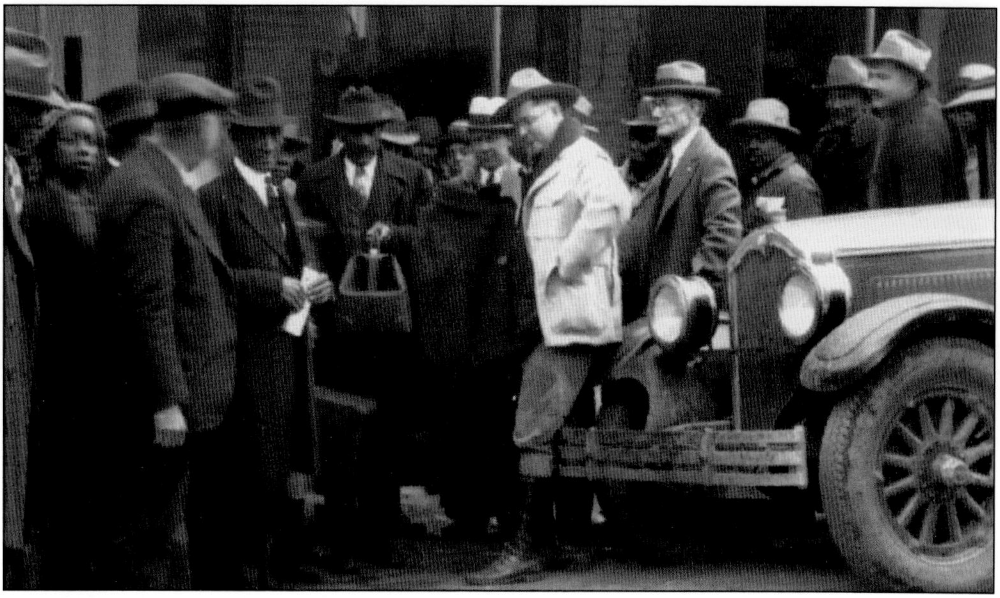

RED CROSS STATION AND CEREMONY C. SEPTEMBER 30. Dr. Coad was very active in seeing that the proper relief was provided to the refugees. Here recipients show their gratitude at a ceremony. (Courtesy of USDA.)

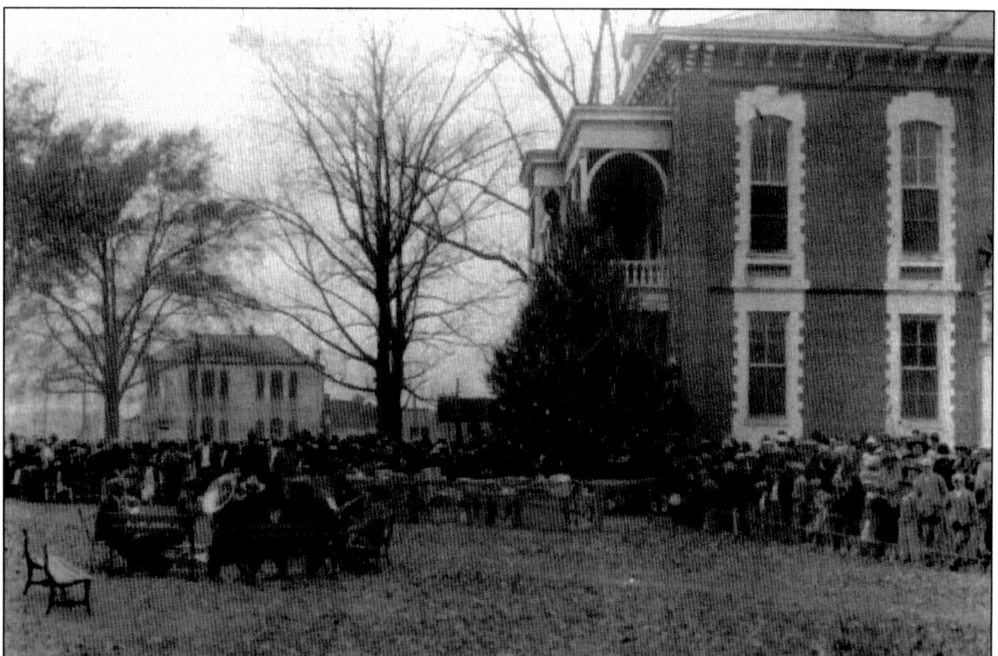

CHRISTMAS TREE FOR MADISON PARISH CHILDREN C. DECEMBER 15. In December, the Red Cross put up a Christmas tree on the Madison Parish courthouse lawn for the children of the parish, most of whom had lost everything in the flood and would likely have received nothing for Christmas. (Courtesy of USDA.)

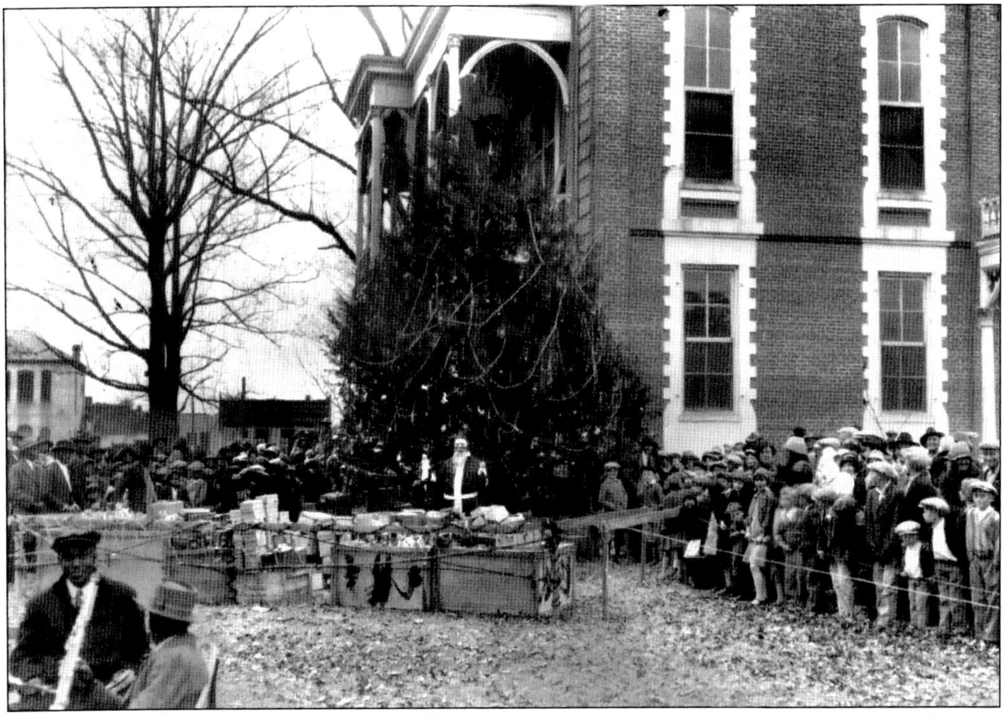

Christmas Tree for Madison Parish Children c. December 15. Before a large crowd Santa Claus prepares to hand out gifts to Madison Parish children. (Courtesy of USDA.)

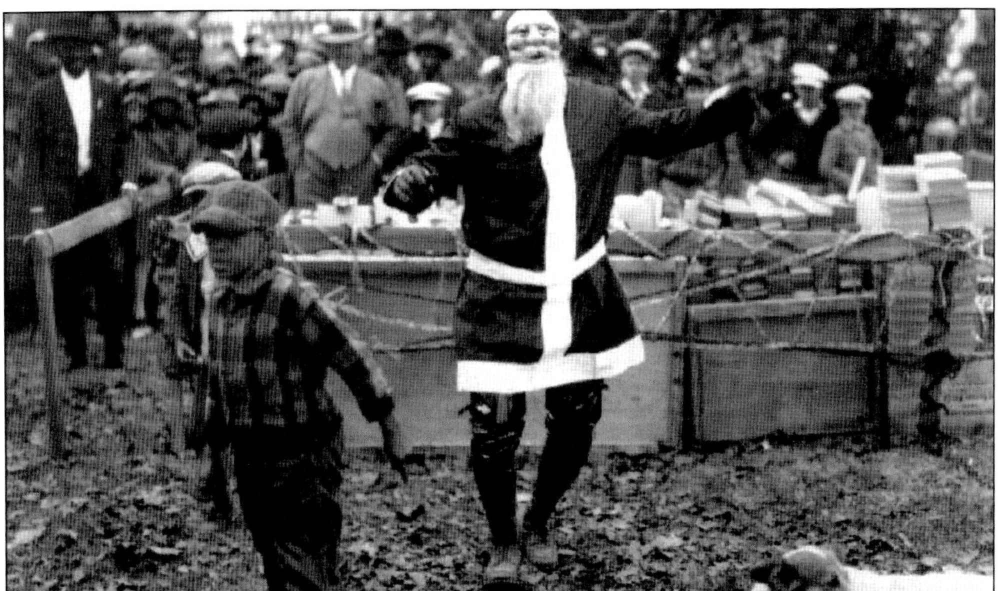

Christmas Tree for Madison Parish Children c. December 15. This young fellow runs off apparently suspicious of Santa's intentions. Santa's gifts may be seen on the table in the center. (Courtesy of USDA.)

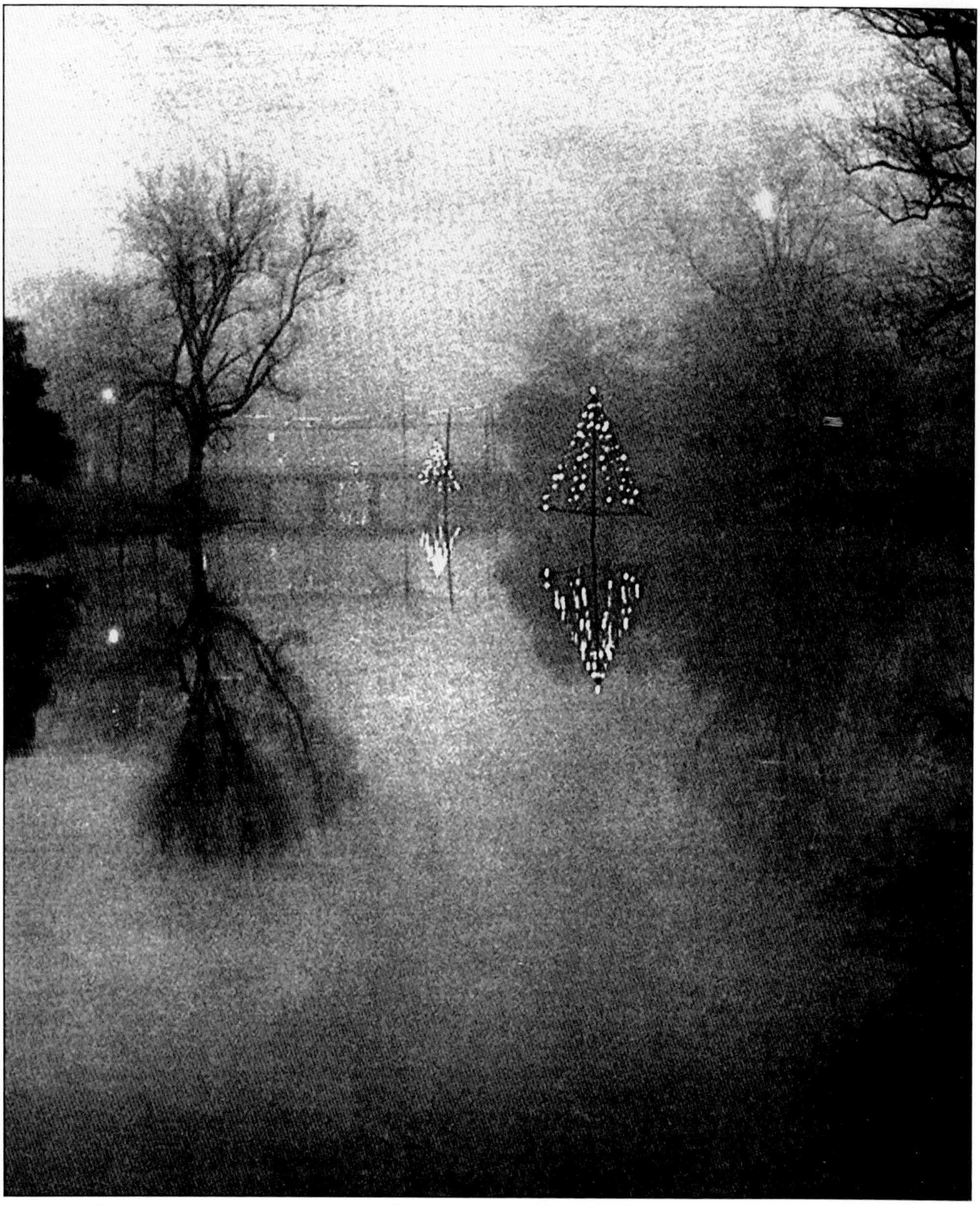

BRUSHY BAYOU CHRISTMAS LIGHTS—TALLULAH. Although this picture does not fit within the 1800–1927 chronology, it is presented here to set the record straight. Ever since childhood I have thought how great it would be for a picture of Tallulah to appear in *Life* Magazine. In 1972 a *Life* photographer was sent to Tallulah to do a story on the town's nationally recognized Christmas lighting along Brushy Bayou. This picture finally appeared in *Life*'s next-to-last weekly issue (December 22, 1972) under the following caption: "In a Mississippi bayou, near Vicksburg, a pole strung with lights glows in the mist of dusk, fragile as a child's dream of Christmas." What a mistake! Mississippi bayou? Vicksburg? The man was probably lost! Unfortunately, there was not enough time to write a letter to the editor since *Life* ceased to exist as a weekly after the December 29, 1972 issue. So 30 years later, *Life*, whether you know it or not, the picture was taken in Tallulah, Louisiana! (Courtesy of *Life* Magazine.)